I would recommend this book very strongly to people serving on boards, academics and postgraduate students interested in corporate governance and corporate law. This unique book is one of the first studies in Australia comparing empirical research and examples with theories on board composition, evaluation and diversity. The book has a very solid scholarly underpinning, but it also provides valuable insights into important issues for all boards.

–**Jean J. du Plessis**, *Professor at Deakin Law School, Deakin University, Australia*

Klettner shows the importance of understanding corporate governance dynamics. Through this book she presents many aspects behind the history and development of corporate governance codes in a thought-provoking and informative way, and provides important management theory-based guidelines for corporate governance development and practices.

–**Morten Huse**, *Professor in the Department of Communication and Culture, BI Norwegian Business School, Norway*

T0361010

CORPORATE GOVERNANCE REGULATION

Corporate governance regulation has been through numerous cycles of reform, and yet we still see instances of companies collapsing suddenly. Codes of corporate governance have been implemented in most developed countries, recommending detailed governance frameworks for publicly listed companies and their boards, but our understanding of how these codes influence behaviour is still limited.

In this book, Alice Klettner draws on the domains of law and business to explore the effectiveness of corporate governance codes. Using interview evidence from company directors and officers, as well as published evidence of companies' corporate governance systems, she discusses the theory and practice of corporate governance and its regulation – with a focus on how corporate governance codes can affect board behaviour and company performance.

This interdisciplinary book will be valuable reading for advanced students and researchers of corporate governance, and will also be directly relevant to governance practitioners and policymakers.

Alice Klettner is a Research Fellow in the Business School of the University of Technology Sydney, Australia and is a qualified lawyer.

Routledge Contemporary Corporate Governance

The *Routledge Contemporary Corporate Governance* Series aims to provide an authoritative, thought-provoking and well-balanced series of textbooks in the rapidly emerging field of corporate governance. The corporate governance literature traditionally has been scattered in the finance, economics, accounting, law and management literature. However, the international controversy now associated with corporate governance has focused considerable attention on this subject and raised its profile immeasurably. Government, financial institutions, corporations and academics have become deeply involved in tackling the dilemmas of corporate governance due to widespread public concerns.

The *Routledge Contemporary Corporate Governance* Series will make a significant impact in this emerging field: defining and illuminating problems; going beyond the official emphasis on regulation and procedures to understand the behaviour of executives, boards, and corporations; analysing the wider impact and relationships involved in corporate governance. Issues that will be covered in this series include:

Exploring the impact of the globalisation of corporate governance
Assessing the ongoing contest between shareholder/stakeholder values
Examining how corporate governance values determine corporate objectives
Analysing how financial interests have overwhelmed corporate governance
Investigating the discourse of corporate governance
Considering the imperative of sustainability in corporate governance
Addressing the contemporary crises in corporate governance and how they might be resolved.

Series Editor

Thomas Clarke, Professor of Corporate Governance, University of Technology Sydney, Australia.

Editorial Board

Professor Bernard Taylor, Executive Director of the Centre for Board Effectiveness, Henley Management College, UK

Dr David Wheeler, Erivan K Haub Professor of Business and Sustainability, Schulich School of Business, York University, Canada

Professor Esther Solomon, Graduate School of Business, Fordham University, New York, US

Professor Jean-Francois Chanlat, CREPA, Director of Executive MBA, Université Paris IX Dauphine, France

Titles available

Governance and the Market for Corporate Control
John L. Teall

Nonprofit Governance
Edited by Chris Cornforth and William A. Brown

Corporate Governance Regulation
The changing roles and responsibilities of boards of directors
Alice Klettner

CORPORATE GOVERNANCE REGULATION

The changing roles and responsibilities of boards of directors

Alice Klettner

Routledge
Taylor & Francis Group

LONDON AND NEW YORK

First published 2017
by Routledge
2 Park Square, Milton Park, Abingdon, Oxon OX14 4RN

and by Routledge
711 Third Avenue, New York, NY 10017

Routledge is an imprint of the Taylor & Francis Group, an informa business

British Library Cataloguing-in-Publication Data
A catalogue record for this book is available from the British Library

Library of Congress Cataloging-in-Publication Data
Names: Klettner, Alice, author.
Title: Corporate governance regulation: the changing roles and
responsibilities of boards of directors / Alice Klettner.
Description: Abingdon, Oxon; New York, NY: Routledge, 2017. |
Series: Routledge contemporary corporate governance
Identifiers: LCCN 2016019636 | ISBN 9781138909991 (hardback) |
ISBN 9781315693644 (ebook)
Subjects: LCSH: Corporate governance. | Boards of directors. |
Corporate governance—Law and legislation.
Classification: LCC HD2741 .K479 2017 | DDC 346/.0662—dc23
LC record available at https://lccn.loc.gov/2016019636

ISBN: 978-1-138-90999-1 (hbk)
ISBN: 978-1-138-91000-3 (pbk)
ISBN: 978-1-315-69364-4 (ebk)

Typeset in Bembo
by codeMantra

CONTENTS

PREFACE AND ACKNOWLEDGEMENTS

This book emerges from 10 years of research conducted at the Centre for Corporate Governance at the University of Technology Sydney between 2005 and 2015. It is based partly on my doctoral thesis but also draws from the experience gained through managing a series of research projects during those years. Each project involved an industry partner – professionals interested in finding out more about corporate governance in practice. All projects were initiated due to a real and pressing need on the part of investors, government and other corporate stakeholders, to better understand how boards of directors function against a background of increasingly detailed, yet mostly voluntary, regulation. In other words, they all touched on the topic of codes of corporate governance. Over that decade these codes proliferated across the globe and yet relatively little academic research was conducted into their practical impact and effectiveness. The global financial crisis in 2008 raised questions over the use of soft regulation in corporate governance but in most countries reforms continued in the same manner. This book explores codes of corporate governance: their development, impact and effectiveness.

Thanks goes to the organisations and individuals who initiated, participated in and provided feedback on the various research projects that paved the way for this book. These include Dibbs Barker Lawyers and Lis Boyce for partnering the Centre for Corporate Governance in an Australian Research Council (ARC) Linkage Grant; Ann Byrne and the Australian Council of Superannuation Investors; Tim Sheehy and Judith Fox at the Governance Institute; Jane Bridge and Boardroom Partners; the Australian Government's Equal Opportunity for Women in the Workplace Agency; and Jo Schofield of Catalyst Australia. Particular thanks must go to the company secretaries and directors who participated in interviews. Last but not least thank you to the academics who were involved in some of the early research, in particular, Thomas Clarke, Michael Adams, Paul Redmond, Marie dela Rama and Martijn Boersma.

Some of the theoretical discussion in Chapters 3 and 9 was developed from ideas published in Klettner A, 2016, Corporate governance codes and gender diversity: management-based regulation in action, *University of New South Wales Law Journal*, vol. 39, no. 2, pp. 715–739. Elements of Chapter 5 on gender diversity were developed from previous work on this topic published in Klettner A, Clarke T, and Boersma M, 2016, Strategic and regulatory approaches to increasing women in leadership: multi-level targets and mandatory quotas as levers for cultural change *Journal of Business Ethics*, vol. 133, no. 3, pp. 395–419 and Klettner, A, Clarke, T, & Boersma, M, 2013, The impact of soft law on social change: measurable objectives for achieving gender diversity on board of directors, *Australian Journal of Corporate Law*, vol. 28, no. 2, pp. 138–165. Similarly some of the material in Chapter 7 on corporate responsibility was developed from work published initially in Klettner A, Clarke T, and Boersma M, 2014, The governance of corporate sustainability: empirical insights into the development, leadership and implementation of responsible business strategy *Journal of Business Ethics*, vol. 122, pp. 145–165. Lastly, the wider implications of the early interview study were published in Klettner A, Clarke T, and Adams M, 2010, Corporate governance reform: an empirical study of the changing roles and responsibilities of Australian boards and directors *Australian Journal of Corporate Law*, vol. 24, no. 8, pp. 148–176.

1

CORPORATE GOVERNANCE CODES

Introduction

Significance of corporate governance and its regulation

Recent years have shown that large and powerful companies can collapse very suddenly causing great damage to national economies and the livelihoods of the people who work and invest in them. As a consequence, corporate governance has become a regular issue on most government policy agendas. Corporate governance regulation, which can include both hard law and softer forms of regulation, has been through several cycles of reform and yet collapses continue to occur. Codes of corporate governance have been implemented in most developed countries recommending detailed governance frameworks for publicly listed companies, yet our understanding of how these codes influence behaviour is still limited. This book explores the development and reform of corporate governance regulation over the last two decades, particularly the impact of corporate governance codes on organisational behaviour.

The book presents research of practical relevance to a wide variety of governance professionals: directors, company secretaries, lawyers and consultants, as well as executives and regulators. It aims to demonstrate the value of corporate governance codes in improving board practices as well as identifying where they might be improved. For researchers and those studying corporate governance, the book places practical problems in the context of academic theory, preparing the ground for future research that will advance our understanding of the relationship between regulation and board performance. Also the book strives to demonstrate the relevance of corporate governance to wider society. The way in which companies are run has the potential to affect individuals across many dimensions. Indeed, we all have daily contact with corporations whether as employees, customers or through our pension fund investments. The manner in which those companies are directed and controlled can impact on our working life, our retirement savings, the products we buy and the air that we breathe.

Thus the gradual development of codes of corporate governance over the last 25 years is of increasing relevance to us all, particularly since codes have expanded their scope to include broad social issues, such as gender diversity and environmental responsibility, as well as the detail of boardroom procedures.

Aims and objectives

The book explores some of the theories behind the different methods of regulating corporate governance, particularly the use of codes of good practice. Its aim is to develop knowledge of how some of these new soft regulatory mechanisms can cause changes in behaviour. One of the practical objectives of the book is to provide evidence and ideas to assist future regulatory reform. It asks whether the policy of regulating through voluntary principles is effective and explores the conditions required for optimal impact: is the 'comply-or-explain' mechanism strong enough to instigate meaningful behavioural change or is it simply a method for improving accountability and information disclosure? Understanding how codes of corporate governance work also assists the companies targeted by such regulation: corporate governance regulation is not intended to be a burden, rather it is designed to assist companies in improving efficiency and decision-making. If this is not the case in practice then we need to understand why and make changes. The novel approach of this book comprises an attempt to bring together the management-based research on the functioning of boards of directors with emerging ideas on regulatory mechanisms. Combining these areas of research enables a more comprehensive view of the aims and objectives of corporate governance regulation. A detailed understanding of the modern role of the board is essential if we are to design regulation that effectively facilitates fulfilment of that role.

Book structure

This Chapter 1 introduces the topic of codes of corporate governance, placing them in the context of corporate governance regulation as a whole. Chapter 2 goes on to detail the history of corporate governance codes: how and why they have been developed over the last two decades. Chapter 3 introduces some of the theories behind corporate governance and the role of the board of directors together with regulatory theory relevant to the use of voluntary codes. Chapter 4 then provides a review of research on corporate governance and its regulation: explaining the different methodological approaches that are possible and the need for more qualitative work of the type presented in this book. The next four chapters are research-based, discussing the response of companies to specific topics covered by corporate governance regulation:

Chapter 5 examines the practice of board performance evaluation and the insights it gives us into the role of the board of directors in corporate governance and the factors contributing to good board performance. All corporate governance codes contain a multitude of suggestions regarding board composition, board committees and board responsibilities: do these correlate with the factors seen in practice as essential for an effective board?

Chapter 6 continues the discussion of board effectiveness in the context of recent code provisions promoting diversity in leadership, particularly gender diversity. It explores the modern dilemma of whether regulation can and should be used to increase the number of women in corporate leadership both for economic reasons and to improve social equity.

Chapter 7 then broadens this discussion to encompass corporate responsibility more widely. The question of whether corporations should be responsible for social and environmental issues, and to what extent, is complex. This chapter notes the increasing integration of corporate responsibility into corporate governance and explores how soft regulation can encourage ethical and responsible behaviour.

Chapter 8 continues the ethical discussion into the area of executive remuneration. Can regulation encourage well-designed remuneration schemes that provide fair reward and encourage executives to strive for long-term sustainable performance rather than short-term gain?

This tour through some of the most topical and tricky areas of corporate governance is then discussed in terms of regulatory theory and the modern role of the board. Chapter 9 goes back to the humble code of corporate governance and its potential for encouraging change in these areas. By comparing and contrasting the effect of code provisions across the four subject areas it is possible to see how the design of codes and their interaction with other institutional forces (law, markets, politics and society) can impact on effectiveness.

Defining corporate governance

First it is important to define corporate governance and hence corporate governance regulation. Early attempts to define the concept of corporate governance appear in the United Kingdom Cadbury Report (1992) and the South African King Report (1994) where it is defined at its simplest as 'the system by which companies are directed and controlled'. Since then, there have been many attempts to elucidate the concept in more detail. Table 1.1 includes a selection of definitions of corporate governance both from academic scholarship and corporate governance codes. The wide variation in these definitions reflects the different approaches of academic disciplines and changing attitudes over time. The OECD definition is often cited as an authoritative, internationally agreed definition. It states:

> Corporate governance involves a set of relationships between a company's management, its board, its shareholders and other stakeholders. Corporate governance also provides the structure through which the objectives of the company are set, and the means of attaining those objectives and monitoring performance are determined.
>
> (OECD 2015, p. 9)

TABLE 1.1 Corporate governance definitions

Academic definitions	
Friedman (1970) Economics	Corporate governance is to conduct the business in accordance with the owner's or shareholders' desires, which generally will be to make as much money as possible, while conforming to the basic rules of the society embodied in law and local customs.
Demb and Neubauer (1992) Management	Corporate governance is the process by which corporations are made responsive to the rights and wishes of stakeholders.
Blair (1995) Law	The whole set of legal, cultural and institutional arrangements that determine what public corporations can do, who controls them, how that control is exercised and how the risks and return from the activities they undertake are allocated.
Monks and Minow (1995) Management	Corporate governance involves the relationships among various participants, including the chief executive officer, management, shareholders and employees, in determining the direction and performance of corporations.
Shleifer and Vishny (1997) Finance	Corporate governance deals with the ways in which suppliers of finance to corporations assure themselves of getting a return on their investment.
Tomasic, Bottomley and McQueen (2002) Law	...the structures, processes and systems, both formal and informal, by which power is exercised, constrained, monitored and accounted for in the management of a corporation.
Tricker (2012) Management	Corporate governance is about the way power is exercised over corporate entities. It covers the activities of the board and its relationships with the shareholders or members and with those managing the enterprise, as well as with the external auditors, regulators and other legitimate stakeholders.
du Plessis, Hargovan, Bagaric and Harris (2014) Law	The system of regulating and overseeing corporate conduct and of balancing the interests of all internal stakeholders and other parties (external stakeholders, governments and local communities) who can be affected by the corporation's conduct, in order to ensure responsible behaviour by corporations and to create long-term, sustainable growth for the corporation.
Mees (2015) Management	Corporate governance is best seen as a movement to improve the performance and standards of the directorial and executive teams at the top of listed companies and to improve the confidence of international investors in local securities markets.

Code definitions

Australian Corporate Governance Principles and Recommendations (2014)	Corporate governance is 'the framework of rules, relationships, systems and processes within and by which authority is exercised and controlled in corporations'. It encompasses the mechanisms by which companies, and those in control, are held to account. Corporate governance influences how the objectives of the company are set and achieved, how risk is monitored and assessed and how performance is optimised. Effective corporate governance structures encourage companies to create value, through entrepreneurialism, innovation, development and exploration and provide accountability and control systems commensurate with the risks involved.
Belgian Code on Corporate Governance (2009)	Corporate governance is a set of rules and behaviours that determine how companies are managed and controlled. A good corporate governance model will achieve its goal by setting a proper balance between leadership, entrepreneurship and performance on the one hand and control as well as conformity with this set of rules on the other hand.
Japan's Corporate Governance Code (2015)	In this Corporate Governance Code, 'corporate governance' means a structure for transparent, fair, timely and decisive decision-making by companies, with due attention to the needs and perspectives of shareholders and also customers, employees and local communities.
OECD Principles of Corporate Governance (2015)	Corporate governance involves a set of relationships between a company's management, its board, its shareholders and other stakeholders. Corporate governance also provides the structure through which the objectives of the company are set and the means of attaining those objectives and monitoring performance are determined.
UK Corporate Governance Code (2014)	Corporate governance is the system by which companies are directed and controlled. Boards of directors are responsible for the governance of their companies. The shareholders' role in governance is to appoint the directors and the auditors and to satisfy themselves that an appropriate governance structure is in place. The responsibilities of the board include setting the company's strategic aims, providing the leadership to put them into effect, supervising the management of the business and reporting to shareholders on their stewardship. The board's actions are subject to laws, regulations and the shareholders in general meeting. Corporate governance is therefore about what the board of a company does and how it sets the values of the company. It is to be distinguished from the day-to-day operational management of the company by full-time executives.

Corporate governance is a broad topic – it covers the structures and processes that define and guide the roles and relationships of the key players in a corporation – including shareholders, directors, managers and wider stakeholders such as employees and creditors. As explained by a respected Australian judge, 'the expression 'corporate governance' embraces not only the models or systems themselves but also the practices by which that exercise and control of authority is in fact effected' (Owen 2003, p. xxxiii).

Mechanisms of corporate governance are often distinguished as either internal or external (Hopt 2011; Kingsford Smith 2012). Internal corporate governance concerns the relationships and balance of powers within a corporation, primarily among the board, managers and shareholders but also other internal stakeholders such as employees. External corporate governance refers to outside forces that exercise a disciplining influence on managers, such as takeover markets, financial markets and regulatory intervention. This is an important distinction because corporate governance codes, as well as comprising an external regulatory force themselves, can be aimed at both improving internal organisational processes and disclosing information to enable other external forces to exert an influence. As Kingsford Smith comments, corporate governance codes, as well as being an external influence ideally have an internal governance effect – 'incorporation into the company's internal rules, norms and culture' (2012, p. 382).

Corporate responsibility

As companies have grown, spread across national boundaries and become hugely powerful, concerns over their social and environmental impact have increased and renewed interest in corporate responsibility has emerged. Corporate responsibility has as its theoretical base the notion that the responsibility of a corporation extends beyond the traditional Anglo-American objective of providing financial returns to its shareholders. Instead, proponents of corporate responsibility argue that the legitimate concerns of a corporation should include broader objectives such as sustainable growth, equitable employment practices and long-term social and environmental well-being (Conley and Williams 2005). The purpose of the corporation is not a new topic, famously debated in 1932 by Berle and Dodd in the *Harvard Law Review*, yet it has arguably been redefined over the last two decades, and there is a growing expectation that companies should take action and report on their efforts to be better corporate citizens.

Corporate governance and corporate responsibility were for many years seen as different issues but, as corporate responsibility has become more mainstream, the overlap between the two has become increasingly evident. Corporate responsibility has moved from being a marketing response to specific events towards being a key element of business strategy. This change requires leadership from the top and integration of corporate responsibility across all aspects of the business. In 2006, John Elkington, co-founder of SustainAbility, wrote about the merging of corporate social responsibility with corporate governance that was then occurring: 'The centre of gravity of the sustainable business debate is in the process of shifting from public relations to competitive advantage and corporate governance – and, in the process, from the factory fence to the boardroom' (2006, p. 524). Confirming this development, a 2008 report by the Conference Board of Canada suggested that 'good corporate governance will be redefined over this decade to include ways in which a board provides oversight and strategic direction on the firm's social and environmental performance'. This process of redefinition is beginning to be seen in codes of corporate governance as they start to incorporate aspects of corporate responsibility. Chapter 7 explores the links between corporate governance and corporate responsibility further, particularly how corporate governance processes and structures can assist boards in developing and implementing corporate responsibility strategies.

Role of the board of directors

Corporate law in most countries provides for a board of directors, formally elected by the shareholders, to act as the mind of the corporation and direct and supervise the managers of the company. In Australia, section 198A(1) of the *Corporations Act 2001* provides that 'The business of a company is to be managed by or under the direction of the directors', reflecting the fact that the historic role of the board was to manage (Farrar 2008, p. 89). Boards of smaller, private companies may still be made up of executive managers, but in large public companies the modern norm is for a separation between board and management, with boards comprised of a majority of independent non-executive members who supervise, monitor and guide the executive management team (Gordon 2007). They lead and represent the company and ensure that it is accountable to its shareholders and other relevant stakeholders. Core board functions include approving executive appointments and remuneration; monitoring the performance of the executive team; and providing advice and resources such as industry knowledge or access to networks (Anderson et al. 2007; Kiel and Nicholson 2003; Roche 2009; Zahra and Pearce 1989). The board plays a vital role in corporate governance reflected in the fact that most regulatory reforms in recent years have been designed to improve board performance. But what are the features of good board performance? Chapter 5 explores whether these reforms have focused on the right areas by reviewing the process of board performance evaluation and what it can tell us about effective boards.

Corporate governance as a whole, including the role of the board within it, is aimed at both creating value and maintaining control. This is reflected in the well-known framework developed by Hilmer and Tricker (1991), which depicts the role of the board as balancing conformance (monitoring and accountability) with performance (strategy and policy). Many scholars have noted the competing nature of the demands placed on directors: to monitor the present while preparing for the future, to act as both advisor and police force (Clarke 2007; Hilmer and Tricker 1991). It is commonly recognised that the role of the board is multi-faceted, combining different functions, each of which may rise in priority depending on the company's circumstances (Lynall et al. 2003). The dilemma for regulatory policy-makers is how to facilitate the fulfilment of these different roles when they may conflict with each other. Academic theories aimed at improving our understanding of the role of the board do not always help. These theories, discussed in Chapter 3, tend to be highly influenced by the discipline in which they are developed (usually economics, law, finance or management) and often take an overly narrow view of the board's role.

Regulation of corporate governance

Corporate governance regulation, at its broadest, encompasses any law, rule, standard or recommendation that is directed at influencing the way companies are controlled and held to account. This includes most corporate legislation but also the codes and standards set by stock exchanges, prudential regulators and accounting bodies, which may be mandatory or voluntary. Kingsford Smith describes corporate governance standards as a new form of soft regulation added to the control of corporate conduct in the last two decades (2012, p. 378). The role of this new soft regulation should not be underestimated, Branson comments that 'at the level of large publicly held and multinational corporations, a principal determinant of corporate behaviour has become 'soft law' rather than law itself (2000, p. 670).

Corporate governance regulation spans jurisdictional boundaries and includes a burgeoning body of international initiatives – principles, frameworks and standards – quasi-legal instruments that do not have any legally binding force. Corporate governance regulation is an area where the regulatory 'rules versus principles' debate is often aired. Some countries, notably the United States, take a more prescriptive, rules-based approach, and others rely on voluntary or semi-voluntary principles. Corbett and Bottomley claim that it is useful to think of corporate governance regulation as a body or category of law as well as a body of governance practices, processes and structures (2004, p. 61).

As discussed further in Chapter 3, corporate governance regulation in many countries involves layers of rules and standards working in parallel, a contemporary form of regulation that falls within the category of 'new governance' or 'meta-regulation' rather than traditional 'command-and-control' regulation (Lobel 2004). John Farrar depicts this as concentric circles of corporate governance regulation: legal regulation at the centre surrounded by stock exchange listing rules, then codes of conduct and business ethics as the outer circle (2008, p. 4).

Codes of corporate governance

The focus of this book is the use of codes of corporate governance as a regulatory policy. Codes deal with the practical aspects of corporate governance such as the composition of the board of directors; its role and responsibilities; and communications with shareholders and other stakeholders. Hong Kong is usually cited as the first country to formally issue a code of corporate governance in 1989 (although a code-like document was published in the United States in 1978) (Small 2011, p. 133). Ireland was the next country to introduce a code in 1991, which was closely followed in 1992 by the UK's influential Cadbury Code. After this there was an amazingly fast diffusion of these codes worldwide· Aguilera and Cuervo-Cazzurra (2004) noted that there were 24 countries with codes in 1999; and López-Iturriaga (2009) reported 63 countries with codes in 2008. The trend has continued with 93 countries providing their codes to the European Corporate Governance Institute in 2015. Cuomo et al. (2016) report that national code proliferation accelerated markedly after the issuance of the OECD Principles in 1999.

Although the legal status of these codes varies from country to country, in the large majority of nations they exist as a form of soft law (Keay 2014). Indeed, Seidl defines a code of corporate governance as 'a non-binding set of principles, standards or best practices, issued by a collective body and relating to the internal governance of corporations' (2006, p. 1). This means that codes of corporate governance do not prescribe behaviour but make suggestions, uptake of which is strongly encouraged but voluntary. The most common regulatory mechanism used is known as 'comply-or-explain' whereby the code requires disclosure rather than mandating specific practices. Companies must explain if they do not adopt a recommended practice but are permitted to choose. Seidl et al. comment that, 'it is the essential genius of comply-or-explain that companies can be said to be in conformance with the code even when deviating from it' (2013, p. 796).

This voluntary and flexible approach to corporate governance is justified on the basis that every company has different needs that change over time making a 'one size fits all' approach inappropriate (Cuomo et al. 2016). The optimal structures and processes for any particular company will depend on contingencies such as size, ownership structure, industry and maturity (Lynall et al. 2003). As a consequence, regulation is designed to give a high level of discretion to companies to permit them to adopt a governance structure that suits their particular needs whilst at the same time forcing accountability and transparency through disclosure (Cuomo et al. 2016). In this way corporate governance codes aim to achieve a balance between permitting flexibility and yet encouraging change. Regulatory theories suggest that this kind of flexible regulation can engage companies to find cost-effective solutions to complex problems (Coglianese & Lazer 2003). However, whether companies fully make use of this flexibility is still open to question: early research on code compliance found a pressure to comply and a tendency for uniformity in corporate responses to codes (Klettner et al. 2010; Hooghiemstra and van Ees 2011). In contrast, recent research has demonstrated not only that code flexibility is utilised, but that it can provide financial benefits to shareholders (Seidl et al. 2013; Luo and Salterio 2014).

The theory behind the comply-or-explain mechanism is that adoption of good corporate governance practices will be enforced by the investment market.

Investors will assess the information disclosed in corporate governance statements and choose companies with good governance over those without. However, several researchers have found that investor engagement over corporate governance has been much less active than expected (MacNeil and Li 2006; Arcot et al. 2010; Keay 2014). Governments are grappling with how to improve investor engagement, with some countries adopting additional 'stewardship' codes for investment organisations (Cheffins 2010). Nevertheless, adoption rates of corporate governance code provisions are generally very good, suggesting that investor engagement may be only one of several elements encouraging code adoption. Certainly, there is a pressing need for more research investigating the purpose and effectiveness of codes including assessment of their content and how they work.

Research on codes of corporate governance

International comparative studies regarding codes of corporate governance have been relatively few and far between. In fact, the only commonly cited study dealing with a significant sample of countries was completed at a law firm in 1998–1999 and developed into a report for the European Union in 2002 (Gregory & Simmelkjaer 2002; Aguilera et al. 2009). With the fast spread of codes worldwide it seems the task of comparing their content has perhaps become too large. López-Iturriaga (2009) includes detailed coverage of 20 countries in his edited book, taking into account their differing national, legal and institutional settings. There have also been reports by professional service firms including a review of European codes by the law firm Clifford Chance in 2011.

Research on codes of corporate governance is reviewed further in Chapter 4. Scholars have recognised that academic research has lagged behind the fast development of codes of corporate governance (Aguilera and Cuervo-Cazurra 2009). This has two consequences: first, code recommendations are not necessarily based on a sound understanding of the role of the board and its influence on company performance; second, research on the theory behind comply-or-explain corporate governance codes is scarce, and we do not fully understand how this mechanism functions (Seidl et al. 2013; Seidl 2007; Aguilera and Cuervo-Cazurra 2009).

With regard to the first point – there is only scattered academic work questioning the substance and content of corporate governance codes and whether, and in what circumstances, adoption of recommended practices has valuable outcomes for corporations and their stakeholders (Finegold et al. 2007). As Finegold et al. put it, 'there is, at best, weak guidance for policymakers on what governance practices will lead to more effective firm performance' (2007, p. 865).

On the second point – other than several surveys of compliance rates, the fact remains that 'very little scholarly research has been carried out on how the comply-or-explain mechanism functions in practice' (Seidl et al. 2013, p. 792). Seidl states: 'Although codes of corporate governance have come to be widely used as a mode of regulating corporations, our understanding of how they function is still rather limited' (Seidl 2006, p. 1s). As introduced above, we do not fully understand why companies voluntarily adopt code provisions or whether they take full advantage of the flexibility inherent in the comply-or-explain system. Even the Organisation for Economic Co-operation and Development (OECD), which has published Corporate Governance Principles since 1999, has made the statement that:

> Although voluntary codes and principles have the advantage of maintaining flexibility and avoiding excessive and costly legal and regulatory measures, the question of their effectiveness does arise.
>
> (OECD 2004, p. 52)

This book accepts the evidence that there are some universal topics covered by most codes internationally (O'Shea 2005). Indeed, it seems that codes converge, to some extent, to the Anglo-American model of corporate governance yet retain divergence due to country-specific factors (Aguilera et al. 2009). Instead of focusing on comparing differences in content, this book explores the operation of a clear similarity – use of the comply-or-explain mechanism that has been adopted by the large majority of codes of corporate governance worldwide (Luo and Salterio 2014). Of course, it is impossible to do this without also reviewing the content of codes. In exploring how the comply-or-explain mechanism takes effect, the book looks at the implementation of some of the common topics dealt with by codes thereby gaining insight into the role of the board and the resources it needs to effectively govern the company.

Qualitative methodology

This book explores the impact of corporate governance codes on organisational behaviour through a detailed examination of the corporate response to code provisions in four topic areas: board performance evaluation, gender diversity, corporate responsibility and executive remuneration. These inter-related topics provide case-studies of how corporate governance regulation, if designed well, can begin to change organisational behaviour. The book draws on interviews with directors and other company officers, as well as published statements describing companies' corporate governance systems, to build knowledge regarding corporate governance and its regulation.

An obvious limitation of this method is that we cannot know whether what companies and their officers say equates to what they actually do in practice. Nevertheless, this kind of qualitative method has several advantages over more traditional quantitative methods discussed further in Chapter 4. Corporate governance researchers have for many years been using quantitative methods to try to find a connection between specific measures of corporate governance (board size, number of independent directors etc.) and firm performance. Bearing in mind the complexity of corporate governance and the number of intermediate factors between board composition and a company's share price, it is not surprising that this research has been inconclusive (Finkelstein and Mooney 2003; Kiel and Nicholson 2003; Levrau and van den Berghe 2007). As a result, there have been repeated calls for 'the use of a more in-depth, qualitative approach involving the direct study of boards and contact with corporate directors' (LeBlanc & Schwartz 2007). A new body of corporate governance research is emerging based on analysis of board processes and behaviour rather than comparison of inputs and outputs (Huse 2005; Roberts et al. 2005). Regulatory scholars have also called for more behavioural research into the effects of regulation, uncommon because of its time-consuming nature (Baldwin and Black 2008, p. 73). It is only through a better understanding of the role of the board and how it is influenced by regulation that we have a chance of implementing reforms likely to have a significant and positive impact on future corporate governance.

Summary of chapter 1

This chapter explains the aims and objectives of this book and introduces some of the key concepts that will be discussed within. It briefly introduces and defines corporate governance and its regulation, including widespread use internationally of comply-or-explain codes of corporate governance as a policy tool. It explains the central role played by the board of directors in corporate governance and the fact that corporate governance codes are often designed to facilitate fulfilment of that role. It justifies the need for research that examines the qualitative impact of regulation on boards and organisational behaviour.

References

Anderson, DW, Melanson, SJ & Maly, J 2007, 'The evolution of corporate governance: power redistribution brings boards to life', *Corporate Governance: An International Review*, vol. 15, no. 5, pp. 780–797.

Aguilera, RV & Cuervo-Cazurra, A 2004, 'Codes of good governance worldwide: what's the trigger?', *Organizational Studies*, vol. 25, pp. 415–43.

Aguilera, RV & Cuervo-Cazurra, A 2009, 'Codes of good governance', *Corporate Governance: An International Review*, vol. 17, pp. 376–87.

Arcot, S, Bruno, V & Faure-Grimaud, A 2010, 'Corporate governance in the UK: is the comply or explain approach working?', *International Review of Law and Economics*, vol. 30, pp. 193–201.

Baldwin, R & Black, J 2008, 'Really responsive regulation', *Modern Law Review*, vol. 71, no. 1, pp. 59–94.

Berle, AA, 1931,'Corporate powers as powers in trust', *Harvard Law Review* vol. 44, no. 7, pp. 1049–74.

Blair, MM 1995, *Ownership and Control: Rethinking Corporate Governance for the Twenty-First Century*, Washington, DC: Brookings Institution Press.

Branson, D 2000, 'Teaching comparative corporate governance: the significance of "soft law" and international institutions', *Georgia Law Review*, vol. 34, pp. 669–98.

Cheffins, BR 2010, 'The Stewardship Code's Achilles' heel', *The Modern Law Review*, vol. 73, no. 6, pp. 985–1025.

Clarke, T 2007, *International Corporate Governance: a comparative approach*, Routledge.

Clifford Chance, 2011, *Core Corporate Governance Issues: a comparative overview*, December 2011.

Coglianese, C & Lazer, D 2003 'Management-based regulation: prescribing private management to achieve public goals', *Law & Society Review*, vol. 37, no. 4, pp. 691–730.

Conference Board of Canada, 2008, *The role of boards of directors in corporate social responsibility.*

Conley, JM & Williams, CA 2005, 'Engage, embed and embellish: theory versus practice in the corporate social responsibility movement', *Iowa Journal of Corporation Law*, vol. 31, pp. 1–38.

Corbett, A & Bottomley, S 2004, 'Regulating corporate governance', in C Parker, C Scott, N Lacey & J Braithwaite (eds.), *Regulating Law*, Oxford: Oxford University Press.

Cuomo, F, Mallin, C & Zattoni, A 2016, 'Corporate governance codes: a review and research agenda', *Corporate Governance: An International Review*, forthcoming.

Demb, A & Neubauer, F 1992, *The Corporate Board: confronting the paradoxes*, Oxford: Oxford University Press.

Dodd, EM 1932, 'For whom are corporate managers trustees?', *Harvard Law Review*, vol. 45, no. 7, pp. 1144–63.

du Plessis, JJ, Hargovan, A & Bagaric, M 2010, *Principles of Contemporary Corporate Governance*, 2nd ed, Cambridge: Cambridge University Press.

Elkington, J 2006, 'Governance for sustainability' *Corporate Governance: An International Review*, vol. 14, no. 6, pp. 522–29.

Farrar, J 2008, *Corporate Governance: theories, principles and practice*, 3rd ed, Oxford: Oxford University Press.

Finegold, D, Benson, GS & Hecht, D 2007, 'Corporate boards and company performance: review of research in light of recent reforms', *Corporate Governance: An International Review*, vol. 15, no. 5, pp. 865–78.

Finkelstein, S & Mooney, AC 2003, 'Not the usual suspects; how to use board process to make boards better', *Academy of Management Perspectives*, vol. 17, no. 2, pp. 101–13.

Friedman, M 1970, 'The social responsibility of business is to increase its profits' *New York Times Magazine*, 13 September 1970.

Gordon, JN 2007, 'The rise of independent directors in the United States, 1950–2005: of shareholder value and stock market prices' *Stanford Law Review*, vol. 59, pp. 1465–1568.

Gregory, JH & Simmelkjaer, TR 2002, *Comparative Study of Corporate Governance Codes Relevant to the European Union and Its Member States*, New York: Weil, Gotshal & Manges LLP.

Hilmer, FG & Tricker, RI 1991, *An Effective Board, from the company director manual* Sydney: Pearson/Prentice Hall.

Hooghiemstra, R & van Ees, H 2011, 'Uniformity as response to soft law: evidence from compliance and non-compliance with the Dutch corporate governance code', *Regulation & Governance*, vol. 5, pp. 480–98.

Hopt, KJ 2011, 'Comparative corporate governance: The state of the art and international regulation', *The American Journal of Comparative Law*, vol. 59, no. 1, pp. 1–73.

Huse, M 2005, 'Accountability and creating accountability: a framework for exploring behavioural perspectives of corporate governance', *British Journal of Management*, vol. 16, pp. S65–S79.

Karmel, RS & Kelly, CR 2009, 'The hardening of soft law in securities regulation', *Brooklyn Journal of International Law*, vol. 34, pp. 883–951.

Karlsson-Vinkhuyzen, SI & Vihma, A 2009, 'Comparing the legitimacy and effectiveness of global hard and soft law: an analytical framework', *Regulation and Governance*, vol. 3, pp. 400–20.

Keay, A 2014, 'Comply or explain: in need of greater regulatory oversight' *Legal Studies*, vol. 34, no. 2, pp. 279–304.

Kiel, GC & Nicholson, GJ 2003, 'Board composition and corporate performance; how the Australian experience informs contrasting theories of corporate governance', *Corporate Governance An International Review*, vol. 11, no. 3, pp. 189–205.

Kingsford Smith, D 2012, 'Governing the corporation: the role of 'soft regulation'', *University of New South Wales Law Journal*, vol. 35, no. 1, pp. 370–103.

Klettner, A, Clarke, T & Adams, M 2010, 'Corporate governance reform: an empirical study of the changing roles and responsibilities of Australian boards and directors', *Australian Journal of Corporate Law*, vol. 24, pp. 148–76.

Leblanc, R & Schwartz, MS 2007, 'The black box of board process: gaining access to a difficult subject', *Corporate Governance: An International Review*, vol. 15, no. 5, pp. 843–51.

Levrau, A & Van den Berghe, L 2007, 'Corporate governance and board effectiveness: beyond formalism', Vlerick Leuven Gent working Paper Series 2007/03.

Lobel, O 2004, 'The renew deal: the fall of regulation and the rise of governance in contemporary legal thought', *Minnesota Law Review*, vol. 89, p. 342.

López Iturriaga, FJ (ed.) 2009, *Codes of Good Governance Worldwide*, Cheltenham: Edward Elgar.

Luo, Y & Salterio, SE 2014, 'Governance quality in a "comply or explain" governance disclosure regime', *Corporate Governance: An International Review*, vol. 22, no. 6, pp. 460–81.

Lynall, MD Golden, BR & Hillman, AJ 2003, 'Board composition from adolescence to maturity: a multitheoretic view', *Academy of Management Review*, vol. 28, no. 3, pp. 416–31.

MacNeil, I & Li, X 2006, 'Comply or explain: market discipline and non-compliance with the combined code', *Corporate Governance: An International Review*, vol. 14, no. 5, pp. 486–96.

Mees, B 2015, 'Corporate governance as a reform movement', *Journal of Management History*, vol. 21, no. 2, pp. 194–209.

O'Shea, N 2005, 'How we've got where we are and what's next', *Accountancy Ireland*, vol. 37, pp. 33–37.

OECD, 2004, *Corporate Governance: A Survey of OECD Countries,* OECD.

OECD, 2015, *OECD Principles of Corporate Governance*, 1970G-20.

Owen, J 2003, *The Failure of HIH Insurance – Volume 1: a corporate collapse and its lessons*, Canberra: Report of the HIH Royal Commission, Commonwealth of Australian.

Ribstein, LE 2002, 'Market vs regulatory responses to corporate fraud: a critique of the Sarbanes-Oxley Act of 2002', *Journal of Corporate Law*, vol. 28, p. 1.

Roberts, J, McNulty, T & Stiles, P 2005, 'Beyond agency conceptions of the work of the non-executive director: creating accountability in the boardroom', *British Journal of Management*, vol. 16, pp. S5–S26.

Roche, OP 2009, *Corporate Governance & Organisational Life Cycle*, New York: Cambria Press.

Romano, R 2005, 'The Sarbanes-Oxley Act and the making of quack corporate governance', *The Yale Law Journal,* vol. 114, no. 7, pp. 1521–1611.

Seidl, D 2006, *Regulating Organizations through Codes of Corporate Governance*, Working Paper No. 338, Centre for Business Research, University of Cambridge, December 2006.

Seidl, D, Sanderson, P & Roberts, J 2013, 'Applying the 'comply-or-explain' principle: discursive legitimacy tactics with regard to codes of corporate governance', *Journal of Management and Governance*, vol. 17, no. 3, pp. 791–826.

Shleifer, A & Vishny, RW 1997, 'A survey of corporate governance', *The Journal of Finance*, vol. 52, no. 2, pp. 737–83.

Small, ML 2011, 'The 1970s: The Committee on Corporate Laws joins the Corporate Governance Debate', *Law and Contemporary Problems*, vol. 74, pp. 129–136.

Tomasic, R, Bottomley, S & McQueen, R 2002, *Corporations law in Australia,* 2nd ed, Federation Press.

Tricker, RI 2012, *Corporate Governance: principles, policies and practices*, 2nd ed, Oxford: Oxford University Press.

Zahra, SA & Pearce, JA 1989, 'Boards of directors and corporate financial performance: a review and integrative model', *Journal of Management*, vol. 15, no. 2, pp. 291–334.

2

DEVELOPMENT OF CODES
OF CORPORATE GOVERNANCE

This chapter describes the background to current corporate governance regulation in Australia and internationally. The focus is on Australia because this is where the research presented in this book was conducted; however, developments elsewhere, particularly in the United Kingdom and United States, are included because they have had a strong influence worldwide. Although there are country-specific differences in corporate governance regulation, many of its core aims and objectives are common to all systems. The comply-or-explain mechanism explored by this book is used by the majority of codes of corporate governance across the globe. When the European Commission conducted a study of corporate governance codes in 2002, comply-or-explain was already used in Brazil, China, Indonesia, Korea, Malaysia and Mexico, as well as many Member States (FRC 2012, p. 25). Table 2.1 lists the 93 countries worldwide that have created a code of corporate governance of any sort at the time of writing (ECGI 2015). It shows that the large majority of countries first introduced a code in the early 2000s, although some of these codes began their life earlier as self-regulatory measures that were subsequently formalised into a code. Approximately 70 percent of those codes are based on the comply-or-explain mechanism, the remainder being split between purely voluntary guidelines and mandatory rules. This proliferation of the comply-or-explain mechanism means that the research described in this book, although based on the Australian code, will have much wider relevance.

Before examining the detail of codes of corporate governance, it is important to understand the wider purpose of corporate governance regulation and how it has developed to be what it is today. As a relatively new and dynamic area of regulation, the aims and objectives of corporate governance have expanded over time as the overall corporate environment has become increasingly complex.

TABLE 2.1 Codes of corporate governance worldwide

Country	Date of first code	Date of current code	Nature of code	Applies to
1. Albania	2008	2008	best practice reference	unlisted joint stock companies
2. Algeria	2009	2009	voluntary	all companies except SCEs
3. Argentina	2007	2013	comply-or-explain	listed companies
4. Armenia	2010	2010	comply-or-explain	listed companies and SCEs
5. Australia	2003	2014	comply-or-explain	listed companies
6. Austria	2002	2012	comply-or-explain	listed companies
7. Azerbaijan	2011	2011	voluntary standards	joint stock companies
8. Bahrain	2010	2010	comply-or-explain	joint stock companies
9. Baltic States (Estonia Latvia, Lithuania)	2010	2010	voluntary guidance	SOEs
10. Bangladesh	2004	2012	comply (must get certificate of compliance)	listed companies
11. Barbados	2013	2013	some mandatory some comply-or-explain	financial institutions
12. Belgium	2004	2009	comply-or-explain	listed companies
13. Bosnia & Herzegovina	2006	2011	comply-or-explain	listed companies
14. Brazil	2001	2009	best practice reference	business organisations
15. Bulgaria	2007	2012	comply-or-explain	public companies
16. Canada	1994	2006	guide to disclosure – some required some voluntary	listed companies
17. China	2002	2002	semi-voluntary – companies experiencing problems can be instructed to implement	listed companies
18. Colombia	2007	2007	comply-or-explain	listed companies
19. Croatia	2009	2010	comply-or-explain	joint stock companies

20. Cyprus	2002	comply-or-explain (some mandatory)	listed companies
21. Czech Republic	2001	comply-or-explain	listed companies
22. Denmark	2000	comply-or-explain	listed companies
23. Egypt	2006	voluntary guidelines	listed companies
24. Estonia	2006	comply-or-explain	listed companies
25. Finland	2003	comply-or-explain	listed companies
26. France	1995	comply-or-explain	listed companies
27. Georgia	2009	comply-or-explain	commercial banks
28. Germany	1998	comply-or-explain	listed companies
29. Ghana	2010	guidelines	listed companies
30. Greece	1999	comply-or-explain	listed companies
31. Guernsey	2011	voluntary	finance sector
32. Hong Kong	1999	comply-or-explain	listed companies
33. Hungary	2002	comply-or-explain	listed companies
34. Iceland	2004	follow or explain	listed companies
35. India	1998	voluntary	public companies
36. Indonesia	2000	voluntary	all companies
37. Ireland	1999	comply-or-explain	listed companies
38. Israel	2006	voluntary	public companies
39. Italy	1998	comply-or-explain	listed companies
40. Jamaica	2006	comply-or-explain	listed companies
41. Japan	1997	comply-or-explain	listed companies
42. Jordan	2007	comply-or-explain	non-listed
43. Kazakhstan	2007	Voluntary	joint stock companies
44. Kenya	2002	apply or explain	listed companies
45. Latvia	2005	Comply-or-explain	listed companies
46. Lebanon	2006	adopt a company code	listed companies
47. Lithuania	2003	comply-or-explain	listed companies

(Continued)

Country	Date of first code	Date of current code	Nature of code	Applies to
48. Luxembourg	2006	2013	comply-or-explain	listed companies
49. Malawi	2001	2010	comply-or-explain	all companies
50. Malaysia	2000	2012	comply-or-explain	listed companies
51. Malta	2001	2005	comply-or-explain	listed companies
52. Mauritius	2003	2004	comply-or-explain	large and listed companies
53. Mexico	1999	2010	comply-or-explain	listed companies
54. Moldova	2007	2007	comply-or-explain	listed companies
55. Mongolia	2007	2007	voluntary	listed companies
56. Montenegro	2009	2009	comply-or-explain	listed companies
57. Morocco	2008	2008	comply-or-explain on voluntary basis	all companies
58. New Zealand	2004	2014	explain how you comply	all entities accountable to public
59. Nigeria	2003	2014	voluntary – indicated level of compliance	public & listed companies
60. Norway	2004	2014	comply-or-explain	listed companies
61. Oman	2002	2010	mandatory, yet it says you can give reasons for any non-compliance	listed companies
62. Pakistan	2002	2013	statutory rules	public sector companies
63. Peru	2002	2013	comply-or-explain	listed, SOEs and family companies
64. Poland	2002	2012	comply-or-explain	listed companies
65. Portugal	1999	2012	comply-or-explain	listed companies
66. Qatar	2009	2009	comply-or-explain	listed companies
67. Republic of Macedonia	2006	2006	comply-or-explain	listed companies
68. Republic of Maldives	2012	2014	mandatory and voluntary sections	listed companies
69. Romania	2000	2015	comply-or-explain	listed companies
70. Russia	2002	2014	comply-or-explain	listed companies

	First year	Latest year	Approach	Scope
71. Saudi Arabia	2006	2010	comply-or-explain (some mandatory)	listed companies
72. Serbia	2008	2008	comply-or-explain	listed companies
73. Singapore	2001	2012	comply-or-explain	listed companies
74. Slovakia	2002	2008	comply-or-explain	listed companies
75. Slovenia	2004	2009	comply-or-explain	listed companies
76. South Africa	1994	2009	adopt or explain	all entities (public, private or NFP)
77. South Korea	1999	2003	comply-or-explain	listed and public companies
78. Spain	2006	2015	comply-or-explain	listed companies
79. Sri Lanka	1997	2013	mandatory code	listed companies
80. Sweden	2004	2010	comply-or-explain	listed companies
81. Switzerland	2002	2014	comply-or-explain	listed companies
82. Taiwan	2002	2010	comply-or-explain	listed companies
83. Thailand	2002	2012	comply-or-explain	listed companies
84. The Netherlands	2003	2008	comply-or-explain	listed companies
85. The Philippines	2002	2009	mandatory provision of manual to regulator	listed and large companies
86. Trinidad and Tobago	2007	2013	apply or explain	public accountability (listed or fiduciary)
87. Tunisia	2008	2008	voluntary guidelines	all companies
88. Turkey	2003	2014	mandatory dependent on size with some comply or explain	listed companies
89. Ukraine	2003	2003	voluntary comply-or-explain	listed companies (open joint stock companies traded on the stock market)
90. United Arab Emirates	2007	2007	comply-or-explain	joint stock and listed
91. United Kingdom	1992	2014	comply-or-explain	listed companies
92. USA	1997	2013	listing rules	listed companies
93. Yemen	2010	2010	voluntary guidelines	all companies

Despite international agreement on the broad nature of corporate governance through organisations such as the United Nations and Organisation for Economic Co-operation (OECD) corporate governance systems vary across countries reflecting cultural, political and economic differences. The problems that any regulation is designed to resolve and the mechanisms likely to be effective at initiating change will also depend on these national differences (Cuervo 2002; Cankar et al. 2010). Having said this, in the last two decades, most developed countries have introduced a code of corporate governance for companies listed on their national stock exchange (Seidl et al. 2013). Research shows that despite some contextual differences most cover the same core set of governance topics (O'Shea 2005). These include: (1) board composition (balance between executive and non-executive directors); (2) separation of the roles of chair and CEO; (3) systems for ensuring information flow to the board; (4) procedures for appointing new directors; (5) accurate financial reporting; and (6) maintenance of a sound system of internal control (O'Shea 2005). Thus we see the dual aims of corporate governance regulation: to improve internal governance practices and to increase transparency and accountability through public reporting.

Development and reform of corporate governance regulation

Henry Bosch, who produced one of the first reports on corporate governance in Australia, refers to the fact that corporate governance is a modern term, nearing 30 years old: 'Before the crash of 1987 the term corporate governance was rarely used in Australia and few people gave much thought to the concepts now covered by it' (2002, p. 273). This is a similar story worldwide: the development of corporate governance regulation is a relatively recent phenomenon and has tended to be a reactive process responding to bouts of corporate scandals and fear of economic downturn. It has involved both a strengthening of legislated hard law and also development of rules, standards and recommendations by many different organisations at national and international levels. Indeed in most countries, corporate governance reform tends to be cyclical, following the boom and bust of the business cycle (Clarke 2004). When the economy is good, corporate regulation will be left alone, but when the economy falters, governments are placed under pressure to strengthen regulation in order to reduce the risk of similar problems in future.

This chapter takes a chronological journey through corporate governance reform. Starting with the emergence of the term corporate governance in the 1980s it charts Australia's course of regulatory developments, drawing on relevant international developments along the way. As Australian law grew from a mix of English and American influences it is not surprising that corporate governance reforms in both the United Kingdom and United States have been highly influential. The work of international bodies such as the OECD, G20 and European Union has also been taken into account in Australian regulatory reform. At times Australia has been at the forefront of corporate governance innovation, and at other times Australian institutions have been slower to react, benefiting from the lessons learnt elsewhere.

There have been three notable economic downturns relevant to the development of corporate governance regulation in Anglo-American jurisdictions. Each economic crisis has involved significant corporate collapses and then a wave of investigations followed by regulatory reform. The first phase, triggered by the corporate scandals of the 1980s, resulted in Australia's first report dedicated to the topic of corporate governance, published in 1991, and the highly influential UK Cadbury Code, published in 1992. Although there had been use of the term corporate governance in America and the United Kingdom during the 1980s it was the 1990s that marked the birth of the code of corporate governance as it is known today (Mees 2012).

A second phase of corporate governance reform was triggered by the collapse of one of Australia's largest insurance firms, HIH, as well as American giants Enron and Worldcom in 2001. At this stage it became clear that the United States was taking a different regulatory path from that of the United Kingdom and Australia by using prescriptive legislation (the *Sarbanes Oxley Act* of 2004) to implement governance changes rather than a voluntary code. Also at this time, Australia witnessed the anti-social behaviour of James Hardie Industries in underfunding its compensation fund for asbestos-related injuries. This led to an important legal debate over the role of the corporation in society and the links between corporate governance and corporate responsibility.

As corporations and their markets have become more globalised so has the economic effect of their failure. Thus the third phase of reform was cause by a crisis that, although originating in the United States' housing market, had impacts that were felt worldwide (Clarke 2012). The 'global financial crisis' (GFC), which started to spread across the world in 2008, was blamed on excessive risk-taking and disproportionate executive remuneration in the finance sector and triggered regulatory reform across many areas including corporate governance. The international reform agenda led by the G 20 included significant corporate governance changes that have been implemented widely. Table 2.2 summarises some of the key developments in Australian corporate governance reform over the last three decades with reference to significant international events.

Phase one: early development 1990s

The corporate governance movement in Australia was triggered by corporate misbehaviour in the 1980s blamed partly on the hotchpotch of regulators at State level, all with different priorities and inadequate resources, giving free rein to Australia's corporate cowboys (Clarke 2007; Redmond 1991; Sarre 2002). The collapse of prominent business enterprises and reports of unethical behaviour led to two Parliamentary inquiries into directors' duties and corporate practices: The 1989 Cooney Report recommended an objective standard of care for directors; and the 1991 Lavarch Report recommended a stronger enforcement role for the

TABLE 2.2 Corporate governance developments in Australia

Phase one – Early development

1989	Cooney Report	• Company directors' duties
1991	Lavarch Report	• Corporate practices and the rights of shareholders
1991	Bosch Report – Corporate practices and conduct	• Working group, chaired by Henry Bosch – established by Australian Merchant Bankers Association, ASX, AICD, Securities Institute.
		• Its aim was to 'improve the performance and reputation of Australian business by encouraging and assisting the general adoption of the highest standards of corporate conduct'.
		• A response to the abuses of the 1980s
1992	*AWA Ltd v Daniels* (1992) 10 ACLC 933	• Recognised the difficulties in applying directors' duties in practice
		• Led to the Hilmer Report
		• Appealed as *Daniels v Anderson*
1992	UK Cadbury Report	• Became the UK Corporate governance code
1993	Hilmer Report – Strictly boardroom	• Triggered by the AWA case
		• Examined the board's role in ensuring good corporate performance
1995	*Daniels v Anderson* (1995) 13 ACLC 614	• High standards of care and diligence expected of directors
1995	ASX Listing Rule	• Requiring companies to disclose in annual reports the main corporate governance practices that they had in place
1999	OECD Principles of Corporate Governance	• First international code
2001	*Corporations Act*	• Federal legislation replacing various state statutes

Phase two – Post-Enron reforms

April 2003	HIH Royal Commission Report	• Unethical accounting practices • Found a lack of independent board oversight
March 2003	ASX Principles of Good Corporate Governance and Best Practice Recommendations	• Drafted by a collaboration of professional and business organisations • 10 principles and 28 recommendations • Comply-or-explain disclosure mechanism • Legal backing through the listing rules
July 2004	*Sarbanes Oxley Act*	• United States' reform legislation in response to Enron and Worldcom, which was highly criticised
July 2004	*CLERP 9* reforms	• Directors' legal obligations under the *Corporations Act* were clarified and extended in areas relating to disclosure of executive remuneration, financial reporting and continuous disclosure
2004	Jackson Report into James Hardie	• Found a narrow interpretation of directors' duties had been relied upon, focusing on shareholder value
June 2006	Parliamentary Joint Commission Report on Corporate Social Responsibility	• Purpose was to examine 'the extent to which organisational decision-makers should have regard for the interests of stakeholders other than shareholders, and the broader community' • No legal reform recommended
December 2006	CAMAC Report on Corporate Social Responsibility	• Advice requested on 'the extent to which the duties of directors under the *Corporations Act* should include corporate social responsibilities' • No legal reform recommended
August 2007	Second Edition ASX Principles of Corporate Governance	• 10 principles consolidated into 8 principles (still 28 recommendations) • Clarified risk management reporting but rejected inclusion of corporate responsibility reporting

(*Continued*)

Phase three – Reform post-GFC

March 2009	CAMAC Report on Board Diversity	• Looked at the role and structure of boards, the state of diversity on boards and possible ways to recruit and develop a more diverse pool of directors.
June 2009	CAMAC Report on Market Integrity	• Investigation into dubious practices brought to light by the GFC including margin loans, insider trading, analyst briefings.
January 2010	Productivity Commission Report on Executive Remuneration	• Triggered by the GFC findings on excessive pay practices • Inquiry into the regulatory framework surrounding remuneration of directors and executives • Recommended independent remuneration committees, simplification of remuneration disclosures, prohibition of executives voting on the remuneration report and a 'two strike' rule in relation to shareholder votes against remuneration reports
April 2010	CAMAC Report on Guidance for Directors	• Triggered by the GFC and international developments, particularly in the UK – Walker Review 2009 • Asked the question of whether directors need more guidance on how to fulfil their role
2010	*Dodd Frank Act*	• United States reforms
2010	Amendments to Second Edition of ASX Principles of Corporate Governance	• Took into account the various reports above • Introduced reporting on gender diversity, recommended that remuneration committees should comprise a majority of independent directors and made suggestions as to analyst briefings
March 2014	Third Edition of the ASX Principles of Corporate Governance	• Took into account governance issues brought to light by the GFC such as risk management • Also introduced reporting on topical issues such as gender diversity and corporate social responsibility risks

Australian Securities Commission (Corbett and Bottomley 2004). It marked the start of corporate governance and director conduct becoming an issue of public rather than only private concern (Redmond 1991; Corbett and Bottomley 2004).

The economic downturn also provided the trigger for a national system of corporate legislation in Australia and the creation of one lead regulator, the Australian Securities and Investment Commission (ASIC) empowered to enforce both the *Corporations Act 2001* and the listing rules of the Australian Securities Exchange (ASX). In recognition of the need for dynamic legislation, the *Corporate Law Economic Reform Program* (CLERP) was commenced involving regular policy reviews and legislative amendments to the *Corporations Act 2001*. A second regulator, the Australian Prudential Regulatory Authority (APRA) remained responsible for regulation of prudential corporations (banks, insurance companies and pension funds) under the *Banking Act 1959*. This resulted in Australia's 'twin-peak' system of regulation, which has since become seen as a particularly successful regulatory model (Jones 2013).

The main effect of the corporate collapses of the 1980s was that it became difficult for companies to raise capital. The law reform process was painfully slow, so while the legislators drafted and debated, the corporate community decided to take action to improve their own prospects through a form of soft regulation. The first set of Australian corporate governance standards was developed by a working group made up of leading business organisations (the Business Council of Australia, the Australian Institute of Company Directors, the Australian Securities Exchange and professional accounting bodies) who collaborated to publish the document, *Corporate Practices and Conduct* in 1991 (Bosch 2002, p. 274). Commonly known as the Bosch Report (after the group's chairman, Henry Bosch) this document was revised and updated in 1993 following publication of the UK's *Cadbury Report on the Financial Aspects of Corporate Governance* in 1992 (Cadbury Report) and revised further in 1995. It marked the beginning of 'soft law' regulation of corporate governance, which continues in Australia today.

Another influential report produced by a working group chaired by Fredrick Hilmer was triggered by a court case (*AWA Ltd v Daniels* appealed as *Daniels v Anderson*), which caused considerable concern amongst Australian directors when it investigated the nature of directors' duties and, on appeal, set a high duty of care. The Hilmer Report, published in 1993, investigated the contemporary role of the board, determining that it was to ensure that management was striving for above-average corporate performance. The five key roles of the board were described as: appointing the CEO and other staff; strategy and policy; budgeting and planning; reporting to shareholders including regulatory compliance; and ensuring their own effectiveness. The role of the board, and factors contributing to its effectiveness, are discussed further in Chapter 5.

During the same period in the UK, Sir Adrian Cadbury was asked to lead an industry-supported committee tasked with examining the financial aspects of corporate governance following the collapse of companies such as Polly Peck and BCCI due to fraud. The Cadbury committee, set up in 1991, drafted the

1992 Code of Best Practice, which provided boards with a checklist to enable them to assess where they stood against best practice. The Code was backed by the London Stock Exchange rules with compliance to be encouraged through comply-or-explain disclosures. Since then, the UK Corporate Governance Code has been regularly reviewed, refined and developed based on the results of several other reviews, notably the Greenbury Report on executive compensation (1995), the follow-up Hampel Report (1998), the Turnbull Report on guidance for directors (1999), the Myners Report on institutional investors (2001), the Higgs Report on the role of non-executive directors (2003), the Smith Report on auditors (2003), the Walker review of the financial sector (2009) and the Davies Report on gender diversity (2011).

Also, in 1999, the first international standard for corporate governance was published. The OECD Principles of Corporate Governance (revised in 2004 and again in 2015) have become an important benchmark for corporate governance, forming the basis for regulatory initiatives in many countries worldwide. Indeed, they have been said to reflect a global consensus regarding the critical importance of good corporate governance in contributing to the economic vitality and stability of our economies (Jesover and Kirkpatrick 2005).

The way in which these early codes of corporate governance came into existence highlights some of the reasons they have become a popular policy choice. First, good corporate governance is valuable to both companies and markets. This win-win nature makes it a topic suitable for soft regulation because there are internal incentives to make changes as well as external. Second, the advantage of codes over law is their ability to be drafted and revised relatively quickly so that they can remain up-to-date and relevant to current practice. The comply-or-explain mechanism has been seen to reflect a cost-effective balance between rules and principles, encouraging change through information disclosure whilst permitting flexibility.

Phase two: post Enron reforms 2001–2007

The next major economic crisis in 2001 was caused by the collapse of large companies HIH Insurance and OneTel in Australia as well as US companies Enron and Worldcom. These corporate collapses were blamed primarily on misleading and unethical accounting practices. In Australia, a Royal Commission headed by Justice Owen was established to investigate the collapse of the HIH Insurance Group. The Commission found that there was a lack of independent board oversight and no testing of the practical effectiveness of the company's governance model.

Corporate governance reforms in both Australia and the US focused on the audit process and better monitoring of corporate managers. There was a strong emphasis on increasing the number of independent directors on boards and improving the independence of auditors. In the US this was done through the *Sarbanes Oxley Act* of 2004 and in Australia, through amendments to the *Corporations*

Act 2001 as well as publication by the Australian Securities Exchange (ASX) of Australia's first official code of corporate governance, the 'Principles of Good Corporate Governance and Best Practice Recommendations' in March 2003. Now revised and updated, this document remains Australia's primary corporate governance standard and has been highly influential in developing corporate practice.

Soft law: corporate governance codes

The Australian corporate governance code provides an extensive framework for good corporate governance by setting out eight broad principles together with more detailed recommendations for putting them into effect. They cover topics such as board composition, director independence, financial reporting, business ethics, market disclosure, communication with shareholders, risk management and fair remuneration. Since its first publication in 2003 the Australian code has been revised three times: a second edition was published in 2007; this was amended in 2010, and a third edition was published in 2014. Table 2.3 summarises the content of the 2010 edition of the Australian code because this was the version in force at the time of collecting the research data for this book. The UK code has been revised more frequently, but its main sections consistently cover the same topics: board composition, remuneration, accountability and audit, and relations with shareholders. The 2015 edition of the OECD Principles covers a similar list of topics: the rights of shareholders and wider stakeholders; timely and accurate disclosure of information; and the responsibilities and independence of the board. As pointed out by researchers, there seems to be a core set of governance topics covered by most codes (Aguillera and Cuervo-Cazurra 2009; O'Shea 2005).

Legal context of the ASX Code

Following the UK approach, the Australian code is not law but was drafted by the ASX Corporate Governance Council (CGC), a body made up of representatives from 21 business organisations promoting the interests of a wide range of groups such as shareholders, directors, accountants and superannuation funds. The CGC reports to the ASX which is a commercial entity licensed under section 795B(1) of the *Corporations Act 2001* as a market operator. The ASX code does not apply to all companies, only those who choose to list on the Securities Exchange. This means that the code provisions do not have direct legal effect – the limited legal force behind them comes primarily from the ASX listing rules. Listing rule 4.10.3 requires listed companies to disclose the extent to which they have adopted the code recommendations and to explain any departures from the code. This does not mean listed companies must adopt each of the recommended governance practices: it is possible to fully comply with rule 4.10.3 by giving an explanation of why each recommendation has not been followed.

TABLE 2.3 The Australian corporate governance principles and recommendations (2nd edition with 2010 amendments)

1	Lay solid foundations for management and oversight
1.1	Companies should establish the functions reserved to the board and those delegated to senior executives and disclose those functions.
1.2	Companies should disclose the process for evaluating the performance of senior executives.
1.3	Companies should provide the information indicated in the Guide to reporting on Principle 1.

2	Structure the board to add value
2.1	A majority of the board should be independent directors.
2.2	The chair should be an independent director.
2.3	The roles of chair and chief executive officer should not be exercised by the same individual.
2.4	The board should establish a nomination committee.
2.5	Companies should disclose the process for evaluating the performance of the board, its committees and individual directors.
2.6	Companies should provide the information indicated in the Guide to reporting on Principle 2.

3	Promote ethical and responsible decision-making
3.1	Companies should establish a code of conduct and disclose the code or a summary of the code as to: – the practices necessary to maintain confidence in the companies' integrity – the practices necessary to take into account their legal obligations and the reasonable expectations of their stakeholders – the responsibility and accountability of individuals for reporting and investigating reports of unethical practices.
3.2	Companies should establish a policy concerning diversity and disclose the policy or a summary of that policy. The policy should include requirements for the board to establish measurable objectives for achieving gender diversity for the board to assess annually both the objectives and progress in achieving them.
3.3	Companies should disclose in each annual report the measurable objectives for achieving gender diversity set by the board in accordance with the diversity policy and progress towards achieving them.
3.4	Companies should disclose in each annual report the proportion of women employees in the whole organisation, women in senior executive positions and women on the board.
3.5	Companies should provide the information indicated in the Guide to reporting on Principle 3.

4	Safeguard integrity in financial reporting
4.1	The board should establish an audit committee.
4.2	The audit committee should be structured so that it:
	– consists only of non-executive directors
	– consists of a majority of independent directors
	– is chaired by an independent chair, who is not chair of the board
	– has at least three members.
4.3	The audit committee should have a formal charter.
4.4	Companies should provide the information indicated in the Guide to reporting on Principle 4.
5	Make timely and balanced disclosure
5.1	Companies should establish written policies designed to ensure compliance with ASX Listing Rule disclosure requirements and to ensure accountability at a senior executive level for that compliance and disclose those policies or a summary of those policies
5.2	Companies should provide the information indicated in the Guide to reporting on Principle 5.
6	Respect the rights of shareholders
6.1	Companies should design a communications policy for promoting effective communication with shareholders and encouraging their participation at general meetings and disclose their policy or a summary of that policy.
6.2	Companies should provide the information indicated in the Guide to reporting on Principle 6.
7	Recognise and manage risk
7.1	Companies should establish policies for the oversight and management of material business risks and disclose a summary of those policies.
7.2	The board should require management to design and implement the risk management and internal control system to manage the company's material business risks and report to it on whether those risks are being managed effectively. The board should disclose that management has reported to it as to the effectiveness of the company's management of its material business risks.

(*Continued*)

7.3	The board should disclose whether it has received assurance from the chief executive officer (or equivalent) and the chief financial officer (or equivalent) that the declaration provided in accordance with section 295A of the Corporations Act is founded on a sound system of risk management and internal control and that the system is operating effectively in all material respects in relation to financial reporting risks.
7.4	Companies should provide the information indicated in the Guide to reporting on Principle 7.
8	**Remunerate fairly and responsibly**
8.1	The board should establish a remuneration committee.
8.2	The remuneration committee should be structured so that it: – consists of a majority of independent directors – is chaired by an independent chair – has at least three members.
8.3	Companies should clearly distinguish the structure of non-executive directors' remuneration from that of executive directors and senior executives.
8.4	Companies should provide the information indicated in the Guide to reporting on Principle 8.

(The only exception to this is in relation to audit committees where listing rule 12.7 requires mandatory compliance for larger companies.)

This comply-or-explain mechanism does not mandate or prescribe good governance but gives guidance on practices likely to amount to good governance. By forcing disclosure, the system allows investors to decide how much importance to place on a company's governance practices. Discretion is granted to the companies: to either follow the code or explain why they have taken an alternative approach. In a strict legal sense, *adoption* of the ASX Principles is entirely voluntary, only *disclosure* is required by the listing rules. The pressure to demonstrate that a company has good governance is designed to come from market forces rather than legal sanctions.

Hard law: CLERP 9 and SOX

Although the ASX code is the primary regulatory mechanism used to influence corporate board structures and processes, there have also been developments in Australia's hard law dealing with corporate governance. At around the same time as the first edition of the ASX code was being developed, the ninth policy paper in the corporate law economic reform program (CLERP 9) proposed various changes to the *Corporations Act 2001* focusing on governance.

CLERP 9 came into force in 2004 and made amendments to the *Corporations Act* in four areas: executive remuneration, financial reporting, continuous disclosure and shareholder participation. The amendments regarding remuneration required companies to include within their annual directors' report a remuneration report setting out details of senior executive and director remuneration. This caused quite a stir as it required previously confidential information to be publicly disclosed. Discussed further in Chapter 8, there was debate over whether it would act as a restraint on excessive remuneration or place pressure on companies to meet higher competitor salaries. When the amendments were introduced, the Regulatory Impact Statement explained that the legislation 'does not seek to intervene in the market by placing limits on the quantum of director or executive remuneration'. Instead the amendments were aimed at ensuring transparency to enable shareholders to make informed decisions about the remuneration policies of companies.

Shareholder activism in Australia had not been strong, and so CLERP 9 also introduced various provisions aimed at encouraging, or at least enabling, shareholder participation in corporate governance. For example, it set out requirements for AGM notices to be clear and concise and for the auditor to be available at the AGM to answer questions. These were hardly radical solutions at a time when practitioners were wondering 'Is the AGM dead?' (Chartered secretaries 2006). It seems likely that the Internet may prove a more effective tool in promoting shareholder participation. Information is readily available on company websites, and many companies now produce web-casts of their AGM and email updates of ASX announcements. Activist groups, representing both shareholders and other stakeholders, can readily communicate their policies and strategies through online forums.

Despite their status as 'hard law', many of the CLERP 9 amendments were based on a similar principle to the Australian corporate governance code – requiring disclosure of practices rather than prescribing those practices. The CLERP 9 provisions do not permit explanations for deviations in practice quite like the ASX code but generally do not prescribe in detail how companies must arrange their internal affairs. The Australian approach overall is one of flexible regulation designed to leave much of the enforcement to the market. As discussed further in Chapter 3, this regulatory approach has been termed decentred, responsive or smart regulation (Black 2002; Braithwaite 2011; Gunningham and Grabosky 1998).

United States' approach

Although the New York Stock Exchange includes a set of core corporate governance requirements in its listing rules, the United States remains unusual in that it has no national code of corporate governance (Haskovec 2012). Instead, the alternative regulatory approach of using black-letter, prescriptive law is used. The *Sarbanes Oxley Act* of 2002 (SOX) prescribes governance practices enforced by way of penalties for non-compliance (McDonnell 2004). As a Federal Act, its introduction marked a significant change in United States corporate regulation as it removed much of the 'contractual choice' that existed previously whereby firms could decide whether to be subject to a body of rules through their choice of which state to incorporate in and on which exchange to list their company (Ribstein 2002). SOX involved some delegation to the Securities and Exchange Commission (SEC), which had to set large numbers of rules to implement the Act.

SOX was a direct response to the collapse of companies such as Enron and WorldCom and was highly criticised as a knee-jerk reaction imposing unreasonable costs on business (Ribstein 2002). In particular, section 404 of SOX, requiring companies to implement internal control systems, was said to be unduly onerous and costly, particularly for smaller companies (Glassman 2006). It was accused of inappropriately shifting the focus of corporate governance from a top-down, risk-based management perspective to a bottom-up 'check the box' auditor perspective. Roberta Romano, in her extensive analysis of the substantive provisions of SOX, concluded that it was destined to fail because its makers did not take into account any of the empirical research that had been carried out in the area. She considers that the more efficacious corporate governance regimes are the product of competitive legal systems that allow legal innovations to percolate from the bottom up by trial and error rather than being imposed from the top down by regulators (Romano 2005). Larry Ribstein (2002) argues that less regulation and more market scrutiny is the answer. Chapter 9 explores these regulatory issues in more detail based on the research findings presented in Chapters 5 to 8.

Corporate social responsibility and directors' duties

The concept of corporate social responsibility (CSR) came to the forefront of the Australian public's consciousness in late 2003, primarily because of media coverage of dubious ethical behaviour on the part of a well-known corporation, James Hardie Industries Limited (Nolan 2007). The parent company, seeking to limit its liability to compensate hundreds of former employees for asbestos-related disease, created a compensation fund that was found to be significantly underendowed. At the same time the company restructured, moving its headquarters to the Netherlands, thereby ensuring that group assets were out of the reach of terminally ill claimants (Redmond 2012).

An Australian Government inquiry, led by David Jackson QC, examined the company's actions and an extensive report was published in late 2004 (Jackson Report). This report identified several deficiencies in Australian law that had permitted, if not encouraged, James Hardie's irresponsible behaviour. These included the use of the corporate group structure to shield future profits from asbestos liabilities and the narrow interpretation of directors' duties focusing entirely on shareholder value (Jackson 2004). Thus it was during Phase 2 of the corporate governance reform movement that the issue of corporate responsibility moved into regulatory focus in Australia. It was alleged that the Hardie directors believed they were under a legal duty to prioritise shareholder value over other stakeholders' interests. This prompted a flurry of intellectual and investigative activity into potential legal reform. In 2005 and 2006 the Australian business community was invited to make submissions to not one but four reviews stemming from the findings of the James Hardie inquiry:

- Corporations and Markets Advisory Committee (CAMAC) inquiry into 'the extent to which the duties of directors under the *Corporations Act 2001* should include corporate social responsibilities'. CAMAC released a discussion paper in November 2005 and then a final report in December 2006.
- Parliamentary Joint Committee on Corporations and Financial Services (PJC) inquiry into corporate responsibility. Its purpose was to examine 'the extent to which organisational decision-makers should have regard for the interests of stakeholders other than shareholders, and the broader community'. The PJC issued its final report in June 2006.
- Australian Stock Exchange (ASX) consultation paper on whether the ASX Corporate Governance Council should include sustainability/corporate responsibility reporting in the ASX corporate governance code.
- Corporations and Markets Advisory Committee's inquiry into long-tail liabilities. A more specific inquiry into how tort law ought to deal with asbestos liability, particularly the long time-gap between cause and effect.

The first two of these were major inquiries into the legal framework surrounding CSR, both focusing on the scope of directors' duties under the *Corporations*

Act 2001 as well as the framework for corporate reporting on CSR. The relevant duties of Australian company directors are 'to act in good faith in the best interests of the company' and 'for a proper purpose'. These duties exist as fiduciary duties under the common law and are codified in sections 180 and 181 of the *Corporations Act 2001*. Until the 1980s these duties, especially the duty of care, were viewed as a relatively undemanding performance standard, used infrequently by shareholders in private actions against directors in circumstances of extreme neglect or obvious wrong-doing (Corbett and Bottomley 2004, p. 67). Only as companies got larger and more powerful did it become obvious that the general public might also be concerned by the actions of directors.

There has been relatively little case law in Australia expanding on the detailed meaning of directors' duties, although it was for many years understood that the 'interests of the company' equated to the interests of its shareholders as a general group rather than the company as a firm (Redmond 2012; Kingsford Smith 2012). This principle of 'shareholder primacy' has been much debated in recent years across all Anglo-American jurisdictions in terms of whether companies and their directors should be accountable, not only to shareholders but to local communities and the environment.

Both Australian inquiry reports suggested there may be an implied duty on directors to take these other stakeholders into account on the basis that doing so is likely to be in the long-term interests of the company and its shareholders. The view was that the law permits flexibility and does not restrict directors from taking non-shareholder interests into account. As the CAMAC report said, 'The established formulation of directors' duties allows directors sufficient flexibility to take relevant interests and broader community considerations into account' (2006, p. 7). This means that taking action to reduce damage to the environment or to treat employees equitably (to the extent this is over and above what is required by environmental or employment law) is an optional choice for companies, motivated by a desire to improve corporate reputation and/or long-term sustainability (Sneirson 2009). Recent case law on the topic supports this view. Justice Owen commented in 2008 that, although the established position is that 'a reflection of the interests of the company may be seen in the interests of shareholders', this does not mean that 'the general body of shareholders is always and for all purposes the embodiment of the company as a whole' (Marshall and Ramsay 2009). In short, directors are permitted to take different stakeholder interests into account but only to the point that this can be argued to be good for long-term shareholder wealth (Redmond 2012, p. 324). It would be hard for directors to make decisions that treat the well-being of employees or the environment as the primary cause for action (unless based on other legal obligations under employment or environmental law). Marshall and Ramsay explain that, 'the extension of *duties* of directors has not been attended by the extension of *rights* for stakeholders' (Marshall and Ramsay 2012). This could potentially make it hard for a director to know what to do when balancing different interests (Redmond 2012). The CAMAC report confirmed that directors have wide discretion in how they interpret their duties: 'it is the role of the directors to determine what is in the best interests of the company, unless no reasonable director could have reached the decision' (2006, p. 91).

What is interesting is that, in the absence of judicial precedent on what it takes for a director to fulfil his or her duties, it can be soft law that fills the gap. In two recent cases surrounding breach of directors' duties, corporate governance guidelines were relevant in determining the responsibilities of a non-executive chairman (*ASIC v Rich* 2003; and *ASIC v Healey (No2)* 2011). Chapter 7 explores the role of the board in corporate responsibility including the influence of corporate governance codes and other soft law instruments on corporate behaviour.

Phase three: reform post-global financial crisis

As already indicated, corporate governance regulation has a tendency to wax and wane in line with the economic fortunes of the time. In times of crisis and collapse there is public pressure to increase regulation to resolve the perceived causes of the crisis. Thus, it was not surprising that internationally there were calls for corporate governance reform following the global financial crisis (GFC) that began in 2008. Australia went through the crisis relatively unscathed as compared to many countries, meaning that most reforms were initiated internationally or in the US and UK.

The GFC had many causes including a lack of oversight of macro-economic risk and a general trend towards excessive risk-taking and overly complex financial products (Clarke 2012). Corporate governance reforms worldwide focused on executive remuneration systems with the objective of ensuring they could no longer encourage irresponsible risk-taking. In the US, the much criticised *Dodd Frank Act* was passed in 2010, whereas in the UK and Australia reforms involved amendments to the stock exchanges' existing corporate governance principles. This confirmed the clear difference in the approach taken to corporate governance regulation in the US as compared to the UK and Australia. Despite criticism of the *Sarbanes Oxley Act*, the United States has continued to pass long and prescriptive legislation, whereas the UK and Australia have dealt with the issues through softer regulation and strong input from the business community.

The GFC was a crisis of such magnitude that corporate governance was not the first priority of most governments. The immediate response in most countries was to take emergency measures to rescue vital institutions and stimulate economic recovery. Only after these initial measures had been put in place was attention diverted to regulatory and financial market reform including issues of corporate governance (Nanto 2009). Indeed, poor corporate governance was identified, in combination with weak supervisory authorities and excessive risk-taking, as one of the causes of the crisis (Kirkpatrick 2009). A good deal of blame was placed on boards of directors for failing to properly supervise risk management and incentive systems. Kirkpatrick, in his report for the OECD, identified credit rating agencies, disclosure regimes and accounting standards as contributing to the problem but considered that a good board ought to have been able to overcome these weaknesses:

> [There were] significant failures of risk management systems in some major financial institutions made worse by incentive systems that encouraged and rewarded high levels of risk-taking. Since reviewing and guiding risk policy is a key function of the board, these deficiencies point to ineffective board oversight.

(Kirkpatrick 2009)

As appropriate for a global crisis, the reform agenda was led by international institutions including the G20 and the OECD. The main corporate governance aspect of the G20 action plan was a focus on remuneration policy that had a strong influence on activity at the national level, particularly in the US where there had been reluctance to regulate in this area. The Financial Stability Forum (FSF) Principles for Sound Compensation Practices, published in April 2009, which all G20 countries agreed to implement, were intended to be applied to significant financial institutions. They required: (1) boards of directors to play an active role in the design, operation and evaluation of compensation schemes; (2) compensation arrangements (including bonuses) to properly reflect risk; and (3) firms to publicly disclose clear, comprehensive and timely information about compensation.

On 18 March 2009, the OECD held a conference in Paris to discuss monitoring, implementation and enforcement of corporate governance as well as possible reforms and improvements to the OECD Principles of Corporate Governance in light of the crisis. Priority areas for reform were listed as including: 'board practices, implementation of risk management, governance of the remuneration process and the exercise of shareholder rights'. However after consideration of these issues, an OECD Steering Group concluded that there was no need to change the Principles, rather, '[a] more urgent challenge for the Steering Group is to encourage and support effective implementation of already agreed standards' (2009, p. 7). Nevertheless, in 2014 a review process was initiated resulting in a revised 2015 version of the Principles. Commentary was added to the introduction regarding the value of flexible soft law including comply-or-explain codes, cementing their place in corporate governance regulation. The main changes stemming from the GFC were additional provisions on the regulation of stock markets, the integrity of supervisory authorities and cross-border co-operation. At a company level the amendments entrenched the G20 recommendations regarding executive remuneration as well as picking up on the emerging norms of incorporating gender diversity and corporate responsibility into codes of governance.

In the US regulatory reforms were effected through hard law. The *Dodd Frank Act 2010* introduced significant changes that applied to all public companies, not just the financial sector:

- 'say on pay' – the Act introduced a non-binding shareholder vote on executive compensation;
- increased disclosure on the relationship between executive compensation and the financial performance of the company, including policy on the recovery of incentive-based compensation (compensation 'claw-backs');
- disclosure of the annual total compensation of the CEO including a comparison of the ratio to the annual median total compensation of all other company employees;
- disclosure of whether any employee or director is permitted to hedge any decrease in the market value of company equity securities;
- a requirement that compensation committees be comprised entirely of independent directors;
- disclosures regarding the independence of any compensation consultants employed;
- disclosure of whether and why a company has chosen to combine or separate the roles of CEO and chairman of the board; and
- a requirement that certain banks and financial companies establish risk committees.

(Brown 2010)

Relatively early on in the process, a Congressional research paper commented that 'a large question for Congress may be how US regulations might be changed and how closely any changes are harmonised with international norms and standards' (Nanto 2009). Interestingly, the introduction of better compensation practices came under the White Paper's 'improve international cooperation' section and was clearly a matter that may not have been included were it not for US involvement in the G20:

> In line with G20 commitments, we urge each national authority to put guidelines in place to align compensation with long-term shareholder value and to promote compensation structures that do not provide incentives for excessive risk-taking. We recommend that the BCBS [Basel Committee on Banking Supervision] expediently integrate the FSB principles on compensation into its risk management guidance by the end of 2009.
>
> (US Treasury 2009)

The UK and Australia already had most of these corporate governance practices in place through either company law or corporate governance codes. Consequently, the focus was more on how the board ought to ensure such practices are implemented and enforced. In February 2009, the UK government announced a review of bank governance led by Sir David Walker. The final recommendations were set out under five headings:

- board size, composition and qualifications;
- functioning of the board and evaluation of performance;

- the role of institutional shareholders: communication and engagement;
- governance of risk; and
- remuneration.

(Walker 2009)

There were recommendations aimed at improving the skills of non-executive directors through professional development to ensure that they are 'ready, able and encouraged to challenge and test proposals on strategy put forward by the executive'. The report acknowledged the pivotal role of the chairman of the board and suggested that chairmen be put forward for election on an annual basis. The review also strongly recommended regular board evaluations and better disclosure to investors regarding such evaluation. It was partly this renewed focus on board performance that led to the research described in Chapter 4, which explores the effectiveness of regulation encouraging board performance evaluations.

As stated above, a comply-or-explain system relies on there being market demand for good corporate governance, monitored by the active engagement of investors. An interesting development stemming from the Walker Review was the introduction of the UK Stewardship code for investors, which aims to enhance the quality of engagement between companies and institutional investors. The Stewardship code complements the UK corporate governance code and, like the corporate governance code, is designed to be applied on a comply-or-explain basis. The Stewardship code comprises seven key principles encouraging investors to monitor their investee companies and disclose their policy on discharging their stewardship responsibilities (including voting policy and guidelines on when and how they will escalate their activities as a method of protecting and enhancing shareholder value). Investors are encouraged to publish, on their websites, statements that explain the extent to which they have complied with the code. The reasoning behind this was a belief that institutional shareholders may have contributed to the global financial crisis by being too short-term in their investment policies and failing to monitor their investments actively enough (Cheffins 2010). Cuomo et al. (2016) note that, by the end of 2014, 20 countries had adopted similar codes directed at institutional investors, suggesting that this lack of engagement was not unique to the UK.

In Australia, post-GFC reforms were focused on the area of executive remuneration. In March 2009, the Productivity Commission was asked by the Federal Government to undertake an inquiry into the existing Australian regulatory framework surrounding remuneration of directors and executives. This request was triggered by the growing recognition internationally that remuneration practices were a contributing factor to the financial crisis:

> Unrestrained greed in the financial sector has led to the biggest global recession since World War II. It has now spread across the world and instigated significant slowdowns in the US, Europe, China and caused more than 50 banks to collapse and millions of jobs to be lost. There is significant

community concern about excessive pay practices, particularly at a time when many Australian families are being hit by the global recession

(Australian Treasury 2009)

The Commission's main recommendations (released in January 2010) were that ASX 300 companies should be required to have a remuneration committee comprised of at least three non-executive directors including an independent chair and majority of independent members. Also, executives should be prohibited from voting their shares in relation to the remuneration report and any related resolutions. The Commission accepted concerns that remuneration reports were becoming increasingly complex and suggested they should include a plain English summary and actual levels of remuneration received (rather than the accounting cost to the company). Lastly, as discussed further in Chapter 8, the Commission put forward some novel proposals to give bite to the non-binding shareholder vote on the remuneration report.

Summary of chapter 2

The aim of this chapter was to explain how codes of corporate governance have developed over the last 20 or more years. This sets the scene for the empirical findings presented in Chapters 5 to 8, which explore the corporate response to specific code recommendations thereby enabling an assessment of their effectiveness. In making such assessment it is essential to keep in mind the broad purpose of corporate governance regulation – to improve long-term corporate performance and reduce the likelihood of corporate failure – as well as the more narrow aims of each recommendation. A strong focus of corporate governance codes is to facilitate and improve board performance; however, in recent years codes have begun to touch on wider issues of corporate responsibility and ethics. Despite ongoing development and reform of corporate governance codes, there is still scant research into how they work in practice and the conditions in which they are most effective. Chapter 4 describes the role of research in furthering our understanding of this relatively new form of regulation.

References

Aguilera, RV & Cuervo-Cazurra, A 2009, 'Codes of good governance', *Corporate Governance: An International Review*, vol. 17, pp. 376–87.

ASX 2007, 'Response to submissions on review of Corporate Governance Principles and Recommendations' (August 2007).

ASX Corporate Governance Council 2014, *Corporate Governance Principles and Recommendations* (ASX, 3rd ed, March 2014).

Australian Government 2009, The Treasury, 'Productivity Commission and Alan Fels to examine Executive Remuneration', Media Release, 8 June.

AWA Ltd v Daniels (Trading as Deloitte Haskins & Sells & Ors 1992, 7 ACSR 759; *Daniels v Anderson* 1995, 13 ACLC 614.

Black, J 2002, 'Critical reflections on regulation', *Australian Journal of Legal Philosophy*, vol. 27, pp. 1–35.

Bosch, H 2002, 'The changing face of corporate governance' *University of New South Wales Law Journal*, vol. 25, no. 2, pp. 270–93.

Braithwaite, J 2011, 'The essence of responsive regulation', *University of British Columbia Law Review*, vol. 44, p. 475.

Brown, M 2010, *The Dodd-Frank Wall Street Reform and Consumer Protection Act, Understanding the New Financial Reform Legislation* (9 July 2010).

CAMAC, '*The Social Responsibility of Corporations*', December 2006.

CAMAC, *Long–tail Liabilities: the treatment of unascertained future personal injury claims*, 12 June 2008.

Cankar, NK, Deakin S & Simoneti, M 2010, 'The reflexive properties of Corporate Governance Codes: the reception of the 'comply-or-explain' approach in Slovenia', *Journal of Law and Society*, vol. 37, no. 3, pp. 501–25.

Chartered Secretaries 2006, *Annual Governance Symposium*.

Cheffins, BR 2010, 'The Stewardship Code's Achilles' heel', *The Modern Law Review*, vol. 73, no. 6, pp. 985–1025.

Clarke, T 2004, 'Cycles of Crisis and Regulation: the enduring agency and stewardship problems of corporate governance', *Corporate Governance: An International Review*, vol. 12, no. 2, pp. 153–161.

Clarke, T 2007, *International Corporate Governance: a comparative approach*, London: Routledge.

Clarke, T 2012, 'Markets regulation and governance: the causes of the global financial crisis', in D Branson and T Clarke (eds.) *The SAGE Handbook of Corporate Governance*, Thousand Oaks, CA: SAGE, pp. 533–55.

Cooney Report 1989, Parliament of the Commonwealth of Australia, Senate Standing Committee on Legal and Constitutional Affairs, *Company Directors' Duties: Report on the Social And Fiduciary Duties and Obligations of Company Directors*, Canberra: Australian Government Publishing Service.

Corbett, A & Bottomley, S 2004, 'Regulating corporate governance', in C Parker, C Scott, N Lacey & J Braithwaite (eds.), *Regulating Law*, Oxford: Oxford University Press.

Cuervo, A 2002, 'Corporate governance mechanisms: a plea for less code of good governance and more market control', *Corporate Governance: An International Review*, vol. 10, no. 2, pp. 84–93.

Cuomo, F, Mallin, C & Zattoni, A 2016, 'Corporate governance codes: a review and research agenda', *Corporate Governance: An International Review*, forthcoming.

Davies, M 2011, *Women on Boards*, Department for Business, Innovation and Skills.

European Corporate Governance Institute, http://www.ecgi.org/codes/all_codes.php.

Financial Reporting Council 2012, *Comply or Explain: 20th anniversary of the UK corporate governance code*, London: London Stock Exchange.

Glassman, C 2006, 'Internal controls over financial reporting – putting Sarbanes Oxley Section 404 in perspective' (Speech delivered at the Twelfth Annual CFO Summit, Tampa, Florida 8 May 2006).

Greenbury, R 1995, *Directors Remuneration Report of a Study Group chaired by Sir Richard Greenbury*.

Gunningham, N & Grabosky, P 1998, *Smart Regulation,* Oxford: Clarendon Press.

Hampel, R 1998, *Final Report – Committee on Corporate Governance*.

Haskovec, N 2012, *Codes of Corporate Governance: A Review*, Working Paper, Millstein Center for Corporate Governance and Performance, June 2012.

Higgs, D 2003, *Independent review of non-executive directors*.

Hilmer, FG 1993, *Strictly Boardroom: improving governance to enhance company performance*, Melbourne: Business Library.

Jackson, D 2004, *Report of the Special Commission of Inquiry into the Medical Research and Compensation Foundation* para. 30.67.

Jesover, F & Kirkpatrick, G 2005, 'The revised OECD principles of corporate governance and their relevance to non-OECD countries', *Corporate Governance: An International Review,* vol. 13, no. 2, pp. 127–36.

Jones, E 2013, 'Australia and the GFC – why did we fare so well?' 15 November, *Sydney Law School*, available at <http://sydney.edu.au/news/law/436.html?newsstoryid=12677>.

Kingsford Smith, D 2012, 'Governing the corporation: the role of 'soft regulation'', *University of New South Wales Law Journal*, vol. 35, no. 1, pp. 378–403.

Kirkpatrick, G 2009, *Corporate Governance Lessons from the Financial Crisis*, OECD.

Lavarch Report, 1991, House of Representatives Standing Committee on Legal and Constitutional Affairs, *Corporate Practices and the Rights of Shareholders*, Canberra: Australian Government Publishing Service.

Marshall, S & Ramsay, I 2009, 'Shareholders and directors' duties: law, theory and evidence' (Melbourne Law School, Legal Studies Research Paper No. 411, June 2009) 10. *Discussing The Bell Group Ltd (in liq) v Westpac Banking Corporation* [No 9] [2008] WASC 239, [4392–3].

Marshall, S & Ramsay, I 2012, 'Stakeholders and directors' duties: law theory and evidence' *University of New South Wales Law Journal,* vol. 35, pp. 291–316.

McDonnell, B 2004, 'Sarbanes-Oxley, fiduciary duties and the conduct of officers and directors' (Research Paper No. 04–13, University of Minnesota Law School, Legal Studies Research Paper Series).

Mees, B 2012, 'Corporate governance as a reform movement', *Journal of Management History,* vol. 21, no. 2, p. 194.

Myners, P 2001, *Institutional Investment in the United Kingdom: A Review*.

Nanto, DK 2009, *The Global Financial Crisis: Analysis and Policy Implications,* Congressional Research Service, 2 October 2009.

Nolan, J 2007, 'Corporate responsibility in Australia, rhetoric or reality?' (Paper 47, University of New South Wales Faculty of Law Research Series).

O'Shea, N 2005, 'Governance: how we've got where we are and what's next', *Accountancy Ireland*, vol. 37, pp. 33–37.

OECD 2009, *Corporate Governance and the Financial Crisis: Key Findings and Main Messages*.

PJC Parliamentary Joint Committee 2006, '*Report on Corporate Responsibility*'.

Redmond, P 1991, 'The reform of directors' duties', *University of New South Wales Law Journal*, vol. 15, no. 1, pp. 86–151.

Redmond, P 2012, 'Directors' duties and corporate social responsiveness', *University of New South Wales Law Journal*, vol. 35, pp. 317–40.

Ribstein, LE 2002, 'Market vs regulatory responses to corporate fraud: a critique of the Sarbanes-Oxley Act of 2002', *Journal of Corporate Law*, vol. 28, p. 1.

Romano, R 2005, 'The Sarbanes-Oxley Act and the making of quack corporate governance', *The Yale Law Journal*, vol. 114, no. 7, pp. 1521–1611.

Sarre, R 2002, 'Responding to corporate collapses: is there a role for corporate social responsibility?', *Deakin Law Review*, vol. 7, no. 1, pp. 1–19.

Seidl, D, Sanderson, P & Roberts, J 2013, 'Applying the 'comply-or-explain' principle: discursive legitimacy tactics with regard to codes of corporate governance', *Journal of Management and Governance*, vol. 17, no. 3, pp. 791–826.

Smith, R 2003, *Audit Committees Combined Code Guidance*.

Sneirson, JF 2009, 'Green is good: sustainability, profitability, and a new paradigm for corporate governance', *Iowa Law Review*, vol. 94, no. 3, pp. 987–1022.

Turnbull, N, *Internal Control: Guidance for Directors on the Combined Code*.

Tyson, L 2003, *The Tyson Report on the Recruitment and Development of Non-Executive Directors*, London: London Business School.

US Treasury 2009, *Financial Regulatory Reform: a new foundation rebuilding financial supervision and regulation*.

Walker, D 2009, *A review of corporate governance in UK banks and other financial industry entities* (July 2009).

3

THEORIES OF CORPORATE GOVERNANCE AND ITS REGULATION

Introduction

This chapter introduces some of the academic theories surrounding corporate governance and its regulation. Theories are put forward by scholars as ways of understanding observed behaviour so as to better predict what might happen in similar situations. Corley and Gioia define theory as 'a statement of concepts and their interrelationships that shows how and/or why a phenomenon occurs' (2011, p. 12). An even broader definition describes theory as 'any coherent description or explanation of observed or experienced phenomena' (Gioia and Pitre 1990, p. 587). There are several reasons a discussion of theory is an essential part of this book. As these definitions make clear, theory and practice are closely connected: empirical evidence both inspires and tests theory. Eisenhardt (1989) reminds us of the importance of empirical research in developing testable, relevant and valid theory. Empirical evidence permits us to develop and improve theories or think about phenomena in a new manner (Bansal and Corley 2011).

This book will present evidence of corporate behaviour in the form of statements made by corporations and their officers about how they practice corporate governance and why. As well as providing an interesting description of the state of play of corporate governance, this data can be compared against some of the common theories regarding corporate governance and its regulation. It can be used to develop and refine these theories so that we can better predict the likely impact of corporate governance codes on organisational behaviour. Two areas of theory are of particular relevance: management theories on the role of the board of directors and regulatory theories on the use of soft law.

The first set of theories presented in this chapter includes those claiming to help us to understand the *role of the board* in directing and controlling the company. Each of these theories has consequences for the practical function of the board – is it primarily to set strategy, to mediate between stakeholders, to monitor managers, to guide them or to provide them with resources? It is likely that the board's role involves a mixture of all of these functions, and yet many commonly used theories explain only one role. The aim of this book is to explore through discussion with directors what boards actually do in practice and how this fits with these theories. It is likely that the importance of each of these functions varies over time and is dependent on company circumstances. If this is true, the task for academics is to better understand the limits of each theory and the conditions that determine whether it will apply (Lynall et al. 2003, p. 420). This will provide a basis for advising policy-makers on how regulation might take into account variations in the role of the board and remain appropriate in all circumstances. Theories regarding the role of the board both explain and guide the *content of corporate governance codes*. Code recommendations on board responsibilities, board composition and committee structures are often influenced by these management theories regarding the role of the board.

This chapter also considers theory that can help us understand the *regulatory mechanisms* used to influence corporate governance practice. As already explained, most corporate governance codes use a comply-or-explain mechanism, yet there is little research demonstrating how this works in changing corporate behaviour (Aguilera and Cuervo-Cazurra 2009; Cuomo et al. 2016). On the basis that regulation can be defined as a 'sustained and focused attempt to alter the behaviour of others' (Black 2002, p. 26) it is vital to understand *how and why behaviour changes* in response to different types of regulation. Theories are only just emerging to explain and predict the way in which organisations respond to soft regulation and how this is different from the response to hard law. We need to understand the conditions within which soft law can be most effective and how it can be designed to mitigate its inherent limitations. By exploring how companies have adopted code recommendations, this book examines the processes through which comply-or-explain regulation has its effects.

The role of the board

When reviewing some of the theories aimed at understanding corporate governance and the role of the board of directors, it becomes clear that they can be aimed at different conceptual levels. Figure 3.1 illustrates the three levels of theory that can provide insights into the role of the board. It shows that at the highest level theories review the board's role in fulfilling overall corporate purpose. These theories are primarily about understanding the corporation as a whole rather than board function and dictate *for whom* the board works. Next come board theories about the functional role of the board, **what** the board does: explaining the need for directors to monitor, strategise, network and mediate. It is at this level of analysis that corporate governance codes often operate: recommending board structures and composition likely to facilitate the

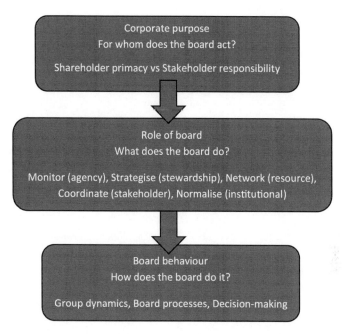

FIGURE 3.1 Theories relevant to the role of the board.

fulfilment of these roles. This chapter introduces five board-role theories that are commonly referred to in the literature: agency theory, stakeholder theory, stewardship theory, resource-dependency theory and institutional theory, though these are by no means the only options. At the third level researchers have begun to develop behavioural or process-based theories of corporate governance that analyse *how* boards fulfil their many functions. This work draws on cognitive psychology to better understand board dynamics and decision-making processes. It moves away from trying to define the role of the board towards an examination of the interactions and relationships at the heart of board function.

Level 1 – purpose of the corporation

Lurking behind questions about the role of the board are more fundamental issues regarding the purpose of the corporation as a whole. There are two competing theories regarding corporate purpose that impact on how a director's legal duty to act 'in the best interests of the corporation' is interpreted. Historically in Anglo-American jurisdictions this phrase has been interpreted as equating to the interests of the shareholders who, as a group, own the corporation's shares. In the Australian context, Corfield states that 'the history of the corporate structure over the last one hundred and fifty years reflects that its fundamental purpose has been to maximise corporate profit with a view to increasing shareholder wealth' (1998, p. 213).

This theory of 'shareholder primacy' can be contrasted with 'stakeholder theory', which has become increasingly popular in recent years and is embodied in the concept of corporate social responsibility or CSR. Stakeholder theory suggests that the corporation should be viewed not through the narrow lens of private ownership of shares but as a network involving multiple stakeholders including employees, customers, suppliers and creditors (Freeman 1984; Donaldson and Preston 1995). The purpose of the corporation is to maximise total wealth creation in the long term rather than just shareholder returns (Blair 1995). The stakeholder approach has long been the model of corporate governance in countries such as Germany and Japan. In Germany, companies with 500 employees or more are required by law to include a certain number of employee representatives on their boards. A propensity for corporations to be financed through debt rather than equity in these countries means that banks, rather than shareholders, often have the strongest stake in a corporation and exercise a level of control over operations through their financing contracts.

The theoretical debate between shareholder primacy and stakeholder theory has been discussed repeatedly in the literature, famously by Berle and Dodd in the *Harvard Law Review* in 1932. Berle believed that directors held their corporate powers in trust for shareholders, whereas Dodd claimed they were held in trust for the whole community. To counter claims that companies should be more socially responsible, Milton Friedman claimed in 1970 that increasing shareholder wealth should be seen as the corporation's social purpose because a profitable corporation has public benefit in terms of maintaining a strong economy.

As Chapter 7 discusses, Australian law has been relatively quiet on this issue leaving wide discretion in the hands of boards of directors. Within the bounds of reasonableness, directors may choose to take a simple shareholder value approach or may take many wider considerations into account. Although there has been case law in the past supporting shareholder primacy, the modern view is that Australian directors are not obliged to pursue only shareholder wealth and may (and probably should) take into account the interests of other stakeholders as long as they simultaneously look after the long-term interests of shareholders (CAMAC 2006). This has been termed the 'enlightened shareholder value' principle and is based on the common sense that maintaining good relations with employees, customers and the local community tends to be of value to the corporation in the long run and therefore is also in the interests of shareholders.

Despite the ongoing lack of consensus over the extent to which shareholders' interests should take priority, directors generally appear able to perform their role effectively. One way or another, it seems this theoretical issue is not a significant problem in daily practice. Nevertheless, there will be instances where deciding on how to balance stakeholder interests is both a strategic and procedural issue that boards must resolve to ensure that they fulfil their legal duties (Klein and du Plessis 2005). Chapter 7 explores whether regulation can assist boards to find methods for mediating between stakeholders and incorporating CSR into core business strategy.

Level 2 – board roles

In their book *Boards at Work* Kiel et al. identify nine key board functions: strategy, CEO oversight, monitoring, risk management, compliance, policy, networking, stakeholder communication and decision-making (2009, p. 259). Academic theorists have divided these practical functions into those that fulfil the control role of the board (monitoring and compliance); those that fulfil the service role of the board (strategy and policy); and those that fulfil its institutional role (networking and stakeholder communication) (Huse 2005; Roche 2009). Different theories help to explain these different roles and are helpful when analysing the purpose of corporate governance regulation. The control or monitoring role of the board is based on agency theory and an economic perspective of corporate governance. The service role is quite different, and a variety of theories, many taking a behavioural perspective of corporate governance, have been advanced to better understand this positive, value-adding function of the board. They include stewardship theory, stakeholder theory and resource-dependency theory. Arguably board roles can be split further to create a third category representing the board's interfacing or institutional role. This includes the board's role in accessing resources for the company but also its role in maintaining corporate legitimacy in the face of changing external expectations.

Agency theory

It was Berle and Means' seminal work in 1932 that described the fact that ownership and control in large Anglo-American companies becomes separated as companies grow and utilise public equity investment. The shareholders, owners of the equity of the company, can comprise a huge number of widely dispersed individuals with little power or knowledge over how the company is being run by its executive team of managers. This distance between the principals/owners of the company (shareholders) and their agents employed on the ground (executive managers) has been seen as a problem for the effective governance of companies for several reasons (Jenson and Meckling 1976; Mallin 2013). First, self-interested managers may not always act in the best interests of the shareholders. Many of the recent corporate collapses can be seen to support this theory. Managers, if not carefully controlled, may become tempted to act in their own best interests, for example, by awarding themselves large bonuses and/or taking unnecessary or fraudulent risks with corporate assets. They are able to do this because of the second agency problem – asymmetry of information – managers have more information and hence more power than most shareholders.

It is this principal-agent problem that much of corporate governance regulation is designed to mitigate (Lan and Heracleous 2010). This means corporate governance regulation is aimed at improving shareholders' control of executive management, both directly through voting powers and indirectly through the board of directors. Reflecting an economic view of corporate governance, some theorists, particularly in the US, define corporate governance as the mecha nisms by which suppliers of corporate finance assure themselves of a return on their investment (Schleifer and Vishny 1997). As listed companies will have a huge number of diverse shareholders unable to monitor management directly, responsibility is placed in the hands of a board of directors elected by the share-holders. In other words, agency theory predicts that the most important role of the board is to monitor management to ensure that they act in shareholders' interests rather than their own.

Agency theory has been very influential in regulatory policy (van den Berghe and Baelden 2005). As Chapter 2 described, much of the thrust of corporate reform in the last two decades, in the Anglo-American world at least, has been to establish and increase board-monitoring capacity, for example, by increasing the number of independent non-executive directors and separating the role of chair and chief executive officer (Langevoort 2001; Anderson et al. 2007). The audit and compensation committees, comprised of a majority of non-executives, are well established as central components of this drive to make boards more in-dependent of executive management. The UK's corporate governance code has been seen to confirm the salience of the board's monitoring role: 'The provisions of the code are intended to make boards more independent and more effective in controlling the chief executive and the executive team' (Taylor 2004, p. 421). In Australia the CLERP 9 Explanatory Memorandum expressly confirmed the agency theory underpinnings of Australian corporate governance regulation:

> Under Australia's corporate regulatory framework, directors and senior company employees exercise control over company resources on behalf of shareholders, who have no direct operational control over the com-pany. While this relationship is the most efficient approach to operating a company that is owned by hundreds or thousands of different parties, a recognised limitation is that it can give rise to a principal-agent problem.
>
> (2003, para. 4.347)

Lazonick and O'Sullivan (2000) explain that one of the consequences of agency theory has been a focus on shareholder value as the measure of managerial per-formance. The agency theory approach to the role of the board tends to meld with economic theories that claim the purpose of the corporation as a whole is to maximise shareholder wealth. Agency theory is based on an assumption that the board is acting on behalf of shareholders rather than any other corporate stakeholders.

The shareholder primacy model of corporate purpose is attractive because of its simplicity and has been incredibly influential. Lazonick and O'Sullivan (2000) note that it became an accepted aim of corporate governance in the 1980s and '90s. Lynn Stout believes the popularity of this idea reached its peak in about 2001 when Kraakman and Hansmann claimed that the dominant corpo-rate ideology of shareholder primacy was likely to spread worldwide (Stout 2012;

Hansmann and Kraakman 2000). Arguably since the spectacular collapses of the 2000s the pendulum has swung towards a more stakeholder-orientated approach to corporate governance. Indeed, Lazonick and O'Sullivan's prediction that shareholder value maximisation was unlikely to be a sustainable ideology in terms of economic prosperity has to some extent been proved true. Many of the companies that collapsed during the global financial crisis were following a business model designed to maximise short-term share price rather than long-term sustainability. Stout (2012) suggests that a focus on shareholder value is a mistake for most companies and can be the cause of reckless and irresponsible behaviours that damage not only corporate performance but also the welfare of employees, communities and investors.

Stakeholder theory

Stakeholder theory is probably the strongest contender to agency theory and shareholder primacy. Although it is first and foremost a theory about corporate purpose, stakeholder theory posits a board role of co-ordination and co-operation whereby the board acts as a mediating body to balance the interests of coalitions of stakeholders (van Ees et al. 2009, p. 308). Hung (1998) states that 'a stakeholder approach to the role of the governing board expects the board to negotiate and compromise with stakeholders in the interest of the corporation'. It is said to have more empirical backing than other theories both in terms of how corporate officers act in practice and how the law has developed in many countries (Donaldson and Preston 1995; Marshall and Ramsay 2012; Romano 2005).

Because stakeholder theory sees the corporation as a social entity involving many different interests, discussion of stakeholder theory lends itself to examination of the overlap between corporate governance and corporate responsibility discussed further in Chapter 7. Stakeholder theory does not change the board's functions in terms of control and service; rather it changes the purpose of board decision-making in fulfilling these functions. Directors must monitor management on behalf of many constituencies – not just shareholders. They must put in place procedures for engaging and communicating with a wide range of stakeholder groups and take the interests of these groups into account when setting strategy or advising management. In theory therefore, a stakeholder approach to corporate governance appears to make the board's role more complicated. Indeed critics of this approach suggest that it can 'blur rather than clarify the purpose that directors are to serve' (CAMAC 2006, p. 111). Certainly it adds an additional board role – that of managing stakeholders and enhancing corporate responsibility (Wang and Dewhirst 1992).

Stakeholder theory supports the need for non-executive directors but for different reasons than agency theory. Rather than emphasising their independence it sees non-executives as potential representatives of external stakeholders. Stakeholder theory also implies a need to engage and communicate with groups other than shareholders. Corporate responsibility reporting is the visible outcome of communication and accountability to stakeholders: regulation that aims to improve CSR reporting can be said to be based on stakeholder theory.

Stewardship theory

Another criticism of agency theory is that it portrays human beings in a very one-dimensional and unrealistic light. Agency theory suggests that managers, if not monitored closely, will pursue their own interests rather than the interests of anyone else. It treats individuals as 'homo economicus', rationally making decisions based purely on economic value. However evidence from the disciplines of psychology and sociology suggests that we are not all opportunistic individuals motivated only by personal wealth maximisation. Fortunately, most of us are also motivated by less egotistical goals. We want to 'do the right thing' and be respected by our peers. We want our colleagues and the organisation where we work to succeed along with ourselves. These common human traits mean that agency theory cannot fully explain managerial behaviour.

Stewardship theory rejects the homo-economicus of agency theory and incorporates a wider range of human characteristics enabling a more complex, but perhaps more accurate, explanation of managerial behaviour (Donaldson and Davis 1994). Stewardship theory does not argue that collective needs should always trump personal needs, rather it demonstrates that the two can be aligned (Davis et al. 1997, p. 21). Interestingly, Justice Owen in investigating the collapse of Australia's HIH Insurance, used the common meaning of stewardship to describe the role that company leaders should aspire to:

> The governance of a public company should be about stewardship. Those in control have a duty to act in the best interests of the company. They must use the company's resources productively. They must understand that those resources are not personal property.
>
> (HIH Royal Commission 2003 vol 1, p. 10)

Stewardship theory suggests that most executives understand that this is their role and will generally act as responsible supervisors of the company rather than personal wealth maximisers. Its consequences for the role of the board are that it does not predict a need for the board to monitor. As Muth and Donaldson have commented '[s]tewardship predictions regarding board independence are directly opposed to those of agency theory' (1998, p. 5). At its extreme, stewardship theory would posit no need for directors to monitor or be independent because managers would be safely working towards the best solution for all. Stewardship theorists focus on corporate governance structures that 'facilitate and empower rather than those that monitor and control' (Davis et al. 1997, p. 26). Stewardship theory would suggest that board structures that facilitate board input into strategic decision-making would be most valuable for improving board performance (Hung 1998, p. 106).

In reality, a team of perfect stewards is no more likely than all managers working selfishly for themselves. Davis et al. suggest that both personal psychological characteristics and external contingencies lead to individuals' choice of whether to act as steward or agent (1997, p. 38). Corporate governance structures and corporate and national cultures will be some of the external contingencies affecting managers' choices. The effect of external contingencies on managerial behaviour was demonstrated quite clearly by the global financial crisis where remuneration structures and a culture of short-termism were found to be incentivising selfish risk-taking by managers in the finance sector. As Chapter 8 describes, recent regulatory reforms have been aimed at removing these agency incentives by requiring better links between remuneration and long-term firm performance. In terms of personal characteristics, stewards are more likely to be motivated by intrinsic rewards such as achievement and opportunity than by external rewards measured in monetary value. They identify with the organisation and its aims and see organisational success as personal success. Governance structures that foster organisational involvement, trust and long-term performance would be likely to foster stewardship behaviour in managers (Davis et al. 1997, p. 37).

On this basis it is important to question whether the recent regulatory focus on the monitoring role of the board is appropriate in all circumstances. It seems that the bad behaviour of a handful of powerful executives may have caused regulatory policy-makers to overlook the positive performance-enhancing role of the board in favour of its role in checking and deterring opportunistic behaviour. Perhaps corporate governance regulation could and should be more active in encouraging trust and collaboration as a method of encouraging good behaviour, rather than focusing on control as a method of discouraging bad behaviour.

Resource-dependency theory

Resource-dependency theory focuses on the role of the board as a link to external resources essential to corporate success (Hillman et al. 2000). These may include access to capital, sources of information or links to key suppliers or customers (Nicholson and Kiel 2007). Resource-dependency theory addresses board members' contributions as 'boundary spanners of the organization and its environment' (Daily et al. 2003, p. 372). Non-executive directors in particular provide skills, experience and information that can expand and improve board decision-making. As such, resource-dependency theory explains the performance side of board function rather than its monitoring role. Management scholars have explored this role of the board including its input into the strategic direction of the corporation (Stiles and Taylor 2001; Judge and Zeithaml 1992). Kiel and Nicholson refer to intellectual capital theory whereby the skills mix on a board is a major determinant of the value-adding that the board brings to the firm (2003, p. 202).

Rather than labelling directors as executive or non-executive, independent or non-independent and building board composition around these categories, resource-dependency theory suggests that director categories based on experience, skills and networks will be more important to board composition. Hillman et al. (2000) put forward four categories based on common resource needs: insiders (executives with in-depth firm knowledge); business experts (with experience running other large companies); support specialists (lawyers and accountants with specialist skills) and community influentials (with experience in politics, regulation or leadership of community groups). The board's role in establishing corporate legitimacy can also be seen through the lens of resource-dependency theory on the basis that directors bring with them their personal reputation and credibility, qualities that add value to the firm in the same way as other resources or skills (Langevoort 2001, p. 802; Subramaniam et al. 2009, p. 321).

Resource-dependency theory has significant consequences for corporate governance regulation as it does not feature independence as a vital board characteristic, something that recent reforms have placed as central to good governance. It casts doubt on the effectiveness of independence requirements, particularly if they reduce a board's ability to recruit other crucial qualities and skills. Aspects of existing corporate governance regulation that support the boards' resource role would include board performance evaluations that assess the overall board skill set, together with effective selection processes designed by the nomination committee.

Institutional theory

Institutional theory explains organisational behaviour as a response to the internal and external environment. It would explain a company's corporate governance structure as emerging from patterns of organisational interaction and adaptation (Selznick 1996). Argote and Greve claim that 'Institutional theory explains how the firm adapts to a symbolic environment of cognitions and expectations and a regulatory environment of rules and sanctions' (2007, p. 340). Institutional theory is evidenced by the fact that firms in similar situations tend to act in the same way – they adopt similar practices and portray themselves in a socially acceptable manner. This is exactly what Hooghiemstra and van Ees (2011) find can occur in response to corporate governance codes: responses become standardised as companies conform to outside expectations.

In this way, institutional theory can explain the spread of 'best practices' for corporate governance and the adoption of voluntary corporate responsibility reporting (Campbell 2007). In terms of the role of the board, institutional theory conceptualises board structures and functions as responses to external pressures including regulation, environmental norms and firm history (Clarke 2004, p. 10). Hung (1998) explains that institutional theory posits a role for the board in legitimising the corporation that usually involves conforming to social rules and conventions. The board's role is to analyse the external environment to better understand changing expectations and then meet them in order to maintain corporate legitimacy (Hung 1998, p. 107). For example, institutional theory might explain the setting up of recommended board committees as necessary to maintain legitimacy whether or not there is internal benefit.

Level 3 – decision-making

Lastly, brief mention should be made of scholarly attempts to move away from defining board roles (*what* the board does) and instead concentrate on board processes (*how* the board fulfils its role). Although they show great promise, these theories, based on board behaviour and dynamics, have not yet reached the same level of development and acceptance as agency theory (van Ees et al. 2009). Daily et al. point out that many behaviour-based theories were intended to complement agency theory rather than provide a substitute for it (2003, p. 372). Van Ees et al. comment that due to the rather scattered nature of behaviour-based research, 'understanding boards and corporate governance in a behavioural framework does not yet provide a coherent alternative to the agency theory perspective in corporate governance' (van Ees et al. 2009, p. 307). They argue that to be a true alternative to agency theory, the behavioural approach needs to be strengthened by developing a core set of concepts that explain the decision-making of boards independently from structures and outcomes. These concepts would include topics from psychology: group decision making and problem solving behaviours and the influence of power and experience.

Van Ees et al. argue that a behavioural theory would conceive of boards of directors as 'problem-solving institutions that reduce complexity, create accountability and facilitate cooperation and coordination between stakeholders' (2009, p. 308). They compare this to agency theory, which views the board, 'primarily as a deterrent to managerial self-interest'. In this sense, the behavioural theory of van Ees et al. posits a very similar role for the board as stakeholder theory: the difference is a focus on decision-making processes rather than on structures and outcomes. They suggest that future research should review actual board behaviour against well-known theories from cognitive psychology such as bounded rationality, satisficing, routinisation and political bargaining. The aim of these advocates of behavioural theory is to move away from trying to define the role of the board and to study board process instead. This involves studying the impact on corporate governance of relationships, trust and emotions; the development of governance norms; and differences in decision-making cultures (Huse 2005).

Role of the board and regulation

In summary, there are many areas of board function where regulation has the potential to facilitate good corporate governance. It can clarify *to whom* directors owe their duty of care and how to balance the interests of different stakeholders. It can suggest *what* the board's responsibilities are and require or recommend board composition and structures to help directors fulfil these responsibilities.

Regulation, if cleverly designed, may also be able to encourage better board processes and decision-making (*how* the board functions) as well as an ethical organisational culture.

The next question is how regulation might best achieve these objectives. Regulatory theories can assist in understanding whether these topics are best tackled using hard law, soft law or one of the many innovative options that lie somewhere in-between. As this book is focused on codes of corporate governance, it focuses on theories that explore the scope and limitations of this kind of soft regulation.

Regulatory theories

Regulatory theories aim to explain and predict the effects of different kinds of soft regulation and the circumstances in which they are most effective (Coglianese and Lazer 2003; Ford and Hess 2011). As with theories on the role of the board, different terminologies are used across different scholarly disciplines and different jurisdictions: it is a body of literature that has yet to be developed into a coherent whole.

Corporate governance provides an interesting case study from a regulatory point of view because novel mechanisms have been used to influence behaviour. As described in Chapter 2, the beginnings of the Australian corporate governance code were a self-regulatory response by companies to the problem of lack of capital and low investor confidence. It was a classic case of self-regulation where 'companies join together to regulate their collective action to avoid a common threat or to provide a common good' (King and Lenox 2000). The development of the ASX code by the Corporate Governance Council had the same underlying purpose: to improve confidence in the share market following periods of corporate collapse and economic downturn. Both companies and governments wish to maintain a healthy economy and prevent corporate collapse. Thus there is an ongoing incentive, for both regulators and businesses, to implement and explain good corporate governance practices that can have the added advantage of maintaining corporate reputation in an environment of scrutiny by both investors and customers. Aguilera and Cuervo-Cazurra describe the key regulatory issue as follows:

> An important debate in the international corporate governance world is whether countries should develop hard laws, such as the United States with the Sarbanes-Oxley Act 2002, or whether soft regulation, such as codes of good governance, are sufficiently effective to improve existing corporate governance practices across countries, as well as to address the pressing issues of corporate accountability and disclosure.
>
> (2009, p. 376)

Against this background, this section introduces some of the theories behind soft regulation including why it is used in certain circumstances, how it works and its limitations. These include theories of 'new governance' or non-legal governance; meta-regulation; and responsive regulation.

New governance

In the United States, 'new governance' appears to be a term that encompasses a wide range of contemporary approaches to regulation. This relatively new paradigm combines many theories regarding non-traditional regulation. In a comprehensive list Lobel includes theories of: 'reflexive law, soft law, collaborative governance, democratic experimentalism, responsive regulation, outsourcing regulation, reconstitutive law, post-regulatory law, revitalizing regulation, regulatory pluralism, decentering regulation, meta-regulation, contractarian law, communicative governance, negotiated governance, destabilization rights, cooperative implementation, and interactive compliance' (2004, p. 346). This is a huge range of theories, reflecting the broad nature of the term 'new governance', which appears to encompass anything that is not traditional hard law. Hess (2008) explains that because new governance is an emerging regulatory approach appearing in a variety of policy domains, there are differences and basic confusion over its theoretical underpinnings. At the same time there appears to be a level of agreement over its practical nature. Karkkainen describes new governance as follows:

> This scholarship endeavours simultaneously to chronicle, interpret, analyze, theorize, and advocate a seismic reorientation in both the public policymaking process and the tools employed in policy implementation. The valence of this reorientation, New Governance scholars argue, is generally away from the familiar model of command-style, fixed-rule regulation by administrative fiat, and toward a new model of collaborative, multi-party, multi-level, adaptive, problem-solving New Governance.
>
> (2004, p. 473)

In other words 'new governance' appears to be another term for soft regulation. Several scholars have noted the close relationship between new governance theories and other contemporary regulatory ideas such as responsive regulation, risk regulation, management-based regulation and meta-regulation (Gilad 2010; Ford and Hess 2011). Ford and Condon explain that new governance involves 'a restructured and more collaborative relationship between the state and regulated entities based on the recognition that regulation may operate most effectively when it incorporates private actors' context-specific experience and relevant expertise' (2011, p. 450). Hess refers to the theory behind this type of regulatory feature as 'democratic experimentalism' whereby government encourages regulated actors to experiment to find tailored solutions to complex problems (2008, p. 450).

Comply-or-explain corporate governance codes fall neatly within these descriptions of new governance. Indeed, they champion two of the features of new governance highlighted by Ford and Condon: (1) giving regulated entities greater autonomy to design their own internal processes to meet broadly defined outcomes and (2) counterbalancing this freedom with mechanisms designed to force transparency and accountability (2011, p. 450). As Figure 3.2 demonstrates,

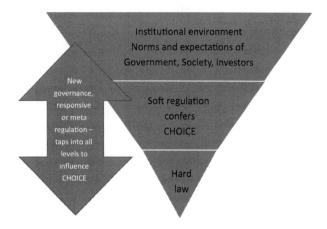

FIGURE 3.2 Theories regarding soft regulation.

the discretion inherent in codes of corporate governance leaves companies with choice in terms of how to respond. Coglianese and Mendelson (2010) point out that this type of regulation is all about levels of discretion, and the key to its effectiveness is to get the targets of regulation (in this case the companies) to exercise the discretion afforded to them consistently with overarching public goals rather than with their own private interests. This may be done by tapping into other coercive influences, perhaps a threat of hard legislation or concerns about reputation. Coglianese and Lazer name this kind of regulation 'management-based regulation' because it permits firms to engage in their own planning and internal rule-making efforts rather than dictating what they must do or what they must achieve (2003, p. 692). The idea is that use of flexible regulation can engage companies to find cost-effective solutions to complex problems.

A special issue of the University of Denver's *Law and Policy* journal in 2011 focused on the implementation of new governance systems by business organisations. It was partly triggered by the global financial crisis because of the way it exposed practical shortcomings in regulatory capacity. Some US scholars still strongly believe that new governance style regulation is not capable of countering the effects of economic self-interest and therefore has limited use in the field of corporate governance (Sarra 2011). Ford and Condon highlight the importance of empirical work in testing new governance theory and understanding its possibilities and limitations (2011, p. 451).

Meta-regulation

Meta-regulation is described as 'the proliferation of different forms of regulation (whether tools of state law or non-law mechanisms) each regulating one another' (Parker 2007, p. 208). Coglianese and Mendelson (2010) review some of the definitions of meta-regulation, finding that they all involve layers of regulation, one institution regulating another, commonly involving state oversight of self-regulation. Bryan Horrigan explains that:

> the modern era is witnessing what prominent regulatory scholars describe as the new regulatory state, accompanied by the 'decentring' of regulation into many more strands than simply self-regulation, on one hand, and government-mandated 'command and control' regulation in the form of 'regulation by the state through the use of legal rules backed by (often criminal) sanctions' on the other.
>
> (2010, p. 59)

Although it is still early days in testing and elaborating meta-regulatory theory, preliminary suggestions are that in sociological conditions of a complex division of labour, it is likely to be more responsive and more effective than direct command-and-control regulation (Braithwaite and Parker 2004, p. 287). Whilst in the past regulation was often perceived in very hierarchical terms as stemming directly from government authority, theories of 'smart regulation' and 'meta-regulation' have shown that regulation can also be carried out by a host of other bodies including professional or trade bodies and voluntary organisations, as well as by the traditional targets of regulation through self-regulatory mechanisms (Gunningham and Grabosky 1998).

The Australian corporate governance code is a good example of this new way of regulating. As described in Chapter 2, the meta-regulatory hierarchy starts with the *Corporations Act 2001,* which sets up the Australian Securities Exchange (ASX) and gives it power to draft the Listing Rules, compliance with which is enforced by sanctions. The Listing Rules require disclosure against the ASX code, drafted by the Corporate Governance Council, which employs a comply-or-explain mechanism. Thus although, in most cases, adoption of the recommendations of the corporate governance code is voluntary, disclosure against them is a contractual condition of listing, and legal sanctions can be imposed for non-disclosure.

Responsive regulation

John Braithwaite would most likely label this layered corporate governance regulation as responsive regulation, which he describes as 'regulation that is responsive to the moves regulated actors make, to industry context and to the environment' (2011). Regulation is much more likely to be effective if its targets perceive it as legitimate and fair:

> According to responsive regulatory theory, what we want is a legal system where citizens learn that responsiveness is the way our legal institutions work. Once they see law as a responsive regulatory system, they know that there will be a chance to argue about unjust laws (as opposed to being forced into a lower court production line or a plea bargain). But they will

also see that game-playing to avoid legal obligations, and failure to listen to arguments about the harm their actions are doing and what must be done to repair it, will inexorably lead to regulatory escalation.

(Braithwaite 2011, p. 486)

Braithwaite's influential regulatory pyramids demonstrate that a regulatory policy ought to start with informal discussions about undesirable behaviour and only escalate to severe penalties if the more respectful methods fail. By going through this process, if and when severe control is exercised it will be seen as more legitimate: '[r]esponsive regulators seek contextual, integrated, joined-up strategies that will work in synergy' (Braithwaite 2011, p. 490). Australia's corporate regulator, ASIC, has certainly attempted a system such as this for listed companies with voluntary comply-or-explain disclosures backed up by legal sanctions. Mandatory legal requirements are also enforced in a responsive fashion with enforcement options ranging from negotiated resolution and infringement notices requiring compliance to punitive action (ASIC 2013).

The objective of responsive regulation is access to justice rather than access to courts. It accepts that justice may best be achieved through self-regulation by civil society and that law should leave room for this to occur in a flexible way that makes contextual sense. Braithwaite and Parker talk of a two-way process of norm-building: 'a justice of the law that filters down into the justice of the people and a justice of the people that more effectively bubbles up into the justice of the law' (2004, p. 285). Many corporate governance codes have been developed over time through a two-way process akin to this description. Corporate governance structures such as independent audit committees have filtered down from being compulsory in the finance sector to being voluntarily adopted in most companies. At the same time, public consultation over amendments to codes has enabled both business and civil society to have a say in the development of regulation. In this way code recommendations represent a codification or reinforcing of commonly used corporate governance practices. Corporate governance codes have also been described as reflexive regulation, explicitly designed to trigger a learning process that will enable companies to incorporate developments from practice (Cankar et al. 2010, p. 510).

Disclosure as regulation

Disclosure of information has long been used as a mechanism of corporate accountability but more recently has also been viewed as a tool of regulation (Spira and Page 2010). The distinction is subtle: if disclosure of information is purely an exercise in correcting for information asymmetries, for example, between corporate managers and shareholders, then disclosure is a regulatory goal rather than a regulatory strategy. If, however, the information disclosure has another purpose, to change the behaviour of the firm and improve corporate governance practices, it can be viewed as a form of management-based regulation

(Coglianese and Lazer 2003). Spira and Page (2010) identify three linked and overlapping objectives of corporate disclosure-based regulation: (1) securing corporate accountability to stakeholders; (2) enabling better investment decisions and smooth-running capital markets; (3) as a form of indirect regulation that achieves the aims of regulators. In the case of corporate governance codes it is easy to see the overlap of these three purposes – the objective of most codes is to improve both investor confidence and corporate governance practices. The third edition of the Australian code describes its recommended practices as 'likely to achieve good governance outcomes' whilst also explaining that disclosures around any non-adoption of the code enable security holders and investors to 'factor that information into their decisions' (ASX 2014, p. 3).

The theory behind comply-or-explain corporate governance codes is that by requiring disclosure they provoke enforcement by the investment market. The assumption is that there is a market for good governance – investors will value it, and good governance will be recognised in the value of the company's shares. Investors will assess the information provided in corporate governance statements and choose companies with good governance over those without. In other words, the theory is based on an assumption that:

> … shareholders will consider non-compliance or unsatisfactorily explained non-compliance negatively. It also assumes that the market responds not just to disclosure or not, but also its content.
>
> (Kingsford Smith 2012, p. 396)

However, several researchers have found that investor engagement over corporate governance has been much less active than expected (Keay 2014; Arcot et al. 2010; MacNeil and Li 2006). Nevertheless, evidence shows that the majority of large companies do adopt code recommendations (Grant Thornton 2012). The ASX has carried out regular reviews of the level of adoption of the Australian code by listed companies, finding that it has increased every year up to levels of 92 percent in 2010, with disclosure improving in its clarity and coverage (ASX 2010). This raises the question of why, if it is not fear of judgment by investors causing this behaviour, what drives companies to implement code recommendations?

Soft law and norms

The relationship between soft regulation and norms of behaviour is important in understanding whether or not a regulatory measure is likely to be effective. Soft law has been defined to comprise 'regulatory instruments and mechanisms of governance that, while implicating some kind of normative commitment, do not rely on binding rules or on a regime of formal sanctions' (Robliant 2006, p. 499). In the area of corporate governance soft-law instruments exist at international, national and industry levels. Examples of international soft-law instruments relevant to corporate governance and corporate responsibility include the

OECD Corporate Governance Guidelines and the UN Guiding Principles on Business and Human Rights.

Norms can be defined as 'observed behavioural regularities', like wearing a suit for office work or forming a queue at the bus stop (Rock and Wachter 2001b, p. 1641). These are unwritten rules or standards of behaviour that are not legally enforceable but are enforced or encouraged by other social means: peer pressure, social acceptance, shaming or concerns about reputation. Norms relevant to corporate behaviour can be both internal and external. Internal norms make up the culture of the organisation and can be developed through either top-down processes (the board communicating its expectations) or bottom up processes (employee agreement on methods of task performance). As Rock and Wachter explain, 'behavioral rules and standards for corporate actors are provided by corporate culture and are essentially norm-based' (2001a, p. 1608). They explain the importance of studying the role played by norms in the corporate arena:

> Norms may help explain the manner in which the law, in the absence of bright line rules, influences corporate governance. Norms may also explain why standards rather than rules work well in a corporate setting.
>
> (2001a, p. 1608)

External norms affecting corporate behaviour are what we might call norms of best practice. As Chapter 7 explores, corporate responsibility is an area where corporations are left with a great deal of discretion in terms of how to react and how to report. Yet a review of annual corporate responsibility reports demonstrates a norm of disclosure across areas such as employee relations, health and safety, environmental performance and community relations. Again there is a close relationship between this observed practice and the development of soft-law initiatives such as the Global Reporting Initiative (GRI) and other reporting guidelines. Black refers to a study that shows that norm-building is often started by a 'small but global community of professionals rather than through the application of established legal rules'. (2010, p. 168). She notes there are only 'scatterings of empirical research' into how norms develop in financial markets despite many scholars noting their influence on behaviour (2010, p. 168).

One of the recurring questions regarding the relationship between soft law and norms is the question of which came first: 'Does soft law evolve into social norms or do social norms generate soft law?' (Morth 2004, p. 4). Most scholars suggest that both of these propositions are correct and that norms and soft law are mutually reinforcing and develop in parallel (Veasey 2001). Using human–rights norms as an example, Moore Dickerson describes a feedback loop whereby 'as the actual behaviour of multinationals becomes increasingly consistent with the evolving human rights norms, the behaviour both reinforces the norms and is reinforced by them' (2002, p. 1460). She goes further to suggest that, despite being rather unstructured, this process is akin to democracy and tends to acquire the type of legitimacy afforded to democratically approved conclusions.

Soft versus hard law

Morth asks, 'to what extent should soft law be seen as a transitional mode of regulation? Or can it be seen as an independent form of regulation?' (2004, p. 3). Certainly in the realm of corporate governance there is no expectation that codes will ultimately be hardened into legislation. Most regulatory theories posit that soft regulation can be a first choice rather than a transitional phase:

> More than one author has claimed that soft law measures may be preferred over legally binding rules when there is a need for flexibility and rapid reactions and when there is a concern about the possibility of non-compliance.
>
> (Morth 2004, p. 3)

Langevoort concludes that 'changing norms have been a more important influence on the structural evolution of board dynamics than law' (2001, p. 817). His point is that corporate governance structures are probably best left to norms rather than law because of the need for flexibility. One of the advantages of soft law is that it can be drafted relatively quickly by organisations with in-depth knowledge of the issues at stake. The flip-side of this is that there is no guarantee of public input or consultation. Ulrika Morth points out that:

> Soft law and governance raise questions of democracy. Is it democratically desirable for soft law to be a first step in the legalization process or should soft law be regarded as separate from traditional legislative methods?
>
> (2004, p. 2)

The Australian government has chosen to enshrine certain aspects of corporate governance in hard law, but as Chapter 2 notes, this has disadvantages because the process of law-making is slow, particularly when compared to the rate of innovation of business models and markets. Depending on how the law is phrased compliance can be costly and the burden on business can be high (as was claimed of the US *Sarbanes-Oxley Act*). Nevertheless, law-making is a public and democratic process unlike the semi-private drafting of the ASX code by a group of organisations each with its own agenda and potential conflicts of interest. Also law can force behavioural change through sanctions for non-compliance whereas softer regulation can be more easily ignored. The advantages of codes of corporate governance include the ability to keep them up-to-date and relevant and the fact that, through relatively informal consultation, they have tended to find an acceptable balance between regulatory burden and benefit (Klettner et al. 2010). Indeed, Nash and Ehrenfeld (1997) suggest that when trying to trigger behavioural change, the need for a threat of sanctions (a feature of hard law) is overstated because the institutional structure of self-regulation can control behaviour through informal means of coercion, the transferal of norms and the diffusion of best practices. Fasterling discusses the value of disclosure-based regulation as a process 'that can initiate a dialogue about norm interpretation, application and norm desirability' (2012, p. 73). Thus even if it cannot effectively discipline a particular behaviour, it can still have a significant influence in defining acceptable standards.

Majumdar and Marcus (2001) find that a key advantage of flexible regulation is that it encourages innovative implementation rather than routine and mechanical compliance. This concept of engaging rather than simply complying with regulation is an important one, especially in complex situations. It is why Braithwaite argues that 'as the regulated phenomena become more complex, principles deliver more consistency than rules' (2002, p. 47). Indeed the popularity of comply-or-explain codes stems from their flexibility, which avoids the costs of a 'one size fits all' regime and recognises that the optimal governance structure may be different for each company and change over time. However there has been little research on whether this flexibility is actually used by companies in the way intended. The few empirical studies conducted suggest that, certainly in the early stages of code adoption, companies tend to take a standardised approach (Cankar et al. 2010; Hooghiemstra and van Ees 2011).

Gunningham and Rees confirm the advantages of self-regulatory systems (often with government backing) are 'speed, flexibility, sensitivity to market circumstances and lower costs', yet these systems are often criticised for being 'a cynical attempt by self-interested parties to give the appearance of regulation (thereby warding off more direct and effective government intervention) while serving private interests at the expense of the public' (1997, p. 370). This type of criticism gained strength after the 2008 global financial crisis, which was seen to be caused in part by poor governance in large financial institutions (Kirkpatrick 2009). The regulatory regime was not strong enough to curb a culture of excessive risk-taking incentivised by personal gain. However, as Tomasic and Akinbami argue, while legislatures and courts must set new directions, effective corporate governance is ultimately best achieved by internal control mechanisms within corporations (2011, p. 238). They have suggested that a more robust and nuanced approach to corporate governance would involve multiple layers of regulation including both internal change processes and external oversight. For some self-regulation is the solution to the limits of 'centred' regulation; for others it is the challenge that has to be addressed: 'regulation of self-regulation is the new challenge' (Black 2001, p. 104).

Empirical research is needed so that we can better understand the advantages and disadvantages of using soft law, hard law or hybrid forms of regulation to influence corporate behaviour. It is through exploring the workings of internal board processes and the impact of corporate governance regulation upon them that qualitative research can contribute to both regulatory theory and policy. Reviewing how companies choose to fill out the flexible framework provided by corporate governance codes can reveal evidence of the processes through which soft regulation takes effect. It is through better understanding of the links between theory and practice, between regulatory recommendations and norms or expectations, that research can contribute to discussion of regulatory policy and its influence on board behaviour.

Summary of chapter 3

This chapter provides a review of the literature relevant to corporate governance and its regulation, particularly with regard to the role of the board and the regulatory mechanisms used by codes of corporate governance. It describes the wide range of responsibilities placed upon the board of directors – to set strategy, to mediate between stakeholders, to monitor managers, to guide them and to provide them with resources. Different theories place different priority on each of these roles whereas in practice it is likely that they are all important at different times in a company's life cycle. This makes the task of the regulator quite difficult: to effectively facilitate the fulfilment of board functions, regulation must be able to take account of these different roles. This is why flexible, principle-based regulation has been the popular choice even though we still do not fully understand how it works. Regulatory theories suggest that soft regulation is cost-effective and can foster innovative problem-solving. However, the design of this kind of regulation requires a fine balancing act that takes into account the cultural norms and expectations in a particular market. The freedom and choice permitted by the regulation must be tempered by mechanisms of accountability and may need to be supported by the possibility of more stringent regulation within an overall system.

References

Aguilera, RV & Cuervo-Cazurra, A 2009, 'Codes of good governance', *Corporate Governance: An International Review,* vol. 17, no. 3, pp. 373–87.

Anderson, DW, Melanson, SJ & Maly, J 2007, 'The evolution of corporate governance: power redistribution brings boards to life', *Corporate Governance: An International Review,* vol. 15, no. 5, pp. 780–97.

Arcot, S, Bruno, V & Faure-Grimaud, A 2010, 'Corporate governance in the UK: is the comply or explain approach working?', *International Review of Law and Economics,* vol. 30, pp. 193–201.

Argote, L & Greve, HR 2007, 'A behavioural theory of the firm – 40 years and counting: introduction and impact', *Organization Science,* vol. 18, no. 3, pp. 337–49.

ASIC Australian Securities & Investments Commission 2013, 'ASIC's approach to enforcement', Information Sheet 151, September 2013 available at <www.asic.gov.au>.

ASX 2010, Analysis of Corporate Governance Disclosures in Annual Reports for year ended 30 June 2010.

Bainbridge, SM 2006, 'The case for limited shareholder voting rights', *UCLA Law Review,* vol. 53, pp. 601–36.

Bansal, P & Corley, K 2011, 'From the editors. The coming of age for qualitative research: embracing the diversity of qualitative methods', *Academy of Management Journal,* vol. 54, pp. 233–37.

Berle, AA 1932, 'Corporate powers as powers in trust', *Harvard Law Review,* vol. 44, p. 1049.

Berle, AA & Means, GC 2009, *The Modern Corporation and Private Property,* originally published in 1932, San Diego, CA: Harcourt, Brace and World.

Black, J 2001, 'Decentring regulation: understanding the role of regulation and self-regulation in a "post-regulatory" world', Current Legal Problems, vol. 54, no. 1, pp. 103–46.

Black, J 2002, 'Critical reflections on regulation', Australian Journal of Legal Philosophy, vol. 27, pp. 1–35.

Black, J 2010, 'Financial markets', in P Cane & H M Kritzer (eds.) The Oxford Handbook of Empirical Legal Research, Oxford: Oxford University Press.

Blair, M 1995, 'Rethinking assumptions behind corporate governance', Challenge, vol. 38, no. 6, pp. 12–17.

Braithwaite, J 2002, 'Rules and principles: a theory of legal certainty', Australian Journal of Legal Philosophy, vol. 27, p. 47.

Braithwaite, J 2011, 'The essence of responsive regulation', University of British Columbia Law Review, vol. 44, p. 475.

Braithwaite, J & Parker, C 2004, 'Conclusion', in C Parker, C Scott, N Lacey & J Braithwaite (eds.), Regulating Law, Oxford: Oxford University Press.

CAMAC, 2006, The Social Responsibility of Corporations, Australian Government Corporations and Markets Advisory Committee, December 2006.

Campbell, JL 2007, 'Why would corporations behave in socially responsible ways? An institutional theory of corporate social responsibility', Academy of Management Review, vol. 32, no. 3, pp. 946–67.

Cankar, NK, Deakin, S & Simoneti, M 2010, 'The reflexive properties of corporate governance codes: the reception of the 'comply-or-explain' approach in Slovenia', Journal of Law and Society, vol. 37, no. 3, pp. 501–25.

Clarke, T 2004, 'Introduction', in T Clarke (ed), Theories of Corporate Governance, New York: Routledge.

Coglianese, C & Lazer, D 2003, 'Management-based regulation: prescribing private management to achieve public goals', Law & Society Review, vol. 37, no. 4, pp. 691–730.

Coglianese, C & Mendelson, E 2010, 'Meta-regulation and self-regulation', in R Baldwin, M Cave & M Lodge (eds.), The Oxford Handbook of Regulation, Oxford: Oxford University Press.

Corfield, A 1998, 'The stakeholder theory and its future in Australian corporate governance: a preliminary analysis', Bond Law Review, vol. 10, pp. 213–40.

Corley, KG & Gioia, DA 2011, 'Building theory about theory building: what constitutes a theoretical contribution?', Academy of Management Review, vol. 36, no. 1, p. 12.

Cuomo, F, Mallin C & Zattoni, A 2016 'Corporate governance codes: a review and research agenda'.

Daily, CM, Dalton, DR & Cannella, AA 2003, 'Corporate governance: decades of dialogue and data', Academy of Management Review, vol. 28, no. 3, pp. 371–82.

Dalton, CM & Dalton, DR 2005, 'Boards of directors: utilizing empirical evidence in developing practical prescriptions', British Journal of Management, vol. 16, pp. S91–S97.

Davis, JH, Schoorman FD & Donaldson, L 1997, 'Toward a stewardship theory of management', Academy of Management Review, vol. 22, no. 1, pp. 20–47.

Dodd, EM 1932, 'For whom are corporate managers trustees?', Harvard Law Review, vol. 45, p. 1148.

Donaldson, L & Davis, JH 1994, 'Boards and company performance – Research challenges the conventional wisdom', Corporate Governance: An International Review, vol. 2 pp. 151–60.

Donaldson, T & Preston, LE 1995, 'The stakeholder theory of the corporation: concepts, evidence, and implications', *Academy of Management Review*, vol. 20, no. 1, pp. 65–91.

Eisenhardt, KM 1989, 'Building theories from case study research', *Academy of Management Review*, vol. 14, no. 4, pp. 532–50.

Fasterling, B 2012, 'Development of norms through compliance disclosure', *Journal of Business Ethics*, vol. 106, pp. 73–87.

Ford, C & Condon, M 2011, 'Introduction to "New governance and the business organisation" Special Issue of Law and Policy', *Law & Policy*, vol. 33, no. 4, pp. 449–58.

Ford, C & Hess, D 2011, 'Corporate monitorships and new governance regulation: in theory, in practice and in context', *Law & Policy*, vol. 33, no. 4, pp. 509–41.

Freeman, RE 1984, *Strategic Management: a stakeholder approach*, Boston: Pitman.

Friedman, M 1970, 'The social responsibility of business is to increase its profits', *New York Times Magazine,* vol. 32, 13 September 1970.

Gilad, S 2010, 'It runs in the family: meta-regulation and its siblings', *Regulation & Governance*, vol. 4, pp. 485–506.

Gioia, DA & Pitre, E 1990, 'Multiparadigm perspectives on theory building', *Academy of Management Review*, vol. 15, no. 4, pp. 584–602.

Gordon, JN 2007, 'The rise of independent directors in the United States, 1950–2005: of shareholder value and stock market prices', *Stanford Law Review*, vol. 59, pp. 1465–1568.

Grant Thornton 2012, *Corporate Governance Reporting Review 2012.*

Gunningham, N & Grabosky, P 1998, *Smart Regulation,* Oxford: Clarendon Press.

Gunningham, N & Rees, J 1997, 'Industry self-regulation: an institutional perspective', *Law & Policy*, vol. 19, no. 4, pp. 365–414.

Hansmann, H & Kraakman, R 2000, 'The end of history for corporate law', *Georgetown Law Journal*, vol. 89, pp. 439–68.

Hess, D 2008, 'The three pillars of corporate social reporting as new governance regulation: disclosure, dialogue and development', *Business Ethics Quarterly*, vol. 18, no. 4, pp. 447–82.

Hillman, AJ, Cannella Jr, AA & Paetzold, RL 2000, 'The resource dependence role of corporate directors: strategic adaptation of board composition in response to environmental change', *Journal of Management Studies*, vol. 37, no. 2, p. 235.

Hooghiemstra, R & van Ees, H 2011, 'Uniformity as response to soft law: evidence from compliance and non-compliance with the Dutch corporate governance code', *Regulation & Governance*, vol. 5, pp. 480–98.

Horrigan, B 2010, *Corporate Social Responsibility in the 21st Century: debates, models and practices across government, law and business*, Cheltenham: Edward Elgar Publishing.

Hung, H 1998, 'A typology of the theories of the roles of governing boards', *Corporate Governance: An International Review*, vol. 6, no. 2, pp. 101–11.

Huse, M 2005, 'Accountability and creating accountability: a framework for exploring behavioural perspectives of corporate governance', *British Journal of Management*, vol. 16, pp. S65–S79.

Jenson & Meckling 1976, 'Theory of the firm: managerial behaviour, agency costs and ownership structure', *Journal of Financial Economics*, vol. 3, pp. 305–60.

Judge, WQ & Zeithaml, CP 1992, 'Institutional and strategic choice perspectives on board involvement in the strategic decision process', *Academy of Management Journal*, vol. 35, no. 4, pp. 766–94.

Karkkainen, B 2004, 'Reply: "New governance" in legal thought and in the world: some splitting as antidote to overzealous lumping', *Minnesota Law Review*, vol. 89, p. 471.

Keay, A 2014, 'Comply or explain: in need of greater regulatory oversight', *Legal Studies*, vol. 34, no. 2, pp. 279–304.

Kiel GC & Nicholson GJ 2003, 'Board composition and corporate performance: how the Australian experience informs contrasting theories of corporate governance', *Corporate Governance: An International Review*, vol. 11, no. 3, pp. 189–205.

Kiel, G, Nicholson, G, Tunny J & Beck, J 2009, *Directors at Work: A Practical Guide for Boards*, Sydney: Thomson Reuter.

King, AA & Lenox, MJ 2000, 'Industry self-regulation without sanctions: the chemical industry's responsible care program', *Academy of Management Journal*, vol. 43, no. 4, pp. 698–716.

Kingsford Smith, D 2012, 'Governing the corporation: the Role of 'soft regulation'', *University of New South Wales Law Journal*, vol. 35, no. 1, pp. 378–403.

Kirkpatrick, G 2009, 'Corporate governance lessons from the financial crisis', OECD.

Klein, E & du Plessis, JJ 2005, 'Corporate donations, the best interest of the company and the proper purpose doctrine', *University of New South Wales Law Journal*, vol. 28, no. 1, pp. 69–97.

Klettner, A, Clarke, T & Adams, M 2010, 'Corporate governance reform: an empirical study of the changing roles and responsibilities of Australian boards and directors', *Australian Journal of Corporate Law*, vol. 24, pp. 148–76.

Lan, LL & Heracleous, L 2010, 'Rethinking agency theory: the view from law', *Academy of Management Review*, vol. 35, no. 2, pp. 294–314.

Langevoort, DC 2001, 'The human nature of corporate boards: law, norms and the un-intended consequences of independence and accountability', *Georgetown Law Journal*, vol. 89, no. 4, pp. 797–832.

Lazonick, W & O'Sullivan, M 2000, 'Maximizing shareholder value: a new ideology for corporate governance', *Economy and Society*, vol. 29, no. 1, pp. 13–35.

Lobel, O 2004, 'The renew deal: the fall of regulation and the rise of governance in con-temporary legal thought', *Minnesota Law Review*, vol. 89, p. 342.

Lynall, MD, Golden, BR & Hillman, AJ 2003, 'Board composition from adolescence to maturity: a multitheoretic View' *Academy of Management Review*, vol. 28, no. 3, pp. 416–431.

MacNeil, I & Li, X 2006, 'Comply or explain: market discipline and non-compliance with the combined code', *Corporate Governance: An International Review*, vol. 14, no. 5, pp. 486–496.

Majumdar, SK & Marcus, AA 2001, 'Rules versus discretion: the productivity con-sequences of flexible regulation', *Academy of Management Journal*, vol. 44, no. 1, pp. 170–79.

Mallin, C 2013, *Corporate Governance*, Oxford: Oxford University Press.

Marshall, S & Ramsay, I 2012, 'Stakeholders and directors' duties: law theory and evi-dence', *University of New South Wales Law Journal*, vol. 35, pp. 291–316.

Moore Dickerson, C 2002, 'How do norms and empathy affect corporation law and cor-porate behavior?: human rights: the emerging norm of corporate social responsibility', *Tulane Law Review*, pp. 1431–60.

Morth, U 2004, 'Introduction', in U Morth (ed.), *Soft Law in Governance and Regulation*, Cheltenham: Edward Elgar Publishing.

Muth, MM & Donaldson, L 1998, 'Stewardship theory and board structure: a contingency approach', *Corporate Governance: An International Review*, vol. 6, no. 1, p. 5.

Nash & Ehrenfeld, J 1997, 'Codes of environmental management practice: assessing their potential as a tool for change', in R H Socolow (ed.), *Annual Review of Energy and Environment,* vol. 22, Palo Alto: Annual Reviews, pp. 487–535.

Nicholson, GJ & Kiel, GC 2007, 'Can directors impact performance? A case-based test of three theories of corporate governance', *Corporate Governance: An International Review*, vol. 15, no. 4, pp. 585–608.

Owen, N 2003, *HIH Royal Commission Report, 'The failure of HIH: a critical assessment'*, tabled to Parliament, 16 April 2003.

Parker, C 2007, 'Meta-regulation - legal accountability for corporate social responsibility', in D McBarnet, A Voiculescu & T Campbell (eds.), *The New Corporate Accountability: corporate social responsibility and the law*, Cambridge: Cambridge University Press.

Roberts, J, McNulty, T & Stiles, P 2005, 'Beyond agency conceptions of the work of the non-executive director: creating accountability in the boardroom', *British Journal of Management*, vol. 16, pp. S5–S26.

Robliant, D 2006, 'Genealogies of soft law', *The American Journal of Comparative Law,* vol. 54, p. 499.

Roche, O P 2009, *Corporate Governance & Organisational Life Cycle*, New York: Cambria Press.

Rock, EB & Wachter, ML 2001a, 'Norms & corporate law', *University of Pennsylvania Law Review,* vol. 149, no. 6, pp. 1607–1700.

Rock, EB & Wachter, ML 2001b, 'Symposium norms and corporate law: islands of conscious power: law norms and the self-governing corporation', *University of Pennsylvania Law Review,* vol. 149, no. 6, p. 1619.

Romano, R 2005, 'The Sarbanes-Oxley Act and the making of quack corporate governance', *The Yale Law Journal*, vol. 114, no. 7, pp. 1521–1611.

Sarra, J 2011, 'New governance, old norms, and the potential for corporate governance reform', *Law & Policy*, vol. 33, no. 4, pp. 576–602.

Sarre, R 2002, 'Responding to corporate collapses: is there a role for corporate social responsibility?', *Deakin Law Review*, vol. 7, no. 1, pp. 1–19.

Selznick, P 1996, 'Institutionalism "old" and "new"', *Administrative Science Quarterly*, vol. 41, no. 2, pp. 270–77.

Shleifer, A & Vishny, RW 1997, 'A survey of corporate governance', *The Journal of Finance,* vol. 52, no. 2, pp. 737–83.

Stiles, P & Taylor, B 2001, *Boards at Work: how directors view their roles and responsibilities,* Oxford; New York: Oxford University Press.

Stout, L 2012, *The Shareholder Value Myth: how putting shareholders first harms investors,* Oakland: Berrett-Koehler Publishers.

Subramaniam, N, McManus, L & Zhang, J 2009, 'Corporate governance, firm characteristics and risk management committee formation in Australian companies', *Managerial Auditing Journal*, vol. 24, no. 4, pp. 316–39.

Taylor, B 2004, 'Leading the boardroom revolution', *Corporate Governance: An International Review*, vol. 12, no. 4, pp. 415–25.

Tomasic, R & Akinbami, F 2011, 'Towards a new corporate governance after the global financial crisis', *International Company and Commercial Law Review*, vol. 22, no. 8, pp. 237–49.

van den Berghe, LA & Baelden, T 2005, 'The monitoring role of the board: one approach does not fit all', *Corporate Governance: An International Review*, vol. 13, no. 5, pp. 680–90.

van Ees, H, Gabrielsson, J & Huse M 2009, 'Toward a behavioural theory of boards and corporate governance, *Corporate Governance: An International Review*, vol. 17, no. 3, pp. 307–39.

Veasey, N 2001, 'Should corporation law inform aspirations for good corporate governance or vice versa?', *University of Pennsylvania Law Review*, vol. 149, pp. 2179–91.

Wang, J & Dewhirst, HD 1992, 'Boards of directors and stakeholder orientation', *Journal of Business Ethics*, vol. 11, no. 2, pp. 115–23.

4

RESEARCHING CORPORATE GOVERNANCE CODES

Disciplines, methods and theories

Research into corporate governance and its regulation can originate in many disciplines and extend in a variety of directions in terms of both method and theory. It is a topic that has been written about by management, law, politics, economics, finance and accounting scholars to name a few. Although early research tended to be quantitative, using statistical methods to try to find a relationship between governance structures and financial performance, there is now an emerging stream of qualitative research that draws on psychology and team dynamics to explore the intermediate processes occurring in the boardroom (Huse et al. 2011). Methods used to explore board process include: questionnaire surveys, interviews, case studies, the collection and analysis of discourses (such as board-life stories) and direct observation of boards and directors in action (Huse 2009).

Scholars braving this methodological shift have begun to develop new theoretical approaches that challenge the predominant agency theory of corporate governance with more complex behavioural theories (Huse et al. 2011; van Ees et al. 2009). To some extent a philosophical divide appears to have arisen between the agency theorists (many in North America) and the behavioural theorists (many in Europe), which is concerned as much with methodology as it is with theory. Overall, however, there is growing consensus of a need for theoretical and methodological pluralism if we are to further our understanding of boards and corporate governance (van Ees et al. 2009, p. 311; Roberts et al. 2005, p. S8).

As introduced in the previous chapter, this book aims to bridge two areas of literature from two academic disciplines – the work of management scholars into the role of the board of directors and the work of legal scholars into regulatory systems. It answers increasing calls for more interdisciplinary work in corporate governance in order to develop richer and more intriguing theoretical frameworks and bring additional perspectives and expertise to bear on common questions (McNulty et al. 2013; Hess 2008; Black 2010). Scholars have pointed to the need to consider empirical evidence in designing and assessing corporate governance regulation. Dalton and Dalton sum this up:

> By considering the empirical evidence, we can better evaluate the promise that lies in current guidelines and prescriptions for effective governance structures.
>
> (2005, p. S92)

This research seeks to advance our understanding of the contemporary role of the board and link this to regulatory effectiveness. Scholars have recognised that academic research has lagged behind the rapid development and proliferation of corporate governance codes (Aguilera and Cuervo-Cazurra 2009; Romano 2005). The purpose of corporate governance regulation is to facilitate effective governance, and yet much recent regulation is based on policies that have little empirical backing regarding their likely effectiveness (Romano 2005). It is not only the content of regulation that is unproven but also the method of regulating. Over the last two decades regulatory scholars have noted the increasing use of decentred layers of soft regulation whilst commenting that we still do not fully understand how such regulation works and in which contexts it is most effective (Braithwaite and Parker 2004). By reviewing the corporate response to the recommendations of the Australian corporate governance code, this book presents a case-study of soft regulation and provides evidence of the processes through which it can effect behavioural change.

Research into boards of directors and their behaviour

The book builds on the work of management researchers such as Stiles and his colleagues (Stiles and Taylor 2001; Roberts et al. 2005, Leblanc and Gillies 2005; Spira and Bender 2004; Pettigrew and McNulty 1995; McNulty and Pettigrew 1999; Pye 2001) who have used interview-based methodologies to explore board processes and behaviour. Although empirical research is common in the discipline of management, corporate governance research was for several decades dominated by research based on quantitative methods. Huse describes this as the 'input-output model' where measures of board composition (numbers of independent directors, board size etc., described by Finkelstein and Mooney (2003) as the 'usual suspects') are statistically compared to measures of firm performance. Interview-based studies are a relatively new approach to studying corporate governance, developed after these traditional quantitative methods failed to find a convincing link between measures of board composition and corporate performance. As Forbes and Milliken neatly put it:

> ... the influence of board demography on firm performance may not be simple and direct, as many past studies presume, but, rather, complex and

indirect. To account for this possibility, researchers must begin to explore more precise ways of studying board demography that account for the role of intervening processes.

(1999, p. 490)

McNulty et al. (2013), in an extensive review of corporate governance research, found that, although research had burgeoned in the last decade, only about 1 percent of all articles used qualitative methods. Nevertheless, qualitative research into corporate governance has great practical value because it 'can assist policy-makers and practitioners to develop more efficient governance mechanisms by shedding light on the efficacy of policy prescription' (McNulty et al. 2013, p. 183). Board-process information is highly relevant when considering the effectiveness of regulation designed to improve board performance. The aim of processual analysis, as described by Pettigrew, is 'to explore the dynamic quality of human conduct and organizational life and to embed such dynamics over time in the various layers of context in which streams of activity occur' (1997, p. 347). The research presented in this book aims to consider, based on empirical evidence, the areas where corporate governance codes are having positive effects and areas where their design and scope could be improved: 'Qualitative research provides a basis for rethinking and challenging some of the dominant assumptions and meanings about how governance actors and institutions actually function' (McNulty et al. 2013, p. 183).

The difficulty when embarking on qualitative research is that boardroom processes are much harder to identify and analyse than measures of board composition. The real-life functioning of a board depends on human relationships, skills and decision-making, which cannot easily be reduced to numbers and statistics (Adams et al. 2008). Also, it is difficult, but not impossible, to gain access to boards to observe them in action or to question them about their decision-making, due to the highly confidential nature of most of their deliberations. Leblanc and Schwartz dedicate an article to the methodological difficulties of conducting research into boards of directors whilst stressing the importance of boardroom-based research: 'What it takes to make a board effective, and what it takes to make a director effective, are constructs that may only be assessed thoroughly from inside boardrooms' (2007, p. 850).

Prior to 1995 there were only three such studies regularly cited: Mace's 1972 study involving 75 interviews, Lorsch and MacIver's 1989 study of 'nearly 100' directors and Demb and Neubauer's research published in 1992 referring to 71 interviews with directors across eight countries. Moving towards the 2000s, there were several UK studies involving interviews with board directors also presented in the literature. McNulty and Pettigrew (1999) interviewed 108 non-executive directors in the UK and explored, amongst other things, their role in influencing corporate strategy. Stiles and Taylor (2001) interviewed 51 directors and used the resulting data to analyse board roles. Annie Pye also interviewed 55 directors from nine organisations in a study designed to investigate change over time. She discusses the interesting methodological issue of whether it is ever possible to repeat this kind of study due to 'changing interpretive frameworks and organizational context' (2001, p. 34). Roche also examined changes over time but by asking 34 directors in Montreal about their views on the changing role of the board over an organisation's life cycle (2009). The 2005 article by Roberts et al. draws on their work for the UK government's Higgs review into the role of non-executive directors. Their study, with its objective of informing government policy with regard to corporate governance regulation had a similar ethos to this book.

Research into codes of corporate governance

A more specific aim of this book is to build knowledge on the topic of corporate governance codes, where research is scarce and somewhat scattered. Aguilera and Cuervo-Cazurra describe a code of good governance as 'a set of best practice recommendations regarding the behaviour and structure of the board of directors' (2009, p. 376). They show how codes proliferated very suddenly in the 1990s and diffused worldwide. Several researchers have called for more studies into how corporate governance codes work in practice, particularly since the global financial crisis highlighted the fact that code compliance did not correlate with actual board effectiveness (Roberts 2012). Aguilera and Cuervo-Cazurra comment that there has been 'little systematic analysis of how codes of good governance have affected how corporations are structured, or how managers behave across different corporate governance systems' (2009, p. 376). Indeed, a 'striking schism' has been noted between the beliefs of business people and academic research:

> All this is resulting in an apparent divergence in development between the real world, where codes continue to be developed and revised, and the academic world, where there is limited theoretical advancement on the topic.
> (Aguilera and Cuervo-Cazurra 2009, p. 377)

Aguilera and Cuervo-Cazurra's 2009 review of the literature on codes of corporate governance divides research into three categories: (1) cross-country comparative work; (2) within-country reviews of compliance; (3) studies of the link between corporate governance and firm performance. The research described in this book does not fall squarely into any of these categories: (1) it provides limited cross-country comparison to set the context for specific code provisions and demonstrate international themes in the reform agenda; (2) it purposely avoids trying to measure code compliance, focusing more on the behavioural changes that compliance can initiate; (3) in this way it examines the links between codes and firm behaviour – a somewhat different concept than firm performance. Its aim is to take a step back from attempts to link governance structures and processes to financial performance, by exploring instead their effect on the board of directors and management. In an updated literature review on the topic, Cuomo et al. (2016) confirm that, although there have been country-level studies on code implementation mechanisms, this has not been studied at firm level. They find that research on codes tends to be empirical without explicit use or development of theory.

Several empirical studies of compliance with corporate governance codes have been conducted (Werder et al. 2005; Akkermans et al. 2007). Although they do not tend to examine the behavioural effects of regulation within corporations, they do assess the effectiveness of the comply-or-explain mechanism in terms of compliance levels and explore the reasons for observed compliance patterns. For example, Hooghiemstra and van Ees (2011) find a uniformity in corporate responses that goes against the logic of the code and casts doubt on the effectiveness of the flexibility of comply-or-explain codes. Keay (2014) also doubts the effectiveness of the comply-or-explain mechanism but due to uninformative company disclosures and lack of shareholder engagement. Keay concludes that codes are not effective because investors, even the large institutional investors, do not assess and engage with companies over their corporate governance practices and ultimately do not base investment decisions on them:

> the idea behind the adoption of comply or explain is that the shareholders and the markets will assess what the company has done and judge it accordingly. ... The problem is that the research suggests that investors do not monitor sufficiently and do not generally bother to engage in any assessment of what companies have done or not done.
>
> (Keay 2014, p. 293)

MacNeil and Li (2006) studied what they termed 'serial non-compliers' in the UK and found that investors would tolerate non-compliance with the corporate governance code if a company was still performing well financially. They also concluded that the benefits of flexibility associated with the code were overstated. On the other hand, Seidl et al., in their recent research based on the UK and German codes, found that 'the sheer number of deviations recorded would seem to suggest that concerns about companies being driven towards full compliance are largely unfounded' (2013, p. 800). Luo and Salterio (2014) also found extensive use of code flexibility in Canada and demonstrated that the ability to tailor corporate governance to a company's needs brings benefits to shareholders. Overall, despite the popularity of comply-or-explain codes, our understanding of how they impact on corporate behaviour is still rather limited (Seidl 2006).

Research reviewing the behavioural impact of codes of corporate governance is particularly scarce. The aim of the research discussed in this book was to examine, in a qualitative way, the corporate response to specific aspects of corporate governance codes – searching for behavioural change of a sort that would demonstrate regulatory effectiveness. As Baldwin and Black discuss, this sort of assessment, of the qualitative output of regulation (as opposed to quantitative assessment of compliance) is important but uncommon because of its time-consuming and difficult nature:

Input based assessment of performance is common: the measurement of numbers of inspectors and inspections, resources devoted to control and other inputs. Process or compliance based assessment is also common: measuring adherence to procedural requirements and other laws, policies or guidelines. What is less common is a qualitative assessment of either output: measuring the extent to which the goals of the specific programme are achieved, or longer term outcomes: evaluating the impact of the regulatory system against the broad objectives of the agency (rather than the specific programme).

(2008, p. 73)

Spira and Page (2010) have empirically examined corporate responses in the area of corporate governance using annual report data. They collected corporate governance statements on risk management and used a process of content analysis to code the data. Although they studied disclosure statements, their aim was to consider 'the possible impact of the disclosure requirements on corporate behaviour' (2010, p. 409). Julia Black identifies one other study that focuses on the behavioural response to regulation and notes the link between methodology and theoretical approach: sociological approaches tend to use qualitative methods, and economic approaches use quantitative methods (2010, p. 170). This study by Larson (2004) found that the amount of interaction between regulatory and market actors influenced whether behaviour was structured more by formal rules or social norms. Langevoort in examining more generally the role of corporate boards from a behavioural perspective concludes:

> Until we discover exactly what directors hear amidst all the [regulatory] noise, we cannot begin to evaluate the wisdom of our bundle of legal and regulatory strategies touching on questions of boards of directors' responsibilities.

(2001, p. 832)

Research into soft regulation and corporate behaviour

Dimity Kingsford Smith is one of few scholars exploring the effectiveness of corporate governance standards in Australia. She notes the fact that corporate governance regulation exhibits many of the characteristics of decentred regulation as described more generally by regulatory scholars (2012, p. 386). Her 2012 article has as its aims:

> ... to map and analyse some of the many ways in which non-state corporate governance norms operate and have effect. The more interesting questions are 'how does SR [soft regulation] operate?', 'what effects does SR have?', and most particularly 'how does SR inter-relate with state regulation and other non-legal orders, to have the effects it does?'

(2012, p. 379)

This book aims to contribute to knowledge in this area by using the Australian corporate governance code as a case study. This is an approach used by other regulatory scholars: by testing theory against empirical case studies researchers have gained understanding of the limits of emerging regulatory approaches and their potential advantages (Ford and Hess 2011; Coglianese and Lazer 2003; Spira and Page 2010). Ford and Hess examined the United States' post-GFC corporate monitorship regulation in order to explore the limitations of 'new governance' style regulation:

> this research, and the example of the recent financial crisis, pushes us to consider larger questions about how and to what degree new governance-style initiatives can consistently and reliably promote better corporate conduct.
>
> (2011, p. 510)

They examined the practical effect of the monitorship regime against its theoretical potential concluding that the monitorship regime did not fulfil its theoretical promise. Importantly they were able to identify some of the reasons, including the sociological and institutional forces at play. Similarly, Gunningham and Sinclair (2009) found that management-based regulation regarding occupational health and safety in the mining sector was only effective where there was an existing culture of trust and commitment. Studies of this nature provide important insights into the effectiveness of regulation of great value for future regulatory design (Majumdar and Marcus 2001). As Ford and Hess comment:

> Understanding how new governance initiatives will play out within the dynamics and institutional processes of particular regulatory regimes is an essential step in making new governance an effective tool for regulatory design.
>
> (2011, p. 538)

Their article was published as part of a special issue of *Law and Policy* dedicated to furthering understanding of how soft regulation or new governance impacts upon business organisations. The case studies used ranged across food safety, privacy, banking and corporate governance and demonstrated the importance of general understanding of how organisations react to these types of initiatives.

However, in order to understand how regulation can improve board performance we need to understand what the board does, what comprises good board performance and to what extent the role of the board differs across different companies. These are important issues for policy-makers when they determine the content of regulation. These issues also impact on the type of regulatory mechanism that is likely to be appropriate. Corporate governance regulation regarding board function has tended to comprise flexible principles rather than strict rules because of the complex and varied nature of the role of the board. The research presented in this book aims to better understand the impact of codes of corporate governance on board behaviour   whether their provisions conflict with or complement the role played by most boards and the mechanisms through which the comply-or-explain mechanism can lead to changes in behaviour.

Research design and methodology

As a whole, the book is based on a case-study methodology where the 'cases' are regulatory provisions, not companies (as management scholars might expect) or court decisions (as legal scholars might expect). Each chapter from 5 to 8 takes a particular recommendation or set of recommendations of the Australian corporate governance code as the unit of study. Each chapter therefore comprises a case-study of the corporate response to a specific element of regulation. Within-case analysis occurs within each of these 'findings chapters' in slightly different ways. In most chapters interview comments and corporate reports were analysed against pre-determined themes. Yin calls this process 'analytic generalisation' in which a previously developed theory is used as a template with which to compare the empirical results of the case study. (2013, p. 31) This process of within-case analysis primarily assesses the effectiveness of the *content* of the regulation, although at times it may also provide insights into the effectiveness of the regulatory *mechanism*.

Cross-case analysis is then presented in Chapter 9. Although the subject matter or content of each of the recommendations studied in Chapters 5 to 8 is different, the regulatory *mechanism* used (comply-or-explain) is the same across each case, enabling cross-case comparison of regulatory effect. Each case also reveals information about the role of the board, which is pooled in Chapter 9 to draw out overriding themes regarding board function and the conditions that foster good board performance. Thus, the process of analytic generalisation is used again in Chapter 9, this time at a higher level, to compare the theories behind both board roles and regulatory mechanisms, set out in Chapter 3, with the themes emerging from the pooled empirical data.

Data collection

The flexible nature of the comply-or-explain mechanism permits variation in the implementation of corporate governance codes. Analysis of companies' implementation choices throws light on the nature of the corporate response to code provisions. This book draws upon two main categories of data to inform its discussion on the effectiveness of codes:

1 Archival data – company annual reports and sustainability reports. Disclosures in these documents, made annually by listed companies, provide evidence of companies' interpretation of the ASX corporate governance code and their governance decisions.

2 Interview data – semi-structured interviews with company officers. Interviews permit a more in-depth understanding of the reasons behind the formal corporate disclosures.

Collection of more than one source of data is a well-known technique for improving the validity of qualitative findings through a process called triangulation (Jick 1979). Triangulation involves cross-verification of findings obtained through different methods. It is possible to be more confident about research conclusions if the findings are replicated across independent data sources. As Huse makes clear, it is best if a variety of methods or tools can be combined to collect data because 'different types of data triangulations may be important for interpreting, embedding and validating results' (2011, p. 21). Tools and methods cited by Huse include: mail-surveys, web-surveys, phone interviews, personal interviews and content analysis of documents.

This book draws on data collected as part of several distinct research projects, and thus the research sample is different for each chapter and explained therein. Most of the interviews were conducted in 2006 and comprise the earliest data source as well as the broadest in scope (see Klettner et al. 2010). The raw interview transcripts with 67 company officers covered all aspects of corporate governance and were re-analysed against each of the four chapter topics. The time difference between collection of this data and much of the archival data (collected between 2010 and 2012 on a topic-specific basis) allowed a level of longitudinal comparison. Chapter 5 on board performance evaluation also includes interview data collected in 2010, increasing the ability to review change over time.

Data analysis

Methods of analysis vary across the chapters as they are closely aligned with the type of data collected. The primary method of analysis was qualitative analysis of text, for example, drawing themes from interview data and coding disclosure statements in annual reports. Strauss and Corbin call this a process of conceptualising and reducing data, elaborating categories in terms of their properties and dimensions and relating through a series of prepositional statements (1998, p. 12). Core terms from the literature can be used as the basis of coding categories when analysing data in this way (Miles and Huberman 1984). The research did not limit coding categories to those pre-determined by theory – where other categories emerged directly from the data, these were included in the research findings (Creswell 2013, p. 185).

Some chapters also use quantitative content analysis where key-word frequency is used as a measure of the prevalence of a theme. Content analysis is 'an empirically grounded method, exploratory in process, and predictive or inferential in intent' (Krippendorff 2012, p. 1). Also defined as 'a technique for gathering data that consists of codifying qualitative information in anecdotal and literary form into categories in order to derive quantitative scales of varying levels of complexity' (Abbott and Monson 1979). It has been widely used in studying corporate website communications and corporate reporting more generally (Paul 2008; Taneja et al. 2011; Jose and Lee 2007).

Research limitations

The research presented here has many of the common limitations faced by research into board behaviour. First, methodologies tend to have to be somewhat opportunistic and creative to overcome the problem of access to elite actors such as directors: not only are they very busy but they will consider many of their activities to be confidential. Response rates to letters mailed to companies ranged from 15 percent to 5 percent. These response rates were similar to those of Leblanc and Gillies (2005) who received expressions of interest from approximately 8 percent of letter recipients. Despite hoping to talk with directors, a large number of the interviews obtained were with company secretaries. In hindsight this may have been an advantage. As Stiles comments:

> The appeal of surveying company secretaries on the role of the board is therefore clear: company secretaries are not typically directors and therefore may be thought to respond in a less self-serving fashion. In other words, responses from company secretaries may be rather more objective than those from directors in questionnaires.
>
> (2001, p. 633)

Personal contacts were also used to obtain interviews, justified on the basis that it was likely to provide a wider range of opinions. Also some of the interviews were obtained by partnering with professional organisations, namely the law firm Dibbs Barker and the Australian Council for Superannuation Investors. This is an effective way to conduct research that is helpful to both industry and academics.

In their 2001 study, Stiles and Taylor used four methods to obtain interviews: (1) direct approach using third-party contact; (2) direct approach via letter; (3) direct approach through personal contact and (4) indirect approach through referral (2001, p. 26). Leblanc and Gillies used a similar mix of methods in their 2005 study including letter, personal contacts and referrals. They observed that the process of negotiating access to directors became easier as the study progressed (2005, p. 843). This was true of the interviews discussed here, for example, once it became possible to (1) tell potential interviewees that similar companies had already been interviewed and (2) have some discussion about the project's preliminary findings, they tended to be more willing to participate. These methods have been described as snowballing techniques and have been criticised on the basis that the resulting sample is not random. However, this limitation is generally accepted by researchers in the field on the basis that a random sample is not essential in qualitative research and can be justified against the alternative of non-access to boards (Leblanc and Schwartz 2007, p. 849; Pettigrew and McNulty 1995, p. 851).

Second, there is the suspicion that some of the information provided by companies and their officers, both in annual reports and at interview, is not entirely candid and may paint a more favourable picture than exists in reality. As mentioned above, validity of data can be improved by triangulating different data sources. Alternatively it can be accepted that both interview and annual report statements may not portray the absolute truth, yet still comprise a valid narrative of events.

Third, like all qualitative studies, there is the risk of subjectivity in interpreting and analysing the information provided: a risk that can be mitigated with a well-designed methodology. As Lillis points out, interviews have great potential but are subject to interviewer bias both during the interview and when transcribing and analysing its detail (1999, p. 84). Using a semi-structured interview template can limit such bias by ensuring that each interview covers pre-determined themes using neutral questions. Also, having more than one person code the data mitigates the risk of subjectivity through a process known as inter-rater reliability.

Lastly, this kind of research, due to limitations of access and resources, is usually based in one country, and findings may not be directly applicable elsewhere. Despite theories of convergence, corporate governance systems are country-specific, and what is applicable in one country may not be effective elsewhere (Cuervo 2002; Gabrielsson and Huse 2004). Nevertheless, the similarity of the Australian corporate governance code to many other nations' codes means the findings may have wider relevance. Yin (2013) explains that case-study research should not aim to generalise directly from one case to another. Instead the objective should be to generalise findings to develop a theory that can then be tested against other cases. Thus, the findings of this research can be compared and contrasted with similar studies based on other nations' corporate governance codes.

Qualitative research

Qualitative methodologies, when compared to proven quantitative methods, have suffered from criticism regarding their validity and reliability, yet their findings can develop rich understanding of complex phenomena in circumstances where quantitative methods can only speculate. The extra time and effort that it takes to conduct qualitative studies can reap great rewards and, with methods becoming more robust, the early criticisms are becoming increasingly weak. Bluhm et al. (2010) believe the field of qualitative research in general is nearing a tipping point at which 'the positivistic stigmatization of qualitative methods and analysis is overturned not only by the value of the unique insights and richness of the knowledge generated through these methods, but also through the near standardization and improved validity of the methodologies themselves'. Leblanc and Gillies differentiate the aims of qualitative research:

> The purpose of qualitative research is not to test hypotheses deductively in the traditional scientific method, nor is it to generalize from a sample to a

> population. The intent of qualitative research is not to generalize findings but to form a unique interpretation of events.
>
> (2005, p. 260)

Thus the next four chapters present qualitative research on corporate governance. The research findings provide unique insights into how regulation can impact on four topical corporate governance issues: board performance, gender diversity, corporate social responsibility and executive remuneration.

Summary of chapter 4

This chapter reviews some of the research on corporate governance and its regulation, explaining the wide variation in methodological approach and the many areas that remain to be explored. This book draws on two, if not three, methodological traditions: (1) interview-based research into the role of the board of directors in corporate governance; (2) research that analyses corporate reporting to understand patterns of adoption of corporate governance codes; (3) regulatory case-studies that explore in depth how particular initiatives impact on behaviour. The research presented in this book combines these approaches using a novel design that analyses both interview and documentary data against objective criteria drawn from the corporate governance literature. It does this for four regulatory case-studies, which are then analysed as a whole to draw out cross-case similarities relevant to future regulatory reform.

References

Abbott, WF & Monson, RJ 1979, 'On the measurement of corporate social responsibility: self-reported disclosure as a method of measuring corporate social involvement', *Academy of Management Journal*, vol. 22, no. 3, pp. 501–15.

Adams, R, Hermalin, BE & Weisbach, MS 2008, 'The role of boards of directors in corporate governance: a conceptual framework and survey' (Working Paper Series, Center for Responsible Business, UC Berkley, 2008) 44.

Aguilera, RV & Cuervo-Cazurra, A 2009, 'Codes of good governance', *Corporate Governance: An International Review,* vol. 17, no. 3, pp. 376–87.

Akkermans, D, van Ees, H, Hermes, N, Hooghiemstra, R, Van der Laan, G, Postma, T & van Witteloostuijn, A 2007, 'Corporate governance in the Netherlands: an overview of the application of the Tabaksblat Code in 2004', *Corporate Governance: An International Review,* vol. 15, no. 6, pp. 1106–18.

Baldwin, R & Black, J 2008, 'Really responsive regulation', *Modern Law Review,* vol. 71, no. 1, pp. 59–94.

Baldwin, R, Cave M & Lodge, M 2012, *Understanding Regulation,* 2nd ed, Oxford: Oxford University Press.

Bansal, P & Corley, K 2011, 'From the editors. The coming of age for qualitative research: embracing the diversity of qualitative methods', *Academy of Management Journal,* vol. 54, pp. 233–37.

Baumann, D & Scherer, AG 2010, 'MNEs and the UN global compact: an empirical analysis of the organizational implementation of corporate citizenship' (Institute of

Organisation and Administrative Science, University of Zurich, IOU Working Paper No. 114, 2010).

Black, J 2010, 'Financial markets', in P Cane & H M Kritzer, (eds,), *The Oxford Handbook of Empirical Legal Research*, Oxford: Oxford University Press.

Bluhm, DJ, Harman, W, Lee, TW & Mitchell, TR 2010, 'Qualitative research in management: a decade of progress', *Journal of Management Studies,* vol. 48, no. 8, pp. 1866–91.

Braithwaite, J & Parker, C 2004, 'Conclusion', in C Parker, C Scott, N Lacey & J Braithwaite (eds.), *Regulating Law*, Oxford: Oxford University Press.

Corley, KG & Gioia, DA 2011, 'Building theory about theory building: what constitutes a theoretical contribution?', *Academy of Management Review,* vol. 36, no. 1, p. 12.

Creswell, JW 2013, *Research Design: qualitative, quantitative and mixed methods approaches*, 4th ed, Thousand Oaks: SAGE Publications.

Cuervo 2002, 'Corporate governance mechanisms: a plea for less codes of good governance and more market control', *Corporate Governance: An International Review*, vol. 10, no. 2, pp. 84–93.

Cuomo, F, Mallin, C & Zattoni, A 2016, 'Corporate governance codes: a review and research agenda', *Corporate Governance: An International Review*, forthcoming.

Dalton, CM & Dalton, DR 2005, 'Boards of directors: utilizing empirical evidence in developing practical prescriptions', *British Journal of Management,* vol. 16, pp. S91–S97.

Finkelstein, S & Mooney, AC 2003, 'Not the usual suspects; how to use board process to make boards better', *Academy of Management Perspectives*, vol. 17, no. 2, pp. 101–13.

Forbes, DP & Milliken, FJ 1999, 'Cognition and corporate governance understanding boards of directors as strategic decision making groups', *Academy of Management Review*, vol. 24, no. 3, pp. 489–505.

Ford, C & Hess, D 2011, 'Corporate monitorships and new governance regulation: in theory, in practice, and in context', *Law & Policy*, vol. 33, no. 4, pp. 509–41.

Gabrielsson, J & Huse, M 2004, 'Context, behaviour and evolution: challenges in research on boards and governance', *International Studies of Management and Organisation*, vol. 34, no. 2, pp. 11–36.

Gioia, DA & Pitre, E 1990, 'Multiparadigm perspectives on theory building', *Academy of Management Review,* vol. 15, no. 4, pp. 584–602.

Gray, R, Kouhy, R & Lavers, DS 1995, 'Constructing a research database of social and environmental reporting by UK companies', *Accounting, Auditing and Accountability Journal*, vol. 8, pp. 78–101.

Gunningham, N & Sinclair, D 2009, 'Organizational trust and the limits of management-based regulation', *Law & Society Review*, vol. 43, no. 4, p. 865.

Hess, D 2008, 'The three pillars of corporate social responsibility reporting as new governance regulation: disclosure, dialogue and development', *Business Ethics Quarterly,* vol. 8, no. 4, pp. 447–82.

Hooghiemstra, R & van Ees, H 2011, 'Uniformity as response to soft law: evidence from compliance and non-compliance with the Dutch corporate governance code', *Regulation & Governance*, vol. 5, pp. 480–98.

Huse, M 2009, 'Exploring methods and concepts in studies of board processes', in M Huse (ed.), *The Value Creating Board: Corporate Governance and Organizational Behaviour*, Abingdon: Routledge, pp. 221–33.

Huse, M, Hoskisson, R, Zattoni, A & Vigano, R 2011, 'New perspectives on board research: changing the research agenda', *Journal of Management and Governance*, vol. 15, pp. 5–28.

Jick, TD 1979, 'Mixing qualitative and quantitative methods: triangulation in action', *Administrative Science Quarterly*, vol. 24, no. 4, p. 602.

Jose, A & Lee, S 2007, 'Environmental reporting of global corporations, a content analysis based on website disclosures', *Journal of Business Ethics,* vol. 72, pp. 307–21.

Keay, A 2014, 'Comply or explain in corporate governance codes: in need of greater regulatory oversight? *Legal Studies,* vol. 34, no. 2, pp. 279–304.

Kingsford Smith, D 2012, 'Governing the corporation: the role of 'soft regulation', *University of New South Wales Law Journal,* vol. 35, no. 1, pp. 378–403.

Klettner, A, Clarke, T & Adams, M, 2010 'Corporate governance reform: An empirical study of the changing roles and responsibilities of Australian boards and directors *Australian Journal of Corporate Law,* vol. 24, pp 148–176.

Kolk, A 2008, 'Sustainability, accountability and corporate governance: exploring multi-nationals' reporting practices', *Business Strategy and the Environment,* vol. 18, pp. 1–15.

Krippendorff, K 2012, *Content Analysis: an introduction to its methodology,* 3rd ed, Thousand Oaks: SAGE Publications.

Langevoort, DC 2001, 'The human nature of corporate boards: law, norms and the un-intended consequences of independence and accountability', *Georgetown Law Journal,* vol. 89, no. 4, pp. 797–832.

Larson, E 2004, 'Institutionalising legal consciousness: regulation and the embedding of market participants in the securities industry in Ghana and Fiji', *Law & Society Review,* vol. 38, no. 4, pp. 737–68.

Leblanc, RW & Gillies, J 2005, *Inside the Boardroom: how boards really work and the coming revolution in corporate governance,* Toronto: John Wiley & Sons.

Leblanc, R & Schwartz, MS 2007, 'The black box of board process: gaining access to a difficult subject', *Corporate Governance: An International Review,* vol. 15, no. 5, pp. 843–51.

Lillis, AM 1999, 'A framework for the analysis of interview data from multiple field research sites', *Accounting and Finance,* vol. 39, no. 1, pp. 79–84.

Luo, Y & Salterio, SE 2014, 'Governance quality in a "comply or explain" governance disclosure regime', *Corporate Governance: An International Review,* vol. 22, no. 6, p. 460.

MacNeil, I & Li, X 2006, 'Comply or explain: market discipline and non-compliance with the combined code', *Corporate Governance: An International Review,* vol. 14, no. 5, pp. 486–96.

McNulty, T & Pettigrew, A 1999, 'Strategists on the board', *Organization Studies,* vol. 20, no. 1, p. 47.

McNulty, T, Zattoni, A & Douglas, T 2013, 'Developing corporate governance research through qualitative methods: a review of previous studies', *Corporate Governance: An International Review,* vol. 21, no. 2, pp. 183–98.

Miles, MB & Huberman, AM 1984, *Qualitative Data Analysis,* Thousand Oaks: SAGE.

Morgan, G, Ryu, K & Mirvis, P 2009, 'Leading corporate citizenship: governance, structure, systems', *Corporate Governance,* vol. 9, no. 1, pp. 39–49.

Paul, K 2008, 'Corporate sustainability, citizenship and social responsibility reporting', *Journal of Corporate Citizenship,* vol. 32, pp. 63–78.

Pettigrew, A 1997, 'What is a processual analysis?', *Scandinavian Management Journal,* vol. 13, pp. 337–48.

Pettigrew, A & McNulty, T 1995, 'Power and influence in and around the boardroom', *Human Relations,* vol. 48, no. 8, p. 845.

Pye, A 2001, 'A study in studying corporate boards over time: looking backwards to move forwards', *British Journal of Management,* vol. 12, p. 33.

Roberts, J 2012, 'Between the letter and the spirit: defensive and extensive modes of compliance with the UK code of corporate governance', in T Clarke & D Branson (eds.), *The SAGE Handbook of Corporate Governance*, London: SAGE, pp. 196–216.

Roberts, J, McNulty, T & Stiles, P 2005, 'Beyond agency conceptions of the work of the non-executive director: creating accountability in the boardroom', *British Journal of Management*, vol. 16, pp. S5–S26.

Roche, OP 2009, *Corporate Governance & Organisational Life Cycle*, New York: Cambria Press.

Romano, R 2005, 'The Sarbanes-Oxley Act and the making of quack corporate governance', *The Yale Law Journal*, vol. 114, no. 7, pp. 1521–1611.

Seidl, D 2006, 'Regulating organisations through codes of corporate governance' (Working Paper No. 338, Centre for Business Research, University of Cambridge, December 2006).

Seidl, D, Sanderson P & Roberts, J 2013, 'Applying the 'comply-or-explain' principle: discursive legitimacy tactics with regard to codes of corporate governance', *Journal of Management and Governance*, vol. 17, no. 3, p. 791.

Spira, LF & Bender, R 2004, 'Compare and contrast: perspectives on board committees', *Corporate Governance*, vol. 12, no. 4, p. 489.

Spira, LF & Page, M 2010, 'Regulation by disclosure: the case of internal control', *Journal of Management and Governance*, vol. 14, pp. 409–33.

Stiles, P 2001, 'The impact of the board on strategy: an empirical examination', *Journal of Management Studies*, vol. 38, no. 5, p. 627.

Stiles, P & Taylor, B 2001, *Boards at Work: how directors view their roles and responsibilities*, Oxford: Oxford University Press.

Strauss, A & Corbin, J 1998, *Basics of Qualitative Research* 2nd Ed., Thousand Oaks: SAGE.

Taneja, SS, Taneja, PK & Gupta, RK 2011, 'Researches in corporate social responsibility: a review of shifting focus, paradigms and methodologies', *Journal of Business Ethics*, vol. 101, pp. 343–64.

Tomasic, R & Bottomley, S 1993, *Directing the Top 500: corporate governance and accountability in Australian companies*, Sydney: Allen and Unwin.

van Ees, H, Gabrielsson, J & Huse, M 2009, 'Toward a behavioural theory of boards and corporate governance', *Corporate Governance: An International Review*, vol. 17, no. 3, pp. 307–39.

Werder, AV, Talaulicar, T & Kolat, GL 2005, 'Compliance with the German corporate governance code: an empirical analysis of the compliance statements by German listed companies', *Corporate Governance: An International Review*, vol. 13, no. 2, pp. 178–87.

Yin, RK 2009, *Case Study Research: Design and Methods* 4th ed, Thousand Oaks: SAGE Publications.

Yin, RK 2013, *Case Study Research: Design and Methods*, 5th ed, Thousand Oaks: SAGE Publications.

5

BOARD EFFECTIVENESS AND PERFORMANCE EVALUATION

Introduction

Regular performance evaluation of the board of directors is a common recommendation of corporate governance codes worldwide on the basis that board evaluations can help identify and resolve any skill gaps, improve board performance and thereby reduce the likelihood of corporate failure (Nicholson et al. 2012; Minichilli et al. 2007; Kiel and Nicholson 2005). As the OECD has explained:

> In order to improve board practices and the performance of its members, an increasing number of jurisdictions are now encouraging companies to engage in board training and voluntary self-evaluation that meets the needs of the individual company.
>
> (2004, p. 66)

Table 5.1 provides some examples of these regulatory provisions from corporate governance codes across the globe. There are some strong similarities: most codes recommend annual evaluation of the full board and also its committees and individual directors; yet there are differences in terms of the level of formality of the evaluation; the appropriate performance criteria and what should be publicly disclosed.

Despite the prevalence of these provisions there has been relatively little research into how board evaluations ought to be designed and carried out and whether they are effective. Minichilli et al. comment that 'the features of board evaluations have been neglected both in theory and practice, and two decades of research on corporate governance has regularly under-estimated the issue of board evaluations' (2007, p. 609). Although this comment is nearly 10 years old it still holds true today.

The board of directors embodies the core of corporate governance, and thus evaluation of board function has the potential to improve both practical and

TABLE 5.1 Code provisions on board evaluation

Code	Provision
Australian Corporate Governance Principles and Recommendations (ASX Corporate Governance Council 2014)	Recommendation 1.6 A listed entity should: (a) have and disclose a process for periodically evaluating the performance of the board, its committees and individual directors; and (b) disclose, in relation to each reporting period, whether a performance evaluation was undertaken in the reporting period in accordance with that process. Commentary The board should consider periodically using external facilitators to conduct its performance reviews. A suitable non-executive director (such as the deputy chair or the senior independent director, if the entity has one), should be responsible for the performance evaluation of the chair, after having canvassed the views of the other directors. When disclosing whether a performance evaluation has been undertaken the entity should, where appropriate, also disclose any insights it has gained from the evaluation and any governance changes it has made as a result.
Denmark Recommendations on Corporate Governance (Committee on Corporate Governance 2014)	3.5 The Committee recommends that the board of directors establish an evaluation procedure where contributions and results of the board of directors and the individual members, as well as collaboration with the executive board, are annually evaluated. Significant changes deriving from the evaluation should be included in the management commentary or on the company's website. Comment: The evaluation should consider the composition, work and results of the board of directors (including the number of members). The need for and usefulness of the committee structure, as well as organisation of work and the quality of material for the board of directors, should also be included in the evaluation.

(Continued)

Code	Provision
French Corporate Governance Code of Listed Corporations (afep-MEDEF, 2013)	Principle 10 For sound corporate governance, the Board of Directors should evaluate its ability to meet the expectations of the shareholders that have entrusted authority to it to direct the corporation, by reviewing from time to time its membership, organisation and operation. The evaluation should have three objectives: • assess the way in which the board operates; • check that the important issues are suitably prepared and discussed; • measure the actual contribution of each director to the board's work through his or her competence and involvement in discussions The evaluation should be performed in the following manner: • Once a year, the board should dedicate one of the points on its agenda to a debate concerning its operation; • There should be a formal evaluation at least once every three years. This could be implemented under the leadership of the appointments or nominations committee or an independent director, with help from an external consultant. • The shareholders should be informed each year in the annual report of the evaluations carried out and, if applicable, of any steps taken as a result.
Japan's Corporate Governance Code (JPX Tokyo Stock Exchange 2015)	Principle 4.11. The board should endeavour to improve its function by analysing and evaluating effectiveness of the board as a whole. 4.11.3. Each year the board should analyse and evaluate its effectiveness as a whole, taking into consideration the relevant matters, including the self-evaluations of each director. A summary of the results should be disclosed.
Maltese Code of Principles of Good Corporate Governance (MFSA 2005)	7.3.1 In effecting the board's performance evaluation, the Performance Evaluation Committee should consider: 7.3.1.1 its performance objectives; 7.3.1.2 testing and development of strategy; 7.3.1.3 the composition and effectiveness of the Board's relations; 7.3.1.4 the board's response to problems; 7.3.1.5 the board agenda; 7.3.1.6 overall board commitment.

Singapore Code of Corporate Governance (Monetary Authority of Singapore 2012)	5.1 Every board should implement a process to be carried out by the NC for assessing the effectiveness of the board as a whole and its Board committees and for assessing the contribution by the Chairman and each individual director to the effectiveness of the board. The board should state in the company's Annual Report how the assessment of the board, its board committees and each director has been conducted. If an external facilitator has been used, the board should disclose in the company's Annual Report whether the external facilitator has any other connection with the company or any of its directors. This assessment process should be disclosed in the company's Annual Report.
	5.2 The NC should decide how the board's performance may be evaluated and propose objective performance criteria. Such performance criteria, which allow for comparison with industry peers, should be approved by the board and address how the board has enhanced long-term shareholder value. These performance criteria should not be changed from year to year, and where circumstances deem it necessary for any of the criteria to be changed, the onus should be on the board to justify this decision.
King Code of Governance for South Africa (Institute of Directors Southern Africa 2009	2.22. The evaluation of the board, its committees and the individual directors should be performed every year.
	2.22.1 The board should determine its own role, functions, duties and performance criteria as well as that for directors on the board and board committees to serve as a benchmark for the performance appraisal.
	2.22.2. Yearly evaluations should be performed by the chairman or an independent provider.
	2.22.3. The results of performance evaluations should identify training needs for directors.
	2.22.4. An overview of the appraisal process, results and action plans should be disclosed in the integrated report.
	2.22.5. The nomination for the re-appointment of a director should only occur after the evaluation of the performance and attendance of the director.
UK Corporate Governance Code (Financial Reporting Council 2014)	B.6 Evaluation: The board should undertake a formal and rigorous annual evaluation of its own performance and that of its committees and individual directors.
	Evaluation of the board should consider the balance of skills, experience, independence and knowledge of the company on the board, its diversity, including gender, how the board works together as a unit, and other factors relevant to its effectiveness.
	B.6.1. The board should state in the annual report how performance evaluation of the board, its committees and its individual directors has been conducted.
	B.6.2. Evaluation of the board of FTSE 350 companies should be externally facilitated at least every three years.
	B.6.3. The non-executive directors, led by the senior independent director, should be responsible for performance evaluation of the chairman, taking into account the views of executive directors.

theoretical understanding of corporate governance: its mechanisms, limitations and outcomes. Consequently, although this chapter spends some time looking at the process of board performance evaluation, it also provides insights into what a well-performing board looks like and how implementation of wider corporate governance recommendations can improve board effectiveness. It also considers the nature and purpose of corporate reporting regarding board evaluation including the type of information companies should be required to disclose in their annual reports.

The research presented in this chapter reveals a series of features that contribute to good board performance and decision-making, arguably the main job of a board. These features are: (1) role clarity; (2) information flow; (3) relevant skills and experience; (4) a culture of open discussion; and (5) an ability to exercise reasoned and independent judgment. Once in place, all of these factors should assist the board of directors to fulfil its legal duty to make decisions in the best interests of the company. Consequently all of these factors should be reviewed as part of a board performance evaluation.

Board performance evaluations

Over the last 10 years, the practice of conducting performance evaluations of boards of directors has become commonplace in large corporations. In 2011, 84 percent of Australia's 200 largest corporations disclosed that they had conducted an evaluation in the past year (Boardroom Partners 2012). This was not the case in the 1990s with several studies reporting that board performance evaluation was relatively unusual at that time (Ingley and van der Walt 2002). This was thought to be due to reluctance on the part of directors rather than lack of awareness. Ingley and van der Walt suggest it may have been because the indicators used to assess board performance were overly simple and viewed as unable to properly take into account the complexities of board dynamics (2007, p. 168). Kazanjian (2000) speculates that there was a level of discomfort on the part of directors due to dislike of rating processes and fear of disruption or embarrassment as a result. Nevertheless, with increased focus on boards in recent years, there has been a level of professionalisation of the role of director and, as a consequence, commitment to performance reviews, training and development. It may be that as evaluation processes have improved so has the willingness of directors to undertake them, a cycle enforced by valuable and rewarding outcomes.

Despite the increasing use of board evaluation processes, investigations into the causes of the global financial crisis concluded that poor board oversight was a contributing factor in the collapse of many financial firms (Kirkpatrick 2009). There was much examination of the boards of directors of failed companies: their composition, skills and dynamics. At a regulatory level, these events led to renewed interest in how board evaluation processes could assist in optimising board effectiveness and whether there ought to be more regulation surrounding board evaluation. In the United Kingdom, the Corporate Governance Code was amended in 2010 to strengthen the recommendations regarding board evaluation and effectiveness. The commentary neatly explained the purpose behind the changes:

- To encourage boards to be well balanced and avoid 'group think', new principles on the composition and selection of the board were introduced, including the need to appoint members on merit, against objective criteria and with due regard for the benefits of diversity, including gender diversity.
- To promote proper debate in the boardroom, new principles were added on the leadership of the chairman, the responsibility of the non-executive directors to provide constructive challenge and the time commitment expected of all directors.
- To help enhance the board's performance and awareness of its strengths and weaknesses, it was recommended that the chairman hold regular development reviews with each director and that board evaluation reviews in FTSE 350 companies should be externally facilitated at least every three years.

(FRC 2010)

These points outline several of the issues that will be explored in this chapter. Board performance evaluations can provide an opportunity to review board composition in light of the board's role and responsibilities and assess the corporate governance structures and processes that support the board. An evaluation also provides a chance to examine the human relationships and board dynamics that comprise a vital but less-discussed feature of effective corporate governance: '[b]oards, like workgroups, are intact social systems that require regular monitoring and feedback in order to work well' (Cascio 2004). The aim of evaluating a board of directors is to improve its performance and make the board more effective at directing the company. Kiel and Nicholson (2005) set out a list of benefits arising from board evaluation, summarised as follows:

- Leadership – if the board is willing to try to improve its performance, this sends a message to the rest of the organisation and sets a culture of a commitment to improve.
- Role clarity – in order to assess the performance of a board, it is first essential to define and clarify what the board's role ought to be and how this is distinguished from the role of management.
- Teamwork – conducting an evaluation should encourage participation and commitment by board members as well as build relationships and iron out any problems.
- Accountability – if the board explains the process and reasons for evaluation well in public disclosures, this can improve relationships with stakeholders. Also, the evaluation process can act as a reminder to directors of their legal duties to shareholders and related performance expectations.

- Decision-making – by clarifying strategic focus and organisational goals and by identifying any skill gaps on the board, an evaluation can improve overall board decision-making ability.
- Communication – the process of board evaluation can improve communication both between directors and between board and management.
- Board operations – a good board evaluation will review the structures and processes used in governing the corporation, which can lead to more efficient meetings and information flow.

It seems that it was the last of these, formal governance structures and processes, that early board evaluations focused on. In 2002, Ingley and van der Walt stated that, 'typically, performance evaluation is concerned with assessing board function and process' and that the more subjective inter-personal and behavioural factors were only just beginning to gain attention (p. 163). Van den Berge and Levrau raised a similar issue in 2004 noting that although these behavioural factors were deemed very important by practitioners, they were nearly absent in the academic literature and governance ratings systems.

Methodology

This chapter first explores how companies conduct board evaluations and, second, what this process can teach us about improving board performance. The research findings presented are based on the 2011 disclosures of the 30 largest listed companies in Australia as well as interviews conducted in 2006 and 2010 with experienced directors, company secretaries and fund managers. Thematic analysis of the data provides insights into (a) how companies have interpreted the Australian regulation on board evaluations and (b) what directors believe are the factors influencing board performance and effectiveness. The evidence reveals directors' views on how regulation, by encouraging processes of board performance evaluation as well as giving guidance on board composition and process, can help to define and ensure fulfilment of board roles and responsibilities. Although the data refers to the Australian corporate governance code, findings will have relevance more widely due to the similarity of other code provisions on board evaluation worldwide.

Findings are presented in two parts:

1 The concept and process of board evaluation, including: who is evaluated, how often, who carries out the evaluation, the process and implementation of outcomes.
2 The factors influencing board performance and effectiveness, including: role clarity, information flow, directors' skills and experience, board culture, decision-making processes and external accountability.

Board evaluation: concept and process

Full board evaluation

Most discussion in interviews, and most disclosure in annual reports, was related to evaluation of the board as a whole rather than committee or individual evaluations. At interview, the earliest board evaluation mentioned by participants was conducted in 1996 with most companies formally starting to evaluate their boards in the early 2000s. This suggests that board evaluation was not suddenly triggered by the publication of the Australian code in 2003 but was an existing practice that was codified and further encouraged by corporate governance regulation.

The ASX conducted a survey of compliance with the code after its first year in operation and found just over 50 percent of companies had disclosed information about their board evaluation process (ASX 2005). Eight years later, in 2012, Grant Thornton found over 90 percent of ASX 300 companies had complied with the recommendation (Grant Thornton 2012). However, because of the wording of the recommendation, compliance equated to disclosure of the 'process' not confirmation that board evaluation had actually taken place. A consultancy firm, Boardroom Partners, reviewed ASX 200 disclosures for 2011 in more detail and found that 84 percent of the ASX 200 had actually undertaken a review in the reporting period. Certainly, over the last 10 years, the practice of conducting performance evaluations of boards of directors has been adopted by most large corporations.

All of the 30 Australian annual reports reviewed included disclosures describing the process for board evaluation and, in the majority of cases, also stating that an evaluation had actually been carried out in the reporting period. Although the comply-or-explain mechanism makes it permissible for a company to explain why it does not have a process for board evaluation, only one company of the 30 took this route, explaining that evaluation was more ad hoc:

> The company does not have a formal process for evaluating the performance of the board or its committees but rather this is done by informal consultation between the Chairman and the CEO and relevant directors as required. The company has held board retreats in the past where evaluation questionnaires have been used to gauge director's views on performance and board effectiveness.
>
> *(Fortescue Metals, 2010)*

Over time it seems that board evaluation processes have been refined and updated and become more formalised. In 2006 there were some interview participants just beginning the process:

> We put our board through the ringer for the first time. It was very confronting for the board. It has resulted in some changes.
>
> *(Company secretary, unlisted company)*

As a contrast, interview participants in 2010 indicated that they had become more comfortable with board evaluation than when it was in its infancy. It seems that the questions posed in evaluations have evolved in line with changing attitudes to governance and the challenges of the moment:

> It is now very much a formalised process rather than an ad hoc process as in the past. There is more rigour around it, and more documentation. As people have become familiar with the process, there is greater willingness to be open about the issues and ask the right questions.
>
> *(Director, ASX 100)*

Individual director evaluations

The apparent acceptance of the concept of whole-board evaluations has not spread quite so convincingly to individual director evaluations. In 2006, interviews showed that individual assessments were in their early stages. Several companies were at the threshold of moving to individual director evaluations, some who had done it for the first time described the process as confronting but useful.

In 2010 most companies stated they were conducting individual evaluations but information disclosed was minimal, focusing mostly on the process used. The Boardroom Partners research found that 79 percent of companies gave information on individual director evaluation (2012, p. 10). Of the 30 Australian companies whose 2010 annual reports were reviewed, most simply stated that the results of individual director performance evaluations would be used when determining whether a director be recommended for re-election. Some companies went further, for example, at Coca Cola Amatil, each director had agreed that he or she would retire if a majority of fellow directors considered his or her performance had fallen below the predetermined criteria. This type of agreement could assist a board to deal with an extreme situation of board dysfunction where it can otherwise be difficult to remove a director who is not willing to resign. It seems the difficulties inherent in trying to 'unappoint' a director contribute to the tendency for boards to appoint candidates already known to them rather than take a risk on someone new. Directors in 2010 explained how dysfunction in the board 'tears at the heart of the company and leads to poor performance' and yet can be difficult to remedy:

> A chair of a dysfunctional board has a lot to do to fix it up. If there is a dysfunctional director, the chair has to act. It is not an easy thing, it is not just 'come and have a cup of tea'. A re-shaping of the board can take up to three years. It can take an average of 18 months if someone digs their heels in.
>
> *(Director, ASX 100)*

The knowledge that all directors will go through a performance assessment that will help to avoid this sort of situation might encourage the appointment of more diverse candidates. Nevertheless, in 2010 interviewees were still divided on the issue of whether individual directors' performances ought to be assessed. Most of the reasons given for the reluctance to assess individuals were related to the fact that the board functions as a team:

> It is much more about the performance of the board as a whole: are we spending time on the right things, are processes working, are we making the right decisions and documenting things well? …. most boards shy away from rating their colleagues because they work in a collegial way.
>
> *(Director, ASX 100)*

> At [our company] it is clear that board evaluations are about the board, not individual directors. You can have the best people on the board, but it does not work. Or potentially you could have the worst people on the board and it works. The board is a team of rowers, or football players. We need to become the best team, to listen, to discuss and make decisions.
>
> *(Director, ASX 100)*

> These people [directors] are elected and are meant to be independent. I think it is very important that there is respect for their independence so I don't engage in personal evaluations. I encourage them to be as different as they want to be, not push them to the average or the middle.
>
> *(Chairman, ASX 100)*

So when it comes to evaluation of individual directors it appears there is still some divergence between recommended practice and actual practice. Company practice, as disclosed in annual reports and these directors' comments, questions the assumption that individual director evaluations increase a board's effectiveness. There appear to be several different reasons for this: first, individual performance may be irrelevant when all decisions have to be made as a team – the team dynamic is more important. Second, assessing individual performance implies that there is some goal or ideal level of performance that every director should aim for, whereas what is more important on a board is diversity and independence. Lastly, if the process of individual assessment involves assessing one's colleagues it can disrupt important relationships; thus, in order to avoid such disruption, participants may self-censor, and information will lack meaning.

All of these arguments could be seen as excuses for tackling a difficult exercise, excuses that are not permitted when considering the performance of an executive team. It may simply be that directors have not yet reached a level of comfort with individual evaluations, or discovered appropriate methods of assessment. Acceptance of individual evaluation may take time in the same way as it has for full-board assessment. In 2012, Boardroom Partners concluded that the fact that over three-quarters of ASX 200 companies made disclosures about individual director review provided 'a strong indication that there is a changed view on the legitimacy and value of assessing individual contributions to the overall performance of a board' (2012, p. 14). Possibly this is an area best handled by an independent consultant so as not to endanger important relationships of trust. As discussed below, a process involving an external facilitator can help to get over some of the initial hurdles – a positive experience can then lead to acceptance and even eagerness to repeat the process.

Frequency of evaluation

As opposed to many codes around the world, the Australian corporate governance code only suggests that board evaluations are 'regular'. Of the 30 Australian companies whose annual reports were reviewed, 21 or 70 percent disclosed that an evaluation was carried out annually. Of the remaining 30 percent, or nine companies: five did not state a particular frequency, commenting only that reviews were regular or giving the date of the last review; two companies did a board evaluation every two years (Origin and Coca Cola Amatil) and two companies (ANZ and IAG) committed to formally review their board only every three years (although less formal reviews would occur between these).

Of the companies conducting annual board evaluations, there were five that alternated the process of evaluation each year such that one year a relatively informal self-evaluation would take place and the next year a more formal process would take place involving an independent consultant. Others alternate a full-board evaluation one year with individual director evaluations the next. This evidence suggests that the frequency of review is closely tied to the nature of the process. It suggests that the flexibility inherent in the word 'regular' is appropriate as it permits companies to set up a schedule of evaluations that suits their circumstances.

External facilitators

When asked about external facilitation of board evaluation, most directors acknowledged the value of using external consultants but considered that the dollar cost may not be justifiable every year. The prevailing opinion was that an external consultant should be used every second or third year or in circumstances where there are sensitive issues that need to be resolved. Comments included the following:

> When we switched to external engagement, with the external facilitator, the quality of responses went high and there was more honesty. When it was done internally the assessment was far more polite.
>
> *(Director, ASX 100)*

> If there are real issues with the board, an external evaluation puts more rigour around the process, and concerns can be professionally identified, which depersonalises the process, and you get more productive discussion.
>
> *(Director, ASX 100)*

It seems external consultants are particularly useful if sensitive issues such as director characteristics and team dynamics need to be discussed. Disadvantages of using external consultants relate to the wide variation in the quality of consultants and the risk of the process or the resultant recommendations causing disagreements within the board. A director concluded:

> Board evaluation has to be a supportive process – if mishandled, it can have unintended consequences. If the process provokes internal bickering and resentment – it is not good. One of the most important things on a board is the quality and openness of discussion – a constructive atmosphere.
>
> *(Director, ASX 100)*

Process of evaluation

Table 5.2 summarises the five stages in an average process of board evaluation: (1) agreeing on the concept; (2) establishing performance criteria; (3) deciding on a method; (4) implementing outcomes; and (5) communicating to stakeholders. Despite the Australian code suggesting a role for the nomination committee in board evaluation, there were no companies that specifically disclosed that it was the nomination committee that had developed the process for board evaluation. However, discussions with directors suggested that this was how the first board evaluations originated, with a particular committee's being tasked with working out how to proceed. However, the research findings did show that the results of board evaluation were often fed back to the board via the nominations committee reflecting the link between evaluation and board composition.

With regard to the code recommendation to disclose the process of board evaluation, it seems most companies interpret this as the data-collection method rather than any other stage of the process. Of the disclosures of the 30 companies reviewed, the majority disclosed the method used to conduct the board evaluation (interviews, external facilitation etc.) and some companies also discussed frequency and the feedback process. However, it seems the aims, criteria and outcomes of board evaluation are generally not interpreted by companies as part of the 'process'.

Similarly, when asked about the process of board evaluation, directors reported that most of their companies use a mixture of questionnaires and one-on-one interviews to collect information. It seems companies often start with relatively informal discussions with the chairman and build up, over the years, to a more formalised process. Interviews with smaller companies in 2006 showed that they were still struggling with how to conduct board evaluation. At that stage, many of the smaller listed companies were searching for information and trying to put together a process internally without spending too much money. They were still testing different processes to find something that was manageable in terms of time, cost and effectiveness:

> It's difficult – last year we had a simplistic process but this year we have developed a full map of responsibilities. A sub-committee is developing criteria to use in judging performance against each of 20 responsibilities.
>
> *(Company secretary, small listed company)*

TABLE 5.2 Stages of board evaluation

Stage	Process	Options
1 Get agreement to the concept of performance management	Agree upon the purpose of the evaluation	To improve board effectiveness and organisational performance To satisfy regulatory requirements and improve accountability/stakeholder relationships
	Agree upon the subjects of the evaluation	Full board, individual directors and/or board committees
2 Establish the criteria for board performance	Agree upon the content of the evaluation	Board composition, governance structures, roles, responsibilities and skills Board process, communication, information flow and external relationships Board teamwork, internal dynamics, leadership and culture
3 Decide on method of board evaluation	Who should conduct the evaluation?	Self-evaluation, committee chair, board chair, company secretary or independent consultant
	What process should be used?	Formal interviews, questionnaire, participant observation or informal mechanisms – how is feedback provided?
	How frequently should evaluations be conducted?	Annually or a cycle linked to board member re-election
4 Implement outcomes	Establish director development plans and board action plans	Link to training/education Link to re-election process Link to succession planning Link to governance and board structures and processes
	Monitor implementation of plans and review evaluation process	
5 Disclose to public	Demonstrate accountability for board performance	Minimal disclosure to comply with regulation Additional voluntary disclosure to explain the value of the process

Table adapted from M Huse (ed), The value creating board: Corporate governance and organizational behavior (Abingdon: Routledge, 2009) and G Kiel, G Nicholson and MA Barclay, Board, director and CEO evaluation (McGraw Hill, 2005).

Most of the questionnaires used by companies were originally developed by external consultants who continue to refine and update their content in order to expose key issues. When evaluation is done internally, the board will use the questionnaire of a preferred consultant or create a hybrid questionnaire that is likely to be self-administered. A standard board-evaluation process, as described by a director, is summarised below:

> The board briefs an outside advisor or internal resources on what it hopes to achieve through a survey and agrees the questions. The board members complete it and it is analysed internally or externally. The findings are presented to the chair and the full board and are blended into anonymous form. In many surveys board members are asked to offer feedback on their colleagues. Information is provided specific to each member in the form of a score or anonymous written comments. The whole process can take 4–8 weeks.
>
> *(Director, ASX 100)*

The information collected is analysed by the chairman, company secretary, a committee chair or external consultant. It is then fed back to the board either in one-on-one meetings or through whole-board discussion. One-on-one meetings will be used for individual director feedback, and it is here that an independent, third party may ease the transmission of any sensitive information:

> I did have a dissident director and I had the one-on-one explaining that he had a conflict and he basically said – yes, tough luck. A third person would have been useful.
>
> *(Director, ASX 100)*

An important point that emerged in the interviews was that the formal annual board evaluation is not the only opportunity for boards to assess themselves and implement improvements. In a good board, evaluation is a continuous process – problems are ironed out as and when they happen, certainly in terms of board processes. For example, directors would not wait until the annual evaluation to tell the company secretary about obvious deficits in the board papers:

> There is a sense that boards go through a process of continuous improvement, that board evaluation is just a helpful complement to what we already do. This doesn't mean that members are opposed to it but that it is not the only way things get surfaced. It just rounds out what already happens.
>
> *(Director, ASX 100)*

Implementation of change

Of the 30 Australian companies whose annual reports were reviewed, only three gave information describing the outcomes of their board-evaluation process. For example, Santos stated:

> As a result of recommendations arising from the external Board review, a number of initiatives have been introduced; for example, increasing time spent on strategic issues and improving the style and format of Board papers.
>
> *(Santos 2010)*

The process of implementation of outcomes is a crucial step that perhaps deserves more attention in descriptions of board-evaluation processes – how actions are followed through and monitored. This was seen by directors as a vital component in whether board evaluations actually lead to better board performance. Changes identified as necessary during the evaluation process can lead to improved board performance only if there is rigour in the follow-up. The commitment of the chair provides another crucial element to success in terms of providing positive leadership and support for change.

Directors commented that public reporting of outcomes can be difficult due to the potentially sensitive and/or confidential nature of performance assessments. There is a fear that the market could misinterpret information in an adverse way when it was intended to convey positive change. However, when asked at interview about outcomes generated from board evaluations, the examples provided were fairly consistent:

- alteration of committee structures (amalgamating committees or clarifying their charters);
- increased number of site visits for non-executives to better understand the business;
- fostering an internal culture that promotes open communication, asking, for example, whether bad news would travel quickly to the board;
- the retirement of directors who were not performing at the right level; and
- improvements in board processes (meeting agendas, format of board papers).

Each of these issues is discussed further below in the context of board performance more generally and the factors that can assist board effectiveness. Lastly, it was pointed out that board evaluation helps not only through identifying areas of change. The simple fact that the board has got together to reflect on its performance has value:

> [Board evaluation] also gets used to strengthen the bonds through whole-board discussion on a different topic to usual – an opportunity to be honest and open about how you are working as a group. It helps the performance of the team in and of itself, not only through the next steps.
>
> *(Director, ASX 100)*

Board performance and effectiveness

The crux of board evaluation is to assess the actual functioning of the board against what it ideally should comprise. However, deciding upon what a board and its directors should be aiming for in terms of performance is not always easy. Despite widely recommending board-performance evaluation, most corporate governance codes do not give a great deal of guidance on the criteria to be used. The Australian code states that board evaluation should be done against 'appropriate measures' but gives no guidance on what these might be. Some countries give more guidance, for example, by suggesting that the board charter (or other statement of the board's role, functions and duties) be used as a performance benchmark. However, in general, companies have flexibility in deciding what it is they want to review in their board evaluation. Only one of the companies reviewed made any disclosure about the performance criteria used, listing the following:

- the board's contribution to developing strategy and policy;
- the board's performance relative to its objectives;
- interaction between the board and management and between board members;
- the board's processes to monitor business performance and compliance, control risks and evaluate management;
- board composition and structure; and
- the operation of the board, including the conduct of board meetings and group behaviours.

(Macquarie Bank 2011)

Interviewees pointed out that having flexibility around board evaluation is important because the type of board evaluation chosen ought to reflect the type of board and the issues facing the company at the time:

> How long the board evaluation takes depends on where the board is at: if there has been a significant changeover, up to half the people are relatively new, then you would adopt a different approach to an experienced board. You need to balance the approach with the longevity of the board – using a prospective evaluation if it is a new board, or a retrospective evaluation if it is an experienced board. The centre of gravity shifts depending on the longevity of the board.
>
> *(Director, ASX 100)*

This supports the argument put forward by Minichilli et al. that 'different contexts and purposes require specific board evaluations' and therefore, to be effective, an evaluation must be tailored to the circumstances of the company (2007, p. 610). The consequence for corporate governance regulation is that it should not be too prescriptive regarding the process or the criteria used for board evaluation.

Nevertheless, each company must choose distinct measures against which to assess its board, and this involves some consideration of what the board is expected to achieve. It requires reflection over what role the board ought to play and whether it has the skills and processes in place to fulfil this role. Table 5.3 summarises the comments of directors in 2010 as to the factors that make a board effective or otherwise, all of which could be used as measures against which to compare any particular board. They relate to culture in the boardroom, director characteristics and experience (particularly the chair), relationships between board and management and board meeting processes.

TABLE 5.3 Features of effective and dysfunctional boards

Features	Effective board	Dysfunctional board
Culture	Collegial atmosphere Honesty, openness and transparency Mutual trust and respect Consensus, common purpose Opportunity to air differing viewpoints Professionalism Strategic insight	Adversarial atmosphere Acrimonious discussion Conformity or group-think Unquestioning or unmotivated Controlled by dominant shareholder Narrow vision Lost in detail
Chair	Experienced – manages the agenda Encourages debate and contribution Professional relationship with the CEO Takes responsibility for effective board	Autocratic Weak Hinders debate Dominated by the CEO
Directors	Diversity (of thought, skills and experience) Right fit for company Work as a team Constructively challenge	Lack of business experience or appropriate skills Not genuinely independent Factional interests or conflicts Disruptive personalities Egos that get in the way
Senior management	Effective communication with board Ask questions and use experience of board members	Withholding information from the board Lack of transparency Lack of trust
Processes	Open discussion Good information flow Effective delegation to committees Board agenda papers (right length and time) Active succession planning	No process to solicit views No process in place to deal with conflict or issues Poor information flow Poorly structured meetings and papers Limited succession planning

The board as a decision-making body

What is clear is that an effective board means an effective decision-making body. The core function of a board of directors, entrenched in most corporate law statutes, is to make decisions in the best interests of the company. Nearly all of the factors in Table 5.3 relate to the process of decision-making: first directors need relevant and comprehensive information; as a group they need the skills and experience required to fully understand the information; they need to be able to discuss and compare ideas and then come to a reasoned decision.

Figure 5.1 shows these factors as a process of board decision-making, each stage supported by governance structures and processes. First, the board (and each committee) must agree on the types of decisions it should make by defining its role and responsibilities. Board and committee charters and a document detailing the authorities delegated to management can help to delineate these roles. Second, the board must ensure it receives or obtains the information it needs to make those decisions: there are many processes within an organisation designed to gather and transmit information to both senior management and board including risk management and internal audit systems. Third, the board must have the skills and experience, as a group, to

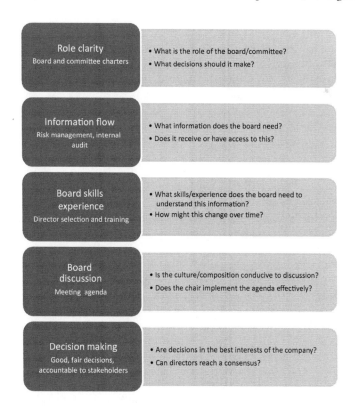

FIGURE 5.1 Process of board decision-making.

understand and digest the information. It is the responsibility of the nomination committee, using skills matrices and succession planning, to maintain an appropriate board composition. Fourth is the board discussion process, which relies on teamwork and culture as well as an appropriate board meeting agenda implemented by the chair. Lastly, decisions must be made 'in the interests of the company', which requires a level of independent judgment and possibly compromise on the part of each director. Directors are accountable for these decisions and ought to be able to communicate their reasoning effectively to shareholders.

At each stage of the process are factors that impact upon board performance and therefore are worth considering as part of a board evaluation. Viewing corporate governance through the lens of board function also provides a way of assessing the value of many other corporate governance code provisions. Figure 5.1 shows how common code provisions dealing with issues such as board composition and director independence are only one aspect of a functioning board. The softer elements such as boardroom culture and dynamics are just as important yet are more difficult to regulate. Each of these five stages of board decision-making will be discussed in turn.

Role clarity

As discussed in Chapter 3 the role of a board is multi-faceted and can include monitoring and checking the actions of management, contributing to strategic plans, advising, networking and communicating on behalf of the company. One of the first things advised by most corporate governance codes is a clear separation between the role of the executive managers and the role of the board (mostly non-executives). Usually the board is responsible for setting the overall direction of the company while managers deal with day-to-day operations. Understanding which decisions should go to the board and which can be made by the managers is important for overall efficiency. Interviewees explained that this is necessary to ensure that a busy board is not overwhelmed with too much detail and yet is in control and accountable to stakeholders for major decisions. One interviewee explained how the process of board performance evaluation can help to clarify these boundaries:

> It has vastly improved the relationship between the board and management. There is better understanding of the roles of the two – much smoother operation of the board and management's interaction with it. Much less harping and carping.
>
> *(Company secretary, ASX 300)*

Another common response was that the evaluation had led to conscious changes to the board's role, often to increase the focus on longer-term strategy rather than immediate operating issues.

It re-focused the board back to what it should be focusing on – most of its time should be on strategy whereas we were dealing with lots of internal compliance issues and getting bogged down in issues regarding the functioning of the board rather than the direction of the company.

(Executive director, small listed company)

Information flow

The second requirement for good board performance is information, which must flow from the operations staff, through to senior management, the executive team and then to the board. Indeed, interviewees mentioned the value of site visits in obtaining first-hand information, as well as requesting presentations from a wide range of staff. Governance processes aimed at improving information flow include risk management and internal audit systems. Chief financial officers, risk officers and the company secretary all have important roles in providing the right amount of information to the board. Again this is a balancing act, the company secretary must provide enough information in the board papers without overwhelming the directors with detail. The directors, in turn, must be confident that they can ask for information and have access to relevant sources.

Of course the main source of information will be the executive team including the CEO and any other executive directors. Thus the relationship between board and management is a vital part of efficient information flow. Solving the information and consequent power asymmetry between full-time employees and non-executives is one of the main tasks of corporate governance systems. It involves implementing systems for information flow but also cultivating good relationships that allow a level of flexibility:

> I've observed a CEO who was very sensitive about the board stepping on his patch. Our CEO here reacts very differently – he is very liberal and if the board wants to get involved he will let them. I think it's much the best way – the relationship should be fluid and open in terms of who gets to decide what matter.
>
> *(Company secretary, small listed company)*

There must be open communication so that the non-executive directors can ask relevant questions and be fully informed in preparation for decision-making. As the following comment makes clear, there should be a two-way communication process: the board can advise management in the early stages of strategy development, it can challenge proposals put forward by management and ultimately agree on a way forward. This two-way dialogue enables the board to monitor what the management team is doing as well as have valuable input:

> … because they are not shrinking violets they do push back and challenge management. They ask for things to be considered again and are not just

a rubber stamp. They are very open and generally discussions occur early in the piece. They act as a sounding board for management so get an early feel before all the forms have been filled out. They have a helicopter view because they are not involved in the business every day. The different backgrounds complement each other and they are all numerate so can discuss the financial information meaningfully.

(Company secretary, ASX 100)

Board skills and experience

The comment above also touches on the need for the board to have certain skills: basic financial literacy is vital in understanding the company's accounts. Other skills or specific industry experience can be very valuable to add different perspectives to discussions around strategy or operations. This is where board composition becomes important and why it has been a focus of corporate governance codes for some time. At interview, the outcomes of board evaluation deemed as most significant to the directors were changes in composition (due to identification of skill deficits or directors contributing to board dysfunction). This confirms the important link between board evaluation and the role of the nomination committee in board renewal and succession planning:

> One of the deliverables of these surveys is to point to gaps in the composition of the board and suggest the skills sets the board should look at. It might point out issues around succession planning or that some directors are short of the mark or that board renewal would be a healthy thing or where board oversight needs to be strengthened, for example, if risk management processes are weak.
>
> *(Director, ASX 100)*

The 2014 edition of the Australian corporate governance code recommends the use of a skills matrix to help ensure that the board as a whole covers the essential skills that it needs. However, all directors interviewed in 2010 already said they used a skills matrix for board evaluation that was linked to the succession process and nomination of new directors. Again this suggests that soft regulation tends to endorse and codify existing practices rather than introduce completely novel concepts. Most directors believed that preparation of a skills matrix is a useful way for boards to identify gaps or weaknesses in their composition:

> With a matrix you can then target your searches. For example looking for regulatory or political skills or financial skills and where gaps will be coming up. It can take up to 3 years to find and induct someone new. While all of us think we are experts, I have found it does take 3 years to get across the detail in order to be credible in a new industry.
>
> *(Director, ASX 100)*

However, the directors acknowledged the complexity of designing and using the skills matrix. It may be asking too much of it to account for all the factors surrounding an effective board. As one participant mentioned, you need both the skills and the 'chemistry' necessary for directors to work well together, another termed it as 'the right strategic fit, skill set fit and culture fit'. Over-reliance on a skills matrix could cause you to overlook someone whose input might be extremely valuable but not fall within the relevant boxes. One director commented that 'there can be some skills that you don't foresee that can be extraordinarily helpful'. Overall, a skills matrix is a useful tool but should not be over-relied upon:

> [The matrix] includes the work experience of all the directors, overlaid with their knowledge. It's really tricky as you want to throw other things in that make people valuable. You can tick a box e.g. international experience but it might not be in the area you want. We do that in terms of looking at potential members.
>
> *(Director, ASX 100)*

> You don't appoint boards on the basis of an expert in each area – narrow expertise can be a disadvantage – if you have, say, a marketing expert who then makes every marketing decision. More important, for skills and experience, is a career and general level of business understanding.
>
> *(Director, ASX 100)*

Rather than discussing skills and experience, most code provisions on board composition tend to focus on the issue of director independence, recommending that boards have a majority of directors who do not work day-to-day at the company and are not connected through shareholdings or other contractual relationships. A more recent focus of regulation has been the issue of diversity, particularly gender diversity, discussed further in Chapter 6. The importance of these aspects of board composition, is related not so much to skills and experience (understanding of business) but to balanced, fair discussion and decision-making:

> For a company our size the balance is good, we've got deep operational knowledge and people who've learnt the lessons. There are enough independents to have a strong voice and neither side can impress their will on the other which is quite useful.
>
> *(Company secretary, small listed company)*

Culture of open discussion

The comments from directors about an effective board often referred to the team dynamics, culture and philosophy. In order to operate effectively, directors valued an honest, transparent board culture conducive to 'healthy, challenging' debate. Mutual respect for each other was seen as vital in order to create an atmosphere within which the board could function effectively as a team. One director stated the importance of differences of view but not acrimony; another referred to the need to discuss matters forcefully but without getting personal. These are subtle but important differences, and it was pointed out that sometimes it can take a while for a board to reach this stage. It requires a certain level of knowledge and understanding of each other that can only be achieved over time:

> Boards are not a loose association of people. A board takes a long time to put together, nurture and develop. The board has a dynamic in its own right that is easily disrupted. A board has a personality of its own you have to manage: is it anxious, does it need reassuring, is it confident?
>
> *(Director, ASX 100)*

Achieving constructive debate also requires a good chair who can mediate and oversee the discussion process and work through the board agenda effectively. Interviews confirmed the role of the chair as pivotal in creating an effective board:

> You certainly need a good chair who encourages debate and draws out contributions from each of the members and doesn't allow the loudest voice to dominate. A chair who drives decisions to a consensus or makes decisions that the board will support.
>
> *(Director, ASX 100)*

A good chair will actively seek the views of all directors and make it clear that opposing views are welcome. Most directors saw the chair as the leader who sets the agenda and the culture of the board, making sure that it stays on track and focuses on relevant issues. An effective chair, who can maintain a constructive relationship with the CEO, is seen as a tremendous asset to the company. As one director stated, 'it's the chair who sets the tone for the board'.

Board size is another feature of board composition affecting board discussion and decision-making. The right size is vital such that the group can cover the skills it needs and yet not be so large that discussion becomes unwieldy and meetings hard to schedule. One company secretary explained that a smaller board (8 rather than 10) can make it much easier to manage the discussion and achieve consensus. On the other hand, if a board gets too small, the workload becomes too high, and it is harder to achieve the right balance of executives to non-executives. A board of between 6 and 8 directors was preferred by most participants reflecting the average ASX 200 board size of 7.2 directors (Clarke et al. 2012). Interestingly this is a small average board size when compared internationally (Spencer Stuart 2015).

Independent decision-making

An interesting finding was that, although directors valued diversity of thought and experience, the ideal outcome was seen to be a consensus decision that all

directors were happy with. One company secretary commented, 'they do disagree and have debates and they occasionally hold votes, although they prefer to
make decisions unanimously'; another commented that, 'generally, well, always,
they can reconcile their views because they respect each other's opinions'. One
company secretary was of the opinion that if a board has frequent arguments or
one regular dissenter, it is not a well-performing board.

It is here that independence becomes important, because decision-making
must be 'in the best interests of the company' not the best interests of a particular director or any one shareholder that he or she might represent. Although
it was pointed out that it is possible for a director to exercise independent
judgment even if he or she is not formally independent from management,
the formal assessment of independence assists in highlighting potential pit-
falls. Most comments supported the regulatory norm of including a majority
of independent directors on a board. Interviewees were conscious that a board
should have a ratio of independents to non-independents that discourages fac-
tions from forming because non-independent directors, particularly as a group,
may be swayed to act in the best interests of a particular shareholder or supplier
rather than in the best interests of the company. As many directors pointed
out, it often comes down to the personality of each director as well as the
mind-set and culture of the board as a whole. A good director will exercise
common-sense and conduct him- or herself with integrity. For example, he or
she should be able to separate personal interests from those of the customer
group or shareholder base:

> I have seen in other places people who haven't been able to separate per-
> sonal interests or those of customers. Here people would politely point
> it out to you. It's one of the things about being a director – you look for
> common sense. A lot of it is about self-monitoring as a group too. I've seen
> people who can say, my view as a customer would be this, but I can see that
> it's not the best thing to do.
>
> *(Company secretary, ASX 100)*

> The dynamics of the board need to be considered too. If you've got a major
> shareholder and you think of the votes around the table, you don't want
> another of theirs appointed to the board.
>
> *(Company secretary, ASX 300)*

Accountability and reputation

Something that does not fit easily into a board-evaluation template and yet appears to affect overall board performance is the personal profile and reputation
of board members. It seems that individual director reputations play a role in
board performance, both internally (directors are careful to exercise independent judgment and declare any conflicts of interest in order to maintain their

reputation) and externally (investors know that this is the case and trust in these directors as individuals):

> The board is very well known in the industry which is a good thing – it means they are very conservative on maintaining independence, for their own personal reputations. It's certainly the most pragmatic, independent and transparent board that I have ever been involved in. There are no raised voices in the boardroom which is quite unusual. I've seen boards where everyone has their own personal views and personal interests.
>
> *(Company secretary, ASX 100)*

> They've got strong views and reputations to protect so they will stand up from an independent point of view.
>
> *(Company secretary, ASX 300)*

This reputation-effect seems to be understood by companies such that the personal profile of a director is an important factor in their appointment to the board. One participant talked of an upgrading of the board, which occurs when a company reaches a stage of maturity at which it can attract higher-profile directors. The external effect of having such directors is particularly important when a company is trying to grow and raise funds:

> We wanted those who were known to the investor community in Australia including a director with a financial background to chair the audit committee. ... Regard and reputation were important both in raising the initial funds and in any follow on funding.
>
> *(Company secretary, recently listed company)*

> If we did need more directors – they have contacts and know people around town – the old boys network. It's an A-grade board and thus you really want high profile directors.
>
> *(Company secretary, ASX 300)*

This empirical evidence links to the literature on trust and social norms, which suggests that good performance by directors may be elicited by social expectations rather than legal rules (Blair and Stout 2001). In cases where social expectations are high (director has good reputation) a director is likely to work hard to fulfil his/her duties for fear of losing that reputation. Blair and Stout argue that it is not only potential shaming that influences behaviour but also the framing of positive expectations (2001, p. 1802). For example, if a director's reputation suggests he/she is trustworthy, other directors are likely to trust each other and act for the group rather than for individual benefit.

Theories regarding the importance of trust amongst directors on boards may also explain the difficulty in moving away from the 'old-boys' network in terms of director selection. It was disappointing to find that in 2006 most companies still used personal networks to identify potential new board members. Without a doubt, the average board member across the sample was a white, Caucasian male over the age of 50. Terms such as comfort and trust were used when justifying this tendency to appoint individuals within existing networks:

> No, we didn't go down the path of using a search agency – we relied on our network and found people that we knew and trusted that were also good additions in terms of their skill set. There is still that network because you need to have trust in people you are working with at director level, especially in a company our size.
>
> *(Company secretary, small listed company)*

Although perhaps understandable in terms of ease of relationships, this practice can result in reduced performance due to groupthink and lack of challenge. Another downside of the search for trust and reputation on boards is that it creates a significant hurdle to accessing unproven talent and the benefits of diversity, discussed more in Chapter 6. Boards appear to be struggling with the conflict between the need for trust and reputation and the need for diversity of skills, characteristics and experience. Certainly trust and reputation have trumped diversity in the past, but a slow process of change may be beginning, encouraged by the most recent amendments to the ASX Principles on gender diversity and encapsulated by a few interviewees:

> So recently we have gone outside the normal area – to people who didn't really have a profile. It's the skill set we want – we are not too worried about profile.
>
> *(Company secretary, ASX 300)*

Communicating board performance

If we move away from director profile as a measure of board performance, we need to ask what other information might be useful for investors or other outsiders to assess a board. When directors were asked this question they suggested it was a 'mission impossible':

> At the end of the day it's about conduct in decision-making and the market has no way of knowing – it just can't tell and is reliant on the judgment of the board – can the market trust the board? If the company's performance was woeful they probably wouldn't trust the board but it is really impossible for anyone else to decide if independent judgment is being exercised. If that is the test, it is impossible for anyone else to know. Thus, for analysts and shareholders – they only have the tick-box things to go on.
>
> *(Company secretary, ASX 100)*

Here again, we see the reliance on trust and reputation rather than company disclosures. All interviewees understood that the link between board performance and company performance is complex and that even the best of boards can be hindered by factors beyond their control. Nevertheless indicators that were listed as being helpful in assessing board performance included:

- willingness of a company to seek and respond to market feedback;
- personal characteristics and credibility of directors;
- professional history of directors;
- company performance within the industry; and
- quality of board decisions, particularly in times of crisis.

For fund managers, assessment of board performance is used only selectively in investment decisions. It is generally not seen as a vital factor in investment decisions because of the difficulty in obtaining information and ambiguity regarding its link to company performance. However, it can be valuable in 'screening' out boards that are perceived negatively:

> This area is not sophisticated enough that it drives our portfolios. There is not a single company where I could say we own it because it has got a great board. Having said that, there are some we would simply not own because their board and management are particularly poor.
>
> *(Fund manager, 2010)*

The UK's Walker review strongly recommended regular board evaluations and better disclosure to investors regarding such evaluations:

> The evaluation statement on board performance and governance should confirm that a rigorous evaluation process has been undertaken and describe the process for identifying the skills and experience required to address and challenge adequately key risks and decisions that confront, or may confront, the board. The statement should provide such meaningful, high-level information as the board considers necessary to assist shareholders' understanding of the main features of the process, including an indication of the extent to which issues raised in the course of the evaluation have been addressed. It should also provide an indication of the nature and extent of communication with major shareholders and confirmation that the board were fully appraised of views indicated by shareholders in the course of such dialogue.
>
> (2009, p. 66)

The findings of this chapter would suggest that even these improved statements may not have great influence on investors. Nevertheless, they are likely to help in further entrenching the process of board performance evaluation in companies and its links to succession planning and board renewal.

Conclusions

Sonnenfeld, in his 2002 article 'What makes great boards great', argues that it's not the rules and regulations but the way people work together on boards that make them great. This sentiment is echoed by Daily and Dalton who state that board effectiveness is a matter of integrity:

> The performance of any board is a function of the character of the individuals that comprise the board. No structural remedy can overcome poor judgment or apathy. At the same time, no amount of individual character can overcome accountability without responsibility.
>
> (2003, p. 43)

The above paragraph summarises the difficulty in assessing board effectiveness. A good board undoubtedly requires members with specific skills and experience; its performance will almost always be assisted by good structure and process; however, the crucial ingredient is the quality of human interaction, and this is much harder for an outsider, especially investors, to know and measure. This is where board evaluation ought to have real value. Only the board itself can really assess its ability to work together, to make decisions efficiently and to identify any problems. As Sonnenfeld observes, a lack of evaluation and feedback can be 'self-destructive'. He states:

> People and organizations cannot learn without feedback. No matter how good a board is, it's bound to get better if it's reviewed intelligently... If a board is to truly fulfil its mission – it must become a robust team-one whose members know how to ferret out the truth, challenge one another, and even have a good fight now and then.
>
> (2002, p. 114)

The evidence discussed in this chapter confirms the value of board evaluation processes and the fact that, if done well, they can contribute greatly to effective board performance. It seems that directors of large corporations are much more willing to engage in board evaluations than they might have been some years ago and recognise their value, especially in times of change. Regulators around the world are also recognising this fact and stock exchange recommendations regarding board evaluation have become more stringent since the global financial crisis.

Outcomes of board evaluation processes range from relatively minor amendments to board processes (meeting agendas, format of board papers etc.) through alteration of committee structures (amalgamation or changes to committee charters) to significant changes in board composition (to fill skill gaps or remove directors contributing to dysfunction). The process of implementing these outcomes of board evaluation is a crucial step that perhaps deserves more attention. It is a vital component in whether a board evaluation process actually leads to better board performance. Equally, the links between the process of board evaluation and other areas of corporate governance such as director re-election, succession planning and director education and development are becoming clearer and more formalised in practice, and these ought to have a tangible impact on overall board performance. The new amendments to the Australian code on diversity and use of skills matrices should begin the process of countering reliance on personal contacts in finding new directors and yet must not underplay the importance of trust and team dynamics.

An important point that emerged in the research interviews was that the formal annual board evaluation is not the only opportunity for boards to assess themselves and implement improvements. In a good board, evaluation is a continuous process – problems are ironed out as and when they happen. Many board members find that board effectiveness can be greatly enhanced if the board members, particularly non-executives, have a chance to get together outside of formal board meetings to discuss issues that might not fall within the formal agenda and to generally get to know each other better. The research demonstrates the importance of board culture in effective decision-making, confirming the need for more behavioural research into corporate governance that takes into account the effects of power and personality.

With regard to increased disclosure of board-evaluation outcomes, there is reluctance amongst board directors due to the risk of such disclosures issuing market-sensitive information. There remains a clear preference towards more informal and direct communication between board members and investors on the basis that disclosures often become standardised and meaningless. Further research exploring investors' views on corporate disclosures would be valuable in determining how regulation might elicit more valuable information. At the very least, investors have the right to know that a rigorous process of board evaluation has taken place against sensible criteria and that the outcomes have been acted upon in an effective way to enhance the board's performance. Codes of corporate governance that recommend board-performance evaluation may not always result in fascinating disclosures, but they do set in train an internal review process that should keep governance alive and relevant. Board evaluation is not a one-off action like drafting a policy; rather, it involves a regular review of many core aspects of corporate governance.

Summary of chapter 5

Most codes of corporate governance recommend regular board-performance evaluation. This chapter first reviews the process of evaluating a board: companies must decide on the criteria against which to assess their boards as well as how to conduct the evaluation and implement its outcomes. The objective of board-performance evaluation is to improve the functioning of the board. The second half of the chapter discusses the elements required for a board to perform effectively: role clarity, access to relevant information, appropriate skills and experience, open discussion and the ability to make decisions that are in the interests of the company. The board must be accountable for its decisions and capable of engaging with stakeholders. The chapter concludes that board-performance evaluation is a valuable process even though this value is difficult to communicate through corporate reporting.

References

ASX 2005, *Analysis of Corporate Governance Practices reported in 2004 Annual Reports*, ASX.

Blair, M & Stout, L 2001, 'Trust, trustworthiness and the behavioural foundations of corporate law', *University of Pennsylvania Law Review,* vol. 149, pp. 1735–1810.

Boardroom Partners 2012, *Anything to Declare? A report examining disclosures about board reviews, identifying good practice and encouraging progress,* Boardroom Partners and Chartered Secretaries Australia.

Cascio, WF 2004, 'Board governance: a social systems perspective', *Academy of Management Perspectives,* vol. 18, no. 1, pp. 97–100.

Clarke, T, Nielsen, B, Nielsen, S, Klettner, A & Boersma, M 2012, *2012 Australian Census of Women in Leadership*, Australian Government, Equal Opportunity for Women in the Workplace Agency.

Daily, CM & Dalton, DR 2003, 'Dollars and sense: the path to board independence', *Journal of Business Strategy,* vol. 24, no. 3, pp. 41–43.

Financial Reporting Council 2010, Revisions to the UK Corporate Governance Code (Formerly the Combined Code) May 2010.

Grant Thornton 2012, *Corporate Governance Reporting Review, 2012.*

Ingley, C & van der Walt, N 2002, 'Board dynamics and the politics of appraisal', *Corporate Governance: An International Review,* vol. 10, no. 3, pp. 163–74.

Kazanjian, J 2000, 'Assessing boards and individual directors', *Ivey Business Journal,* vol. 64, no. 5, pp. 45–50.

Keay, A 2014, 'Comply or explain: in need of greater regulatory oversight', *Legal Studies,* vol. 34, no. 2, pp. 279–304.

Kiel, GC & Nicholson, GJ 2005, 'Evaluating boards and directors', *Corporate Governance: an International Review,* vol. 13, no. 5, pp. 613–31.

Kirkpatrick, G 2009, *Corporate Governance Lessons from the Financial Crisis*, OECD.

Leblanc, R & Schwartz, MS 2007, 'The black box of board process: gaining access to a difficult subject', *Corporate Governance: An International Review,* vol. 15, no. 5, pp. 843–51.

MacNeil, I & Li, X 2006, 'Comply or explain: market discipline and non-compliance with the combined code', *Corporate Governance: An International Review,* vol. 14, no. 5, pp. 486–96.

Minichilli, A, Gabrielsson, J & Huse, M 2007, 'Board evaluations: making a fit between the purpose and the system', *Corporate Governance: An International Review,* vol. 15, no. 4, pp. 609–22.

Nicholson, G, Kiel, G & Tunny, JA 2012, 'Board evaluations: contemporary thinking and practice', in T Clarke & D Branson (eds.), *The SAGE Handbook of Corporate Governance,* Thousand Oaks: SAGE, pp. 285–324.

OECD 2004, Survey of Corporate Governance.

Sonnenfeld, JA 2002, 'What makes great boards great', *Harvard Business Review,* September, pp. 106–14.

Spencer Stuart, *International Comparison Chart*, 2015.

Van den Berghe, LAA & Levrau, A 2004, 'Evaluating boards of directors: what constitutes a good corporate board?', *Corporate Governance: An International Review,* vol. 12, no. 4, p. 461.

Walker, D 2009, 'A review of corporate governance in UK banks and other financial industry entities, Final recommendations, 26 November 2009.

6

GENDER DIVERSITY IN CORPORATE LEADERSHIP

Introduction

Women make up a very small proportion of the total number of directors on corporate boards. This is true, not only in Australia where the 2012 level (when this research was conducted) was 12.3 percent, but for most countries across the globe. The US organisation Catalyst regularly takes data from surveys done in 44 countries, and the median percentage of women on boards as at mid-2013 was approximately 8.4 percent (Catalyst 2013). This low level of women on corporate boards has been highlighted over the last 10 years as a problem that needs to be addressed. Although there are arguments both for and against taking action to increase board-gender diversity there is now a political and regulatory trend worldwide promoting women in leadership (du Plessis et al. 2014). With the aim of overcoming glacial progress, many governments around the world have begun to develop policies to promote and/or mandate increased female representation on corporate boards. Many countries in Europe have implemented mandatory quotas through hard law while others around the world have set voluntary targets by way of corporate governance codes (often supported by government recommendations as well as business and not-for-profit initiatives). Gender diversity in leadership has moved from being an issue of equality and sociology squarely into the realm of corporate governance.

This chapter explores this relatively new objective of corporate governance regulation: to encourage more women into corporate leadership. It explores the likely effectiveness of including gender-diversity provisions in codes of corporate governance and the mechanisms through which they might encourage change. Table 6.1 provides extracts of code provisions referring to diversity in a sample of countries worldwide. There is wide variety in the content of these provisions: some simply state that diversity should be considered when determining board composition; others set targets (40 percent in the French code and 50 percent

TABLE 6.1 Code provisions on gender diversity

Code	Date of inclusion	Provision
Australian Corporate Governance Principles and Recommendations (ASX Corporate Governance Council 2014)	The gender diversity recommendation was first added in 2010 (no reference to diversity in the 2007 edition). Consolidated in 2014 after introduction of the WGE Act in 2012.	Recommendation 1.5 A listed entity should: (a) have a diversity policy that includes requirements for the board or a relevant committee of the board to set measurable objectives for achieving gender diversity and to assess annually both the objectives and the entity's progress in achieving them; (b) disclose that policy or a summary of it; and (c) disclose as at the end of each reporting period the measurable objectives for achieving gender diversity set by the board or a relevant committee of the board in accordance with the entity's diversity policy and its progress towards achieving them, and either: (1) the respective proportions of men and women on the board, in senior executive positions and across the whole organisation (including how the entity has defined 'senior executive' for these purposes); or (2) if the entity is a 'relevant employer' under the Workplace Gender Equality Act, the entity's most recent 'Gender Equality Indicators', as defined in and published under that Act.
Denmark Recommendations on Corporate Governance (Committee on Corporate Governance 2014)	Reference to diversity was first introduced in 2008 and in 2011 the concept of setting measurable objectives was added. In 2013 this was removed from the code in relation to boards due to the introduction of a legal quota in 2012.	2.1.6 – The committee recommends that once a year the board of directors discuss the company's activities to ensure relevant diversity at management levels, including setting specific goals and accounting for its objectives and progress made in achieving the objectives in the management commentary on the company's annual report and/or on the website of the company. Diversity includes e.g. age, international experience and gender. It would be appropriate to prepare action plans describing the company's efforts in respect of diversity at management levels addressing the needs and future development of the company. Such action plans may supplement statutory requirements on target figures and policies for the gender-related composition of management and reporting in this respect. 3.1.2 When assessing its composition and nominating new candidates, the board of directors must take into consideration the need for integration of new talent and diversity in relation to age, international experience and gender.

(Continued)

Code	Date of inclusion	Provision
French Corporate governance code of listed corporations (afep-MEDEF, 2013)	Reference to gender diversity introduced in 2010.	6.3 Each board should consider the desirable balance within its membership and within that of the committees of board members it has established, in particular as regards the representation of men and women, nationalities and the diversity of skills…. 6.4 With regard to the representation of men and women, the objective is that each board shall reach and maintain a percentage of at least 20 percent of women within a period of three years and at least 40 percent of women within a period of six years from the shareholders' meeting of 2010 or from the date of the listing of the company's shares on a regulated market, whichever is later. When the Board comprises fewer than nine members, the difference at the end of six years between the number of directors of each gender may not be in excess of two.
Greece – Hellenic Corporate Governance Code for Listed Companies (Helenic Corporate Governance Council 2013)	Diversity provisions first introduced in 2013.	Principle II Diversity in the board's and senior executive team's composition is essential to broaden the perspective of the company and enable it to read effectively the social (and customer) context in which the company operates and inspire confidence in its stakeholders. … the company should pursue the optimal diversity, including gender balance, in the composition of its board and senior executive team. Such composition aims at the efficient achievement of the company's targets on the basis that the company gains access to a wider talent pool, thus increasing the company's competitiveness, productivity and innovation 2.8 The diversity policy including gender balance, for board members, as adopted by the board, shall be published on the company's website. The corporate governance statement shall make specific reference to the diversity policy applied by the company in relation to the composition of its board and the percentage of each gender represented in the board and senior executive team.
Japan's Corporate Governance Code (JPX Tokyo Stock Exchange 2015)	First included in 2015 (no reference to diversity in previous 2009 version)	Principle 2.4 Ensuring diversity, including active participation of women. Companies should recognise that the existence of diverse perspectives and values reflecting a variety of experiences, skills and characteristics is a strength that supports their sustainable growth. As such, companies should promote diversity of personnel, including the active participation of women.

Singapore Code of Corporate Governance (Monetary Authority of Singapore 2012)	2012 (no reference to diversity in previous 2005 version)	Principle 2 board composition 2.6 The board and its board committees should comprise directors who as a group provide an appropriate balance and diversity of skills, experience, gender and knowledge of the company.
Spanish Unified Good Governance Code (Special Working Group on the Good Governance of Listed Companies, 2006)	Introduced in 2006 and then removed in the 2015 version due to legislation	Recommendation 15 When women directors are few or non-existent, the board should state the reasons for this situation and the measures taken to correct it; in particular, the nomination committee should take steps to ensure that: (a) the process of filling board vacancies has no implicit bias against women candidates (b) the company makes a conscious effort to include women with the target profile among the candidates for board places
The Swedish Corporate Governance Code (Swedish Corporate Governance Board 2015)	This has been in the code since at least 2005.	4.1 The company is to strive for equal gender distribution on the board.
UK Corporate Governance Code (Financial Reporting Council 2014)	Reference to gender diversity first included in 2010 (only general B.2 statement) B2.4 disclosure requirements added in 2012.	Principle B.2 The search for board candidates should be conducted, and appointments made, on merit, against objective criteria and with due regard for the benefits of diversity on the board, including gender. B2.4 The annual report should include a description of the board's policy on diversity, including gender, any measurable objectives that it has set for implementing the policy and progress on achieving the objectives.

in the Swedish code) or ask companies to set and disclose their own targets. In each case it is important to understand the wider context of the code in terms of national law and policy. In the UK, code provisions have become more detailed over time, but this is because there is no hard law on the topic. As a contrast, code provisions on gender diversity in Denmark and Spain have become weaker due to an overall strengthening of regulation through the introduction of legislation. In Australia, code provisions operate in parallel with equal opportunity legislation, which, since 2012, has required corporate reporting of gender-diversity information.

This variation in the type of regulation used by different nations is an interesting phenomenon in itself. The choice of whether to regulate via a corporate governance code or hard law can be related to the desired strength of the regulation, but it may also be a function of the desired target population: stock exchange codes apply only to companies listed on the exchange, whereas legislation can set its own limits based on company size or type. Legislation may also be chosen in order to enable the implementation of legal sanctions for noncompliance; however, this should not be assumed. In countries where mandatory quotas have been set for female board representation, there is wide variation in the sanctions. For example, in Spain there are no penalties for failure to comply despite the quota's mandatory label (Villiers 2010).

The inclusion of gender diversity in corporate governance regulation is a phenomenon of the last 10 years. In keeping with its progressive policies on equality more generally, Northern Europe has led the way. Norway was the first country to introduce a mandatory quota, which resulted in women's participation on boards increasing from 25 percent in 2005 to 40 percent in 2009. France, Italy and Belgium introduced quota legislation in 2011 and Germany more recently in 2015. Spain's quota is softer, framed as a recommendation without formal sanctions, whereas Sweden and the Netherlands rely on comply-or-explain codes. Outside of continental Europe soft regulation is the common choice: Australia, South Africa and the United Kingdom introduced comply-or-explain disclosure requirements in 2009/2010 rather than quota legislation.

Benefits of gender diversity in leadership

There are many reasons for the desire for more women on boards, the most oft-cited being the economic benefits that stem from gender equality. Aside from the desire for social justice and equal opportunity, the loss of women from the workforce is a terrible waste of resources. Research suggests that lifting the proportion of women in the Australian workforce by 6 percent could increase Australia's GDP by around $25 billion (Daley et al. 2012).

With respect to women at board level, there is some evidence that companies with women on their boards perform better, although a direct link is hard to prove (Adams and Ferreira 2009; McKinsey 2007; McKinsey 2008). Nevertheless, it has been suggested that if there had been more women on the boards of large banks, the global financial crisis may have been less severe (Adams and Funk 2012; Rost and Osterloh 2010). Certainly, board effectiveness can be improved by including a diverse range of views in decision-making, including those of both men and women (Carter et al. 2003). In their study of Norwegian boards, Nielsen and Huse found that '[t]he presence of women on corporate boards seems to increase board effectiveness through reducing the level of conflict and ensuring high quality of board development activities' (2010, p. 136).

There is also evidence that women directors are more prepared than men to tackle 'tough issues' and thereby help boards avoid the problems of groupthink and conflict avoidance (McInerney-Lacombe et al. 2008). Also women tend to ask challenging questions (Huse and Solberg 2006), one of the keys to board effectiveness identified by the Walker report in the UK (2009, p. 52). Several other studies have linked aspects of 'good governance' to the presence of women on a board, for example better monitoring of strategy implementation and conflict of interest policies; improving succession planning; and supporting board performance evaluation (Sealy and Vinnicombe 2012, p. 326). Overall, the weight of evidence suggests that the presence of women on boards is a matter of good corporate governance and can improve board performance (du Plessis et al. 2014, p. 47).

Current lack of gender diversity in leadership

The reasons behind the lack of women in leadership are complex but important to understand when considering regulatory action. In Australia, there have been more females entering higher education than men since 1989 (ABS 1998). In addition, more females complete their degrees successfully than men (Olsen 2011). Thus, for many years it was expected that these women would trickle through to senior leadership positions over time. However, research has shown that despite female achievement in education, there has not been a proportionate increase in women attaining senior career success (Sealy and Vinnicombe 2012; Kang et al. 2007). A major loss of female talent from corporations occurs at mid-management level. This is at great cost to the economy and to the companies that have invested time and resources in their training (Daley et al. 2012; Goldman Sachs 2009). Although the obvious biological causes (child bearing and rearing) are an important contributor, they are not the only factor. The most common reasons for the under-representation of women at board level cited by the UK Davies report were issues with work-life balance and workplace culture (2011). Although also important, issues of lack of opportunity or bias in recruitment came lower in the list. Branson describes these issues as more subtle de facto or second-generation discrimination:

> ... such as late day and Saturday managers' meetings, emphasis on office 'face time' and insistence on frequent travel which have a disproportionate effect on women as they move up into the ranks of middle and senior management. The thought is that persistent enshrinement of such practices

cause women, especially those with children, to opt out of the work force, leading to a depletion of the pool from which women director candidates could be chosen 10 years hence.

(2012, p. 11)

Even if there are some talented women rejecting corporate careers, there is evidence that the pool of women who are searching for such positions is still large enough to permit an immediate increase in numbers in leadership. In the UK, Sealy and Vinnicombe identified a pool of 2551 women in pipeline executive positions and suggested that if only 200 of these women found their way onto FTSE 100 boards it could transform the landscape of women directors (2012, p. 330). A survey by GMI Ratings regarding newly appointed female directors in France found that most were highly qualified professionals many new to board service in France and most serving only on one board:

> ... the French experience seems to be validating the theory of many diversity advocates: there are many women who are well-qualified to serve as public company directors, but who are not routinely recruited.
>
> (Gladman and Lamb 2013, p. 12)

The distinction between women who genuinely choose to reject corporate careers and those who are effectively forced out or overlooked is not as simple as it may seem. Peters et al. (2010) found that in male-dominated work environments, the lack of successful female role models directly affects women's levels of ambition. If women cannot identify with those working above them or cannot reconcile their own values and needs with what they see, their career progression inevitably stalls. Instead women choose to set up their own businesses or move to the public sector, academia or not-for-profits as these sectors tend to have more flexible work arrangements and values based more on output than desk-time.

What is clear is that the lack of gender diversity in the higher echelons of corporations has a complex mix of causes. Regulation can either try to tackle these causes, their outcome (low numbers of women on boards) or both. While many countries in Europe are implementing legislative quotas to force companies to appoint more women to the board, Australia and the UK have chosen a softer approach whereby companies are asked to set their own targets for gender diversity and implement policies to achieve those targets. Quota legislation is aimed directly at outcomes whereas use of a comply-or-explain corporate governance code is directed at the underlying workplace policies and culture (GDC 2013, p. 2). Peta Spender succinctly lays out the terms of the debate:

> Debates about women on boards have focused on measures designed to achieve equality of access and across countries governmental approaches may be categorised as 'hard' or 'soft'. Hard strategies involve more coercive means of achieving equality of outcomes such as legislation for affirmative

action and quotas. The soft strategies involve persuasion of market actors to achieve equality of access.

(2012, p. 23)

What this chapter aims to do is to explore in more depth how Australia's chosen soft strategy for encouraging gender diversity is affecting corporate behaviour in practice. It examines the corporate response to the amendments made to the ASX corporate governance code in 2010. Empirical review of how these recommendations function in practice is vital to the international debate on women in leadership. The debate over whether hard or soft law is likely to be most effective at increasing women in corporate leadership can only be answered by reviewing the evidence as it emerges (du Plessis et al. 2014; Klettner et al. 2016).

Methodology

This chapter explores the early impact of the Australian corporate governance recommendations designed to promote gender diversity in corporations. The recommendations were added to the second edition of the Australian code in 2010 as follows:

- **Recommendation 3.2** – Companies should establish a policy concerning diversity and disclose the policy or a summary of it.
- **Recommendation 3.3** – Companies should disclose in each annual report the measurable objectives for achieving gender diversity set by the board in accordance with the diversity policy and progress towards achieving them.
- **Recommendation 3.4** – Companies should disclose in each annual report the proportion of women employees in the whole organisation, women in senior executive positions and women on the board.

These recommendations were consolidated in the 2014 edition of the code and renumbered as recommendation 1.5. However, the research findings presented in this chapter are based on the 2011 disclosures of ASX 200 companies made against the 2010 version of the code, as well as interviews with experienced company officers conducted in 2006. Through presenting evidence of the corporate response to the diversity recommendations this chapter demonstrates how the comply-or-explain mechanism of corporate governance codes can initiate a process of cultural change within corporations. It also draws on the opinions of company officers to discuss the role of gender diversity in board performance. At the heart of this regulation is a belief that by increasing women on the board (and in the executive pipeline) boards will be better equipped to fulfil their role in governing the corporation.

It should be noted that recommendations 3.2 to 3.5 came into force for a listed entity's first financial year commencing on or after 1 January 2011. This means that, at the time of collecting data, compliance statistics were not greatly meaningful because the new code recommendations were only formally in force for companies with a December financial year-end (only 17 percent of ASX 200 companies). Nevertheless, the ASX encouraged early adoption of the recommendations and thus many companies voluntarily made disclosures. In their 2011 annual reports, 57 percent of ASX 200 companies stated that they had a diversity policy in place in accordance with recommendation 3.2; 51 percent had made an attempt to set measurable objectives in accordance with recommendation 3.3 (although less than half of these measurable objectives comprised numerical targets), and 46.5 percent had reported against all three of the gender metrics in recommendation 3.4 (Klettner et al. 2013).

Important also in assessing the response of companies is the fact that the Australian government strengthened its overall stance on gender diversity in corporations through the *Workplace Gender Equality Act* 2012 (WGE Act), which requires companies with over 100 employees to disclose against six 'gender equality indicators'. These supplement the ASX corporate governance code as they also require disclosure of gender statistics and whether a company has a diversity policy. Although the WGE Act was not in force at the time of collecting data, companies would have been aware of the government's desire to move towards stricter reporting requirements.

Clearly the broad objective of all of this regulation is to increase the number of women in corporate leadership. This is a long-term objective, and yet numbers of female board members increased almost immediately following the introduction of the ASX recommendations, from 8.4 percent of ASX 200 directorships in 2010, to 12.3 percent in 2012, rising to 21.7 percent in 2015 (Clarke et al. 2012; AICD 2016). Although this indicates a measure of regulatory success in terms of outcomes, this chapter will focus on the effectiveness of the more direct objectives of the ASX recommendations, which may work towards deeper change. The code recommendations encourage companies to consider how they might improve overall workplace diversity, particularly gender diversity, through: (1) measuring the number of women across their organisations; (2) setting targets for improving gender diversity; and (3) drafting and implementing diversity and other policies to achieve these targets. Indeed, it is this last objective of altering workplace policies and processes that this chapter will focus on.

Thus the aim of the research presented here was not to measure code compliance or numbers of women but to explore, in a qualitative way, the sorts of changes being implemented within companies as a result of having diversity policies (or the sorts of changes disclosed as *intended to be* implemented). In other words its objective was to delve a little deeper to analyse the workplace changes that companies were planning to put in place to achieve their diversity targets. Whether or not a diversity policy is properly implemented is core to whether soft regulation can change behaviour both at board level and throughout an organisation.

Content analysis was used to analyse the disclosures of ASX 200 companies in their 2011 annual reports to understand how they were planning to make changes to support increased diversity. The diversity disclosures generally comprised a well-delineated section of text within the corporate governance statement of the company's annual report, which was copied into a software program for text analysis.

The Australian corporate governance code provides suggestions for the content of a diversity policy, and these were consolidated into five categories (A to E) representing potential workplace policy/strategy changes. For each of the issues A to E, keywords were identified and then searched for across all of the ASX 200 diversity disclosures. Cresswell recommends that if a 'prefigured' coding scheme such as this is used in content analysis, researchers should still remain open to additional codes emerging during the analysis (2013, p. 185). On this basis a further 'emergent' category F was added because the data revealed that many companies had set up a committee to lead and monitor diversity. The final categories were as follows:

A. Articulation of the corporate benefits arising from diversity
B. Inclusion of diversity in recruitment and selection processes
C. Executive mentoring or training programmes
D. Promotion of a culture that supports diversity and recognises domestic responsibilities
E. Tying measurable objectives to Key Performance Indicators
F. Setting up a board or management committee responsible for diversity policy

For each incidence of each keyword, the surrounding paragraph was taken as the unit of analysis, and if the meaning of the paragraph corresponded with the relevant category it was included in the score for that policy change (Krippendorff 2004). The policy and process changes identified were generally described as being part of the diversity policy or as amounting to 'measurable objectives' set in accordance with the policy. The keywords and overall results are summarised in Table 6.2 and discussed in turn below. As described further below, for some categories, statements were also classed as 'well-articulated' or 'basic' in terms of the quality of information provided, an approach taken by other studies of disclosure statements (Spira and Page 2010, p. 418).

A. Articulating the benefits of diversity

The benefits of diversity were articulated well by 38 companies, and a very basic statement was provided by a further 33 companies, making a total of 71 companies or 35.5 percent of the ASX 200 attempting in 2011 to explain why diversity is important. The examples of well-articulated statements demonstrated that thought had gone into the reasons behind diversity policies and the specific benefits for the company. These benefits included better problem solving and innovation; improved understanding of the company's customer base; access to the widest talent pool; more effective and efficient decision-making and competitive advantage.

TABLE 6.2 Policy and process changes to support gender diversity

Content	Search words	Number of companies
A Articulation of the corporate benefits arising from diversity	'benefit' 'advantage' 'value'	71 (35.5 percent)
B Inclusion of diversity in recruitment and selection processes	'recruit' 'appoint' 'select'	34 (17.0 percent)
C Executive mentoring or training programmes	'mentor' 'train' 'develop'	50 (25.0 percent)
D Articulation of a culture that supports diversity and recognises domestic responsibilities	culture leave flexi	54 (27.0 percent)
E Linking diversity objectives to executives KPIs	'key performance' 'KPI' 'remuneration' 'compensation'	4 (2.0 percent)
F Responsibility for diversity objectives allocated to a specific committee or other body	'committee' 'council'	60 (30.0 percent)

A basic statement, recognising the benefits but not actually articulating what they are, included the following sentence, notably used by at least three different companies – a classic example of legal 'boiler-plate' and the use of standardised precedents:

> The company values diversity and recognises the benefits it can bring to the organisation's ability to achieve its goals.
>
> *(Bathurst Resources; Billabong International; Extract Resources)*

Other basic statements simply stated that diversity provides an advantage, or is in the company's best interests, without explaining further. Statements that only said that the company 'values diversity' or that it was an 'important consideration' were not counted as 'articulating' the benefits of diversity. Categorising statements in this way naturally involves a level of subjectivity, and hence the validity of results can be limited. However this type of qualitative analysis is important in understanding that there is a spectrum of responses and wide variation in the level of sophistication of diversity policies.

Interview participants in 2006 were also asked about the benefits of diversity, and 13 interviewees (23 percent of the 57 participants) actively said that their boards would benefit from more diversity of background. Some wanted specific backgrounds or skills to be represented on the board e.g. government, finance or medical experience. A technology company thought that younger directors would be of benefit, whereas a company about to expand overseas was looking for international experience on the board. Their responses made clear the need for a company's leaders to understand and represent the company's market and customers. This evidence supports resource-dependency theories of the board as a provider or link to essential skills and resources. Certainly the perceived value of diversity on the board is to enhance the board's performance role rather than its monitoring role, through improved problem-solving, innovation and market knowledge. Two interviewees explained how gender diversity can also improve board performance at the level of board interaction and decision-making – the behavioural processes at the core of board effectiveness:

> In 2000 when [first female] came on the board there was definitely a feeling she was a token woman, a PC choice, but she has been very impressive. She was from a marketing and communications background and has added a lot of value. She tends to speak up on issues where you wouldn't expect a lot of dissent. She does think differently.
>
> *(Male company secretary, ASX 300)*

> I don't think a female director expresses her views any differently from a male so I'm not sure if it adds to the quality of the board. It does add to the way the board interacts and I think it changes their approach and the way they interact informally. Diversity of background is important in order to get a broad range of views.
>
> *(Female company secretary, ASX 100)*

B. Including diversity in recruitment and selection

There were 34 companies in the ASX 200 that expressly stated that they had made changes in 2011 to recruitment, selection or appointment policies in order to include diversity considerations. Here a company was counted if it stated that it had reviewed or incorporated recruitment practices into its diversity strategy or had made changes to policies to ensure diverse/female candidates were included. Common changes were a commitment to include female candidates in the pool for selection and to include female employees on the interview panel. Recruitment training for leaders was also being implemented to ensure effectiveness in sourcing a wide range of candidates. Although there was certainly a focus on gender diversity several companies also mentioned recruitment policies in relation to specific racial or geographic groups.

Changes that actively encouraged the recruitment of a diverse range of candidates were included in the score but not those that confirmed recruitment practices were non-discriminatory. Anti-discrimination and equal employment opportunity legislation has been in place for many years and has not improved gender diversity in corporate leadership. Thus, a company was not scored if it confirmed that it had equal opportunity policies or recruited only on merit or was transparent in recruitment decisions. The intended effect of the ASX recommendations and of the creation of a diversity policy is to go further and attempt to remove the unconscious bias that tends to exist in recruitment practices (Collins 2007). It is an example of how soft regulation can influence behaviour in areas where prescriptive law has failed. Indeed, three companies expressly mentioned the need to address unconscious bias and were changing recruitment processes or implementing training on the topic, such as the 'Consciously Addressing Unconscious Bias' program!

Some companies explained that changes to recruitment practices were part of a formal policy review to ensure all existing policies were updated in accordance with the diversity policy. Others expressed changes to recruitment practices as measurable objectives, for example:

> Implement recruitment policy that all executive recruitment briefs include a guideline that 50 per cent of shortlisted candidates are to be female.
>
> *(Mirvac)*

> Where multiple entry level operational roles are being recruited at least one will be reserved for a female applicant (including graduate/apprenticeship/cadetship positions) commencing 1 January 2011.
>
> *(OzMinerals)*

This is an appropriate moment to broach the issue of positive discrimination because targets to increase female participation should not be discriminatory to men. There is a fine line between, on the one hand, encouraging women and removing unconscious bias, and, on the other hand, a form of affirmative action. As Wheland and Wood comment, the most common objection to gender quotas and targets is the merit principle: that recruitment and promotion should be based purely on merit, such that the best person for the job is selected irrespective of gender or any other characteristic (2012, p. 9). This was the most common response from company officers interviewed in 2006. Fourteen of 57 participants (24.6 percent) emphasised that they appointed on the basis of merit – that it was most important to find the skills and background needed rather than searching for a specific gender:

> My view is that we should pick the best person for the job. It depends on the needs and requirements of the board at the time. Diversity is part of it – you do need to get the right blend of backgrounds.
>
> *(Male company secretary, ASX 300)*

> The chairman gave a firm response at the AGM – we pick just on merit and not gender – there would be no point appointing a woman just for the sake of gender.
>
> *(Male CFO, ASX 100)*

There is an under-representation of females and we are cognisant of it. While we want to foster diversity, it is most important to get the best candidate. Our board has diversity in terms of skills, experience, nationality – there are directors from the US, Australia, UK and South Africa – it is reasonably diverse although it could be more. The Chairman is committed to enhancing it.

(Male company secretary, ASX 100)

It was interesting to see how many companies put forward the merit principle in their 2011 diversity disclosures in the same way as these interviewees in 2006. In fact, only 16 companies in the ASX 200 (8 percent) stressed that they recruited based only on merit. Most of these companies simply made a positive statement about equal opportunity, for example, we select, retain and develop the best people for the job on the basis of merit and job related competencies – without discrimination. There were only a handful of companies that appeared to be defending the status quo or making a statement against gender targets:

At year end, 39 percent of management positions were held by women, an increase of 7 percent on last year's figure. Rather than employing bias in promoting women, this result has been achieved through our merit based promotion system.

(Kingsgate Consolidated)

Qube policy requires that all positions at Qube are filled on the basis of merit. This means that applicants for positions for which a formal recruitment process is undertaken will be assessed on the basis of the competencies they possess in relation to the requirements of the job. Merit-based selection ensures the opportunity exists for all applicants for such positions to demonstrate their competencies for the position being offered. As such, Qube's diversity policy does not include a requirement on the board to establish measurable objectives for achieving gender diversity or to assess any such objectives or progress towards achieving them and the Qube board has not set any such objectives. Qube believes that such objectives would be inconsistent with its policy on positions being filled on the basis of merit.

(Qube Logistics)

Both of these companies, Kingsgate Consolidated and Qube Logistics, had no female directors in 2011. Interestingly, Qube's board was still all-male in 2015 and although the company had set measurable objectives, they did not comprise numerical targets and were stated to be 'non-gender specific…. directed to promoting diversity through equal employment opportunities'. This perhaps demonstrates that that there is still some resistance to the concept of gender targets, even if few companies are bold enough to say so. In 2015 Kingsgate had one woman on its small board of five but still gave a 'why not' explanation regarding measurable objectives.

> Because the Company, at this stage of its development, has a small Board of Directors and a small management team which is geographically dispersed and because of the industry in which the Company operates, the Board does not consider it to be practicable to set measurable objectives to achieve greater gender diversity at this time.
>
> *(Kingsgate)*

Difficulty in finding female leaders in certain industries was also raised by many interview participants in 2006. Interviewees claimed that although they would like more women in leadership, there was a lack of suitable female candidates. Sixteen interviewees (28 percent) actively said their board would benefit from more women, and yet 11 of them said that it was difficult to find suitably qualified candidates for the job. Sealy and Vinnicombe have also found this to be a common response from CEOs and chairmen (2012, p. 329). However, research by Sheridan and Milgate suggests that these answers may reflect the gender of the interviewees. In interviews in 2000, they found that 'while most of the male respondents focused on the shortage of experienced and/or committed women, the female respondents tended to focus on the nature of the process' (Sheridan and Milgate 2003, p. 150). All of the comments about a lack of female candidates in 2006 interviews were from male participants; however, most were in industries that tend to have fewer females at all levels such as mining or engineering:

> If anything the board believes greater gender balance would be appropriate. However there aren't as many females on the circuit especially with backgrounds in resources or mining.
>
> *(Male company secretary, ASX 100)*

> We've got females in a lot of areas including high up in the executive tree so there are some very good ladies coming through, for example in environmental operations and investor relations. Mining is only just coming of age in terms of getting females into the industry. At board level we are not there yet – there are not yet many females coming through because we've tended to appoint directors who were formerly MDs of mining companies. However, we do get feedback through the females within the organisation.
>
> *(Male company secretary, ASX 100)*

> There is a lack of women in senior positions in this company which is a problem. There is not a single female [unit head]. Engineering is heavily skewed but we do need to do something. There are more women on the advice/consulting side of the business – we are aiming for an engineering-consulting ratio of 60:40 so that should help. On our regional

board the IT manager is a lady and our marketing director. She started off as our receptionist and has worked her way up – so there is certainly an openness to give the opportunity but there's no-one pushing at the door.

(Male general counsel, private company)

I believe there is value in diversity. In reality it is difficult to find women with the depth of business experience to operate well at board level. At senior executive level I'd pick a woman over a man all other things equal – they bring a very different mindset and perspective to a team.

(Male chairman, small listed company)

Several years later, in 2011, there were still a few companies that referred to low numbers of women in their industry as a barrier to gender diversity, for example:

One of the challenges for Adelaide Brighton, and other heavy manufacturing companies, is the traditional low levels of female representation due to the nature of the work performed. In an effort to make our company more attractive to women we sponsor the Women in Engineering programme at the University of Wollongong as well as providing an undergraduate scholarship.

(Adelaide Brighton)

At present 30 percent of our direct workforce (excluding subcontractors) is female. This reflects the reality of the industry in which the Group operates and the generally low participation rates of women in the engineering and manual trades workforce across Australia and the world. The available pool of female candidates for engineering and manual roles is limited and consequentially constrains the ability of the Company to increase female participation through internal promotion and external recruitment both across the workforce generally and at senior executive level.

(UGL)

Historically, the industry in which APA operates has been dominated by men, to a greater degree than some other industries. Today, approximately 75 percent of APA's employees are involved in operating and maintaining APA's and third parties' gas and pipeline and infrastructure assets and that many of those roles require physical, field-based work has meant they have been predominantly filled by men.

(APA)

There is certainly some truth to these statements as all past government surveys have shown that there are low numbers of women in the senior executive ranks of listed companies, particularly these sectors, and that many of the women

currently on boards have come from a background of law, accounting or investment banking rather than the traditional path of first being a senior executive
(Clarke et al. 2012). Industry differences in gender composition suggest that use
of flexible regulation to encourage diversity is appropriate in Australia. However,
across all sectors it seems that women are falling out of the pipeline for board
positions at an early stage in their career, and the complex reasons for this need
to be explored and, if possible, resolved. The following sections regarding talent
development, culture and working conditions will examine how companies are
proposing to encourage women to enter non-traditional fields and retain them
across the corporate workforce more generally.

C. Mentoring, development and training programs to increase diversity

There were 50 companies in the ASX 200 in 2011 (25 percent) that referred to
the use of mentoring, development or training programs designed to increase
diversity. Programs were included in the score for this category if they were designed to develop leadership capabilities, skills development, career progression
or were described as 'talent management' for increasing diversity. These schemes
were only included if they were expressly linked to the objective of increased diversity. Several companies were sponsoring women to attend internal or external
mentoring programs; others were ensuring that women identified as 'high talent'
were offered training and ongoing professional development coaching.

Excluded from the score were general training schemes involving diversity
awareness and the diversity policy, which in some cases were described as an
addition to existing equal opportunity, anti-discrimination or general induction
training. The aim of the research was to identify positive changes rather than
maintenance of the status quo. So if a company simply emphasised existing equal
opportunity measures this was not included. It is accepted that this methodology
involves a level of subjectivity and scores are only approximate. However, the
purpose of the research was not to obtain precise statistics, rather to understand
the types of workplace changes being developed and implemented. Indeed, qualitative analysis of the data revealed that the way in which mentoring or training
programs for diversity were presented by companies was quite varied, including:

- brief mention of programs when summarising the content of a diversity
  policy;
- a more detailed description of diversity programs as areas of current activity
  whether led by a policy or otherwise;
- framing of programs as stand-alone measurable objectives for improving
  gender diversity – targets included numbers of women trained or changes in
  attrition rates; and
- describing programs as part of a bundle of initiatives supporting a company's
  numerical gender-diversity targets.

The ASX's diversity policy suggestions specifically link these types of programs to board gender diversity and the development of executive talent; however, some companies were also using mentoring schemes to encourage indigenous employees, local citizens (particularly in relation to overseas mining operations) and young graduates.

D. Creating a culture that supports diversity

As discussed in the introduction to this chapter, it is thought that many corporations have developed a culture that is unfriendly, if not subtly discriminatory, towards women. For this reason many women choose to leave and pursue their careers in a more accepting environment. The ASX's suggestions as to the content of a diversity policy recognise the need for a culture that accepts employees' domestic responsibilities and in doing so enables more carers (who in Australia still tend to be women) to remain employed and progress their careers. Only one interviewee in 2006 expressly recognised this issue:

> I would like to see a more balanced board but the reality is that there are not that many women who want to deal with the commitments of the job e.g. the ad hoc meetings at strange hours during acquisitions etc. And it's a male-dominated industry. As an organisation we don't do too badly – about 27–30 percent female but it's not represented at board level.
>
> *(Male company secretary, ASX 300)*

In their 2011 annual reports, 54 ASX 200 companies (27 percent) referred to the use of flexible working and leave policies, as well as general cultural change as a way of increasing diversity. Here is evidence of the use of soft regulation as a tool to encourage cultural change in complex situations where prescriptive regulation would be inappropriate (Coglianese and Lazer 2003). As with changes to other policies and processes, some of these changes were framed as measurable objectives for increasing gender diversity, whereas others were presented in a general discussion of the company's approach to diversity. Insurance Australia Group disclosed a particularly impressive set of policies to support the needs of its workers including: parental leave for both parents; programs aimed at mature aged people; a variety of options for flexible working; and leave arrangements to address both personal and family needs. Interestingly, the insurance industry is the only industry to be consistently in the top five industries for female representation at board level (Clarke et al. 2012). Whether this is a result of this kind of policy or a reason for the existence of this kind of policy is worthy of further research.

E. Linking diversity to key performance indicators

Only four companies included mention of key performance indicators (KPIs) in their 2011 disclosures on diversity and, of these, only two stated that KPIs had actually been linked to diversity objectives as opposed to this possibly happening in future. BHP Billiton explained that diversity plans form part of performance requirements for each business and are taken into account in assessing bonus remuneration. QBE Insurance stated that it had included measurable objectives for fostering inclusive, diverse workgroups in the performance objectives for senior leaders.

It must be noted that many companies only provided a short summary or introduction to their diversity policy in their annual report, referring the reader to the company website for the full policy. It may be that more companies are intending to link diversity objectives to executive remuneration but did not disclose this in their annual report statement. Downloading and analysing each company's full diversity policy was beyond the scope of this research. In short, it seems that few companies have gone this extra step, although a review of full-disclosure policies and remuneration reports would be required to be sure of exact numbers. Even if diversity targets are tied to executive remuneration, it is possible (see the findings in Chapter 7 regarding tying pay to sustainability objectives) that there may be little transparency of the dollar amounts involved and whether they would amount to a real incentive.

Another positive initiative wending its way into remunerations policies is the concept of gender pay equity. Triggered by the WGE Act's gender-equality indicators, many companies have conducted a review of pay equity and are putting in place programs to ensure that the considerable gender pay gap (measured as 17.3 percent in Australia) is reduced over time (WGEA 2016).

F. Committee responsibility

An interesting finding was evidence that 60 companies in the ASX 200 (30 percent) had considered the lines of accountability and responsibility for diversity and disclosed the fact that they had allocated responsibility to a particular board–sub-committee (usually nomination or remuneration) or to a group such as a dedicated Diversity Council. This was not suggested in the ASX recommendations and therefore is a clear sign of companies taking the initiative and incorporating diversity into their corporate governance framework. Some companies explained that this had involved formal amendment of the board and committee charters to allocate responsibility to the committee to review and report progress to the board on a regular basis. Others detailed a more complex hierarchy of governance structures whereby an executive diversity committee would report to the board committee.

In counting the number of companies that had done this, those that said that the nomination committee considers diversity when considering new candidates were not included. This is a statement about the general role of the nomination committee. Only statements that allocated specific responsibility and account-ability for setting diversity strategy and objectives (and progress towards those objectives) to a named group were included. The board as a whole has ultimate responsibility for these objectives, but it was interesting to see how companies had used existing corporate governance structures (or created new ones) to clarify responsibility and presumably increase efficiency. This corroborates the evidence in Chapters 5 and 7 regarding the value and efficiency gains that board committees can bring to overall board function and performance.

Several companies specifically mentioned that their diversity committee or policy had been in place for several years and had not been set up simply as a response to the ASX recommendations. For example, ANZ set up its Diversity Council in 2004 and has been setting gender targets since that time; both Telstra and Commonwealth Bank set up Diversity Councils in 2006; Downer EDI mentioned that it had been reporting on diversity in the sustainability report since 2009 and Qantas since 2007; Macquarie has had a female mentoring scheme since 2009; NAB stated its first gender pay audit was in 2007; Orica approved its formal diversity strategy in 2009. This confirms the theory that soft regulation tends to follow and support emerging practices or norms rather than set them. It is also interesting that many of these companies are banks and that the banking and finance sector has one of the higher levels of women in leadership (Clarke et al. 2012). This may indicate that attention to the issue of diversity can have positive results.

Discussion and conclusions

The Australian corporate governance code recommendations on gender diversity provide an interesting example of soft law in action: they not only suggest that companies draft a diversity policy and disclose gender metrics but ask companies to set their own targets for increasing gender diversity and report annually on progress towards those targets. They demonstrate how well-designed comply-or-explain regulation can do more than simply suggest the one-off implementation of specific governance structures and procedures. These code provisions set up a cycle of self-measurement, self-set policy and self-monitoring, made public through disclosure.

The recommendations came into effect for financial years starting on or after 1 January 2011, and the majority of data presented in this chapter was collected in the first half of 2012. It therefore presents a picture of companies' initial response to the recommendations. At the time of collecting the data, the recommendations were formally in force for only 34 or 17 percent of all companies in the ASX 200, and yet change was afoot in many more companies than this. In 2011, just over half of all companies in the ASX 200, 102 companies, made some attempt at setting measurable objectives for increasing gender diversity. KPMG reported that this had increased to 82 percent of the ASX 200 in 2012 and then to 86 percent in 2013. This demonstrates the force of code recommendations and the fact that they have a strong influence on behaviour despite their soft and voluntary nature. Although these compliance figures suggest that change may slow after initial implementation, the clever design of the recommendations includes progress-reporting. Table 6.3 shows some examples of

TABLE 6.3 Targets for women on the board

	Company	Target 2011	Actual 2015
	Billabong	43%	17% (1/6)
	Mirvac	35% by 2015 and 50% by 2020	50% (4/8)
	Woolworths	33% by 2015	33%
	Coca Cola	30% by 2014	33% (2014)
	Brambles	30%	33%
	Telstra	30% by 2013	3/11 women, 30% of non-execs
	NAB	30% by 2015	20%
	BHP Billiton	25%	3/11 (27%)
	Envestra	25% by 2014	Delisted
	Virgin	25% by 2013	20% (2/10)
	Leighton Holdings	20% by 2016	12.5% (restructured to CIMIC)
	PanAust	2 on board by 2014	2 women or 22% (2014) but taken over, delisted and zero women in 2015
	Industrea	15% board in next 2 years	Delisted
	Sims Metal	1 female director	30% (3/10)
	QR National	1 female director	22% (2/9)(renamed Aurizon

Note: Dark shading = target achieved; light shading = target failed; white = company restructured

numerical targets set by companies for women on the board in 2011 together with actual figures reported in 2015. These demonstrate that, of the 11 companies still in existence, eight of them had achieved their targets.

It is worth bearing in mind that the average board size for the ASX 200 in 2011 was 7.2 members (Clarke et al. 2012). A board of this size could meet a target of 25 percent by having two female members; a small board of four would need only one woman to meet this target, whereas a large board of nine would need three women. Torchia et al. (2011) have investigated the need for a critical mass of women on a board before behavioural advantages are seen. In this context the actual numbers of women rather than percentages can be important with three female members being put forward as the magical number. Some companies appear to be cognisant of this and have a target to maintain a certain number of women rather than a particular percentage.

Certainly, the recommendations have caused most companies to consider the issue of diversity, particularly gender diversity, in the context of their organisation. This is a phenomenal development in itself – that a corporate governance code has caused companies to take some responsibility for a complex issue of social equality and economic importance. Some of the more comprehensive company statements show good understanding of the business case for diversity and will help to spread the message that encouraging diversity can provide advantages to an organisation both at board level and below. Company statements for the 2011 financial year show that organisations recognise that increased diversity in leadership teams can improve problem-solving, innovative capacity and understanding of customers. Interview comments also touch on the way in which women can change the behavioural dynamics of board discussion and decision-making in a way that is in the best interests of the company.

The research indicates that the practical effect of the ASX recommendations includes changes to recruitment, training, leave and remuneration policies as well as increased awareness of diversity in a cultural sense. All of these issues have previously been identified as possible reasons for the lack of women in leadership (CAMAC 2009). In interviews with women directors in 2000, Sheridan identified the tendency for 'like to promote like' as one of the barriers continuing to limit women's opportunities to access board positions (Sheridan and Milgate 2003, p. 147). Sheridan and Milgate found that the main difference between men and women in attaining board positions was that women felt they needed a level of 'high visibility' whereas men did not:

> women's competence has to be widely acknowledged in the public domain before boards, or their nominating committees, will be prepared to 'risk' having a woman on the board.
>
> (2006, p. 854)

Burgess and Fallon (2003) used social identity theory to test the idea that, to be successful, women have to adapt themselves to fit with the board's male 'ingroup'. They did not find that, once on a board, women strive to fit in; however, they suggest that this testing of 'fit' is likely to occur in the lead up to the offer of a board position and is why many women who attain board positions are already a 'known' quantity. Supporting women's networking groups and changing selection procedures so that women are included on interview panels ought to help this situation. In fact, research has found that women directors are less likely than men to be on a board nomination committee (whereas there is almost no gender difference for audit and remuneration committees) (Clarke et al. 2012, p. 22; Kesner 1988). In 1994, Bilimoria and Piderit found that the only committee where women had a higher likelihood of membership than men was the public affairs (or corporate social responsibility) committee suggesting that women are favoured for the 'softer' areas of the board's work rather than the more central functions. With regard to membership of the nominating committee, they found that men holding business occupations were favoured over similar women (1994, p. 1466). Certainly, a common sense first step towards increasing the numbers of women on boards would be to increase the numbers on nomination committees. This ought to help women to attain board positions by reducing unconscious bias and tapping into women's networks.

The need for cultural change has also been well documented. The CAMAC report (2009) discussed the 'corporate culture for executive positions that values long hours in the office' and its possible role in longer-term supply-side issues 'concerning the number of women with relevant qualifications who are seeking or are otherwise open to board appointments' (2009, p. 28). Although the issue of culture is often listed as one of the barriers to women's progression in the executive ranks, what is not made clear is the exercise of choice. Rather than being turned down for positions because of discrimination, women are turning their backs on the corporate world and finding other ways to use their skills. Ryan et al. found that women opting out of senior executive life did so due to a mix of 'pull' factors – motivating them to leave organisations voluntarily, like family and lifestyle; as well as 'push' factors – aspects of the work environment compelling women to leave (2008, p. 158). However, Lewis and Simpson (2010) argue that these 'choices' are not really free choices but are constrained by circumstances not of women's choosing. For example, the study by Anderson et al. (2010) of women partners who left a management consultancy firm showed that the choice to leave was often forced by the lack of flexibility and excessive time demands placed on partners. Whatever the reasons behind women opting out of work, it is a huge loss of talent, and if these women could be tempted back into service, they would contribute greatly to both corporate performance and the economy (Goldman Sachs 2009). If the ASX recommendations can begin the long-awaited process of cultural change towards more female-friendly work environments, it will be a remarkable achievement.

There is also evidence to suggest that there could be a tipping point at which a critical mass of women in leadership is able to make cultural changes within an organisation that permit many other women to follow in their footsteps. Nielsen and Huse (2010) have shown that one of the impacts of increased gender diversity at board level is to change corporate behaviour and attitude. If workplace culture could be altered to temper negative attitudes towards, for example, flexible working, there would likely be a large increase in the pool of female candidates for executive jobs. Gender targets and changes to recruitment processes can be seen as a first step towards creating the critical mass of women at leadership level necessary for more substantial workplace culture change. As Sealy and Vinnicombe comment:

> Having good numbers of women in leadership positions contributes to an organisation in terms of mentors, role models and female retention from a better understanding of the issues women face at work.
>
> (2012, p. 327)

There is also some evidence that having more female directors in an organisation increases the level of female executives (Matsa and Miller 2013). However, the evidence is not strong, and it will be interesting to see what will be revealed as future research delves into the longer-term effects of the quotas recently implemented in Europe. Despite women now making up 40 percent of Norwegian company boards, there has not yet been a significant increase in women senior executives (Teigen 2012). It is to be hoped that the Australian approach of encouraging practical changes and voluntary targets will aid the progress of women at all stages of their careers. Certainly companies are setting targets at many levels of the organisation. Indeed, in 2011 there were more targets set for management teams than for boards (Klettner et al. 2013).

Overall this Chapter shows that in companies that are taking the issue of diversity seriously, substantial cultural change may be afoot. Branson sums up the potential effect of the recommendations:

> Despite grumbling about the unprecedented reach of the ASX regulations, and the increase in workload compliance entails, most Australian corporations will comply and disclose what steps they have taken, adding to the pressure both to enlarge the pool from which women candidates to the board may be chosen and to name additional women to the board.
>
> (2012, p. 16)

It will be very interesting to see how numbers of women change over the next few years, particularly in senior management, and whether the push for change stalls at a certain point or in certain industries. Although the measuring of women in the organisation and the setting of a diversity policy are important steps in the setting of a strategy on diversity, at the heart of the ASX recommendations is the setting of measurable objectives for gender diversity and the reporting of progress against these objectives. It is only through active implementation of practical workplace changes that the ultimate aim of increasing women in leadership is likely to occur. As discussed further in Chapter 9, the inclusion in the design of the recommendations of public progress reporting against self-set targets is innovative and potentially highly effective.

Summary of chapter 6

The aim of this chapter was to discuss the effectiveness of corporate governance codes in promoting gender diversity. Rather than focusing on numbers of women on boards or compliance with the code, the chapter reviews evidence of the intermediate processes of organisational change. It explores whether the Australian code has been effective at achieving its immediate, short-term aims: to encourage companies to consider how they might improve workplace diversity, particularly gender diversity, through setting targets and drafting and implementing policies to support those targets. The findings are positive. The data reviewed showed that, even before the recommendations were fully in force, companies were beginning the process of altering their recruitment, promotion, training and leave processes with the aim of making the workplace more conducive to female career development.

References

ABS, Australian Bureau of Statistics 1998, *Australian Social Trends*, cat. no. 4102.0, Canberra.

Adams, R & Ferreira, D 2009, 'Women in the boardroom and their impact on governance and performance', *Journal of Financial Economics*, vol. 94, no. 2, pp. 291–309.

Adams, RB & Funk, P 2012, 'Beyond the glass ceiling: does gender matter?', *Management Science,* vol. 58, no. 2, pp. 219–35.

AICD, Australian Institute of Company Directors, *Board Diversity Statistics.*

Anderson, D, Vinnicombe, S & Singh, V 2010, 'Women partners leaving the firm: choice, what choice?', *Gender in Management*, vol. 25, no. 3, pp. 170–83.

Bilimoria, D & Piderit, SK 1994, 'Board committee membership: effects of sex-based bias', *Academy of Management Journal*, vol. 37, no. 6, pp. 1453–77.

Branson, DM 2012, 'An Australian perspective on a global phenomenon: initiatives to place women on corporate boards of directors', *Australian Journal of Corporate Law*, vol. 27, pp. 2–21.

Burgess, Z & Fallon, B 2003, 'A longitudinal study of women directors in Australia', *Women in Management Review*, vol. 18, no. 7, pp. 359–68.

CAMAC 2009, 'Corporations and Markets Advisory Committee, 2009', *Diversity on Boards of Directors*, Australian Government, March.

Carter, DA, Simkins, BJ & Simpson, WG 2003, 'Corporate governance, board diversity and firm value', *Financial Review,* vol. 38, no. 1, pp. 33–53.

Catalyst, Women on Boards Quick Take, 31 May 2013.

Clarke, T & Klettner, A 2010, 'Governance Issues for SMEs', *Journal of Business Systems, Governance and Ethics*, vol. 4, no. 4, pp. 23–40.

Clarke T, Nielsen, BB, Nielsen, S, Klettner, A & Boersma, M 2012, *Australian Census of Women in Leadership*, Sydney: Australian Government, Equal Opportunity for Women in the Workplace Agency.

Coglianese, C & Lazer, D 2003, 'Management-based regulation: prescribing private management to achieve public goals', *Law & Society Review,* vol. 37, no. 4, pp. 691–730.

Collins, BW 2007, 'Tackling unconscious bias in hiring practices: the plight of the Rooney rule', *New York University Law Review*, vol. 82, pp. 870–912.

Creswell, J 2013, *Qualitative Inquiry and Research Design: choosing among five approaches,* Thousand Oaks: SAGE.

Daley, J, McGannon, C & Ginnivan, L 2012, *Game-Changers: economic reform priorities for Australia*, Melbourne: Grattan Institute.

Davies, M 2011, *Women on Boards*, London: Department for Business, Innovation and Skills.

du Plessis, J, O'Sullivan J & Rentschler, R 2014, 'The multiple layers of gender diversity on corporate boards: to force or not to force diversity?', *Deakin Law Review*, vol. 19, no. 1, pp. 1–50.

GDC, Guidelines Development Committee 2013, *Guidelines for Gender Balance Performance and Reporting Australia*, Chartered Secretaries Australia and Women on Boards.

Gladman, K & Lamb, M 2013, *2013 Women on Boards Survey*, GMI Ratings, April 2013.

Goldman Sachs & JBWere 2009, *Australia's Hidden Resource: The Economic Case for Increasing Female Participation*, Research Report, 26 November 2009.

Huse, M & Solberg, A 2006, 'Gender related boardroom dynamics: how Scandinavian women make and can make contributions on corporate boards', *Women in Management Review*, vol. 21, no. 2, pp. 113–30.

Kang, H, Cheng, M & Gray, SJ 2007, 'Corporate governance and board composition: diversity and independence of Australian boards', *Corporate Governance: An International Review*, vol. 15, no. 2, pp. 194–207.

Kesner, IF 1988, 'Directors' characteristics and committee membership: an investigation of type, occupation tenure and gender', *Academy of Management Journal*, vol. 31, pp. 66–84.

Klettner, A, Clarke, T & Boersma, M 2013, 'The impact of soft law on social change: measurable objectives for achieving gender diversity on board of directors', *Australian Journal of Corporate Law*, vol. 28, no. 2, pp. 138 65.

Klettner, A, Clarke, T & Boersma, M 2016, 'Strategic and regulatory approaches to increasing women in leadership: multilevel targets and mandatory quotas as levers for cultural change', *Journal of Business Ethics*, vol. 133, no. 3, pp. 395–419.

KPMG, *ASX Corporate Governance Council Principles and Recommendations on Diversity': Analysis of 31 December 2011 year end disclosures*, ASX, July 2012.

Krippendorff, K 2004, *Content Analysis: An Introduction to its Methodology*, Thousand Oaks: SAGE.

Lewis, P & Simpson, R 2010, 'Meritocracy, difference and choice: women's experiences of advantage and disadvantage at work', *Gender in Management*, vol. 25, no. 3, pp. 165–69.

Matsa, A & Miller, AR 2013, 'A female style in corporate leadership? Evidence from Quotas', *American Economic Journal: Applied Economics*, vol. 5, no. 3, pp. 136–69.

McInerney-Lacombe, N, Bilimoria D & Salipante, PF 2008, 'Championing the discussion of tough issues: how women corporate directors contribute to board deliberations', in S Vinnicombe, V Singh, RJ Burke, D Bilimoria & M Huse (eds.), *Women on Corporate Boards of Directors: international research and practice*, Cheltenham: Edward Elgar.

McKinsey & Company 2007, *Women Matter: gender diversity, a corporate performance driver*.

McKinsey & Company 2008, *Women Matter 2: female leadership a competitive edge for the future*.

Nielsen, S & Huse, M 2010, 'The contribution of women on boards of directors: going beyond the surface', *Corporate Governance: An International Review*, vol. 18, no. 2, pp. 136–48.

Olsen 2011, *The Gender Agenda: gender differences in Australian higher education*, Strategy Policy and Research in Education.

Peters, K, Ryan M & Haslam, A 2010, 'Achieving the possible: Ambition and the under-representation of women surgeons', University of Exeter, unpublished presentation, cited in R Sealy & S Vinnicombe 'Women and the Governance of Corporate Boards', in T Clarke & D Branson (eds.), *The SAGE Handbook of Corporate Governance* (2012), Thousand Oaks: SAGE, pp. 325–44.

Rost, K & Osterloh, M 2010, 'Opening the black box of upper echelons: drivers of poor information processing during the financial crisis', *Corporate Governance: An International Review*, vol. 18, no. 3, pp. 212–33.

Ryan, M, Kulich, C, Alexander, S, Haslam, M, Hersby, D & Atkins, C 2008, 'Examining gendered experiences beyond the glass ceiling: the precariousness of the glass cliff and the absence of rewards', in S Vinnicombe, V Singh, R J Burke, D Bilimoria & M Huse (eds.), *Women on Corporate Boards of Directors, International Research and Practice*, Cheltenham: Edward Elgar Publishing.

Sealy, R & Vinnicombe, S 2012, 'Women and the Governance of Corporate Boards', in T Clarke & D Branson (eds.), *The SAGE Handbook of Corporate Governance,* Thousand Oaks: SAGE, pp. 325–44.

Sheridan, A 2001, 'A view from the top: women on the boards of public companies', *Corporate Governance*, vol. 1, no. 1, pp. 8–14,

Sheridan, A & Milgate, G 2003, '"She says, he says": women's and men's views of the composition of boards', *Women in Management Review*, vol. 18, no. 3, pp. 147–54.

Sheridan, A & Milgate, G 2006, 'Accessing board positions: a comparison of female and male board members' views', *Corporate Governance: An International Review*, vol. 13, no. 6, pp. 847–55.

Spender, P 2012, 'Gender diversity on boards in Australia – Waiting for the great leap forward?', *Australian Journal of Corporate Law*, vol. 27, pp. 22–38.

Spira, LF & Page, M 2010, 'Regulation by disclosure: the case of internal control', *Journal of Management and Governance*, vol. 14, pp. 409–33.

Teigen, M 2012, 'Gender quotas for corporate boards in Norway: innovative gender equality policy', in C Fagan, MC Gonzalez Menendez & S Gomez Anson (eds.), *Women on Corporate Boards and in Top Management: European trends and policy*, New York: Palgrave-MacMillan, pp. 70–90.

Todnem, R 2005, 'Organisational change management: a critical review', *Journal of Change Management*, vol. 5, no. 4, pp. 369–80.

Torchia, M, Calabro, A & Huse, M 2011, 'Women directors on corporate boards: from tokenism to critical mass', *Journal of Business Ethics*, vol. 102, no. 2, pp. 299–317.

Villiers, C 2010, 'Achieving gender balance in the boardroom: is it time for legislative action in the UK?', *Legal Studies*, vol. 30, no. 4, pp. 533–57.

Walker, D 2009, *A Review of Corporate Governance in UK Banks and Other Financial Industry Entities, Final Recommendations*.

WGEA, Workplace Gender Equality Agency 2016, *Gender Pay Gap Statistics*, Australian Government.

Wheland, J & Wood, R 2012, *Targets and Quotas for Women in Leadership: a global review of policy, practice and psychological research*, Gender Equality Project, Centre for Ethical Leadership, Melbourne Business School.

7

GOVERNANCE AND CORPORATE RESPONSIBILITY

Introduction

This chapter examines the role of corporate governance codes in encouraging corporate responsibility, also known as corporate social responsibility or CSR. It explores the role of the board in corporate responsibility and how soft regulation can assist the board in fulfilling that role. At its simplest, corporate responsibility can be defined as a company operating in an economically, socially and environmentally sustainable manner or at least 'considering, managing and balancing the economic, social and environmental impacts of its activities' (PJC 2006, p. xiii). There is a wide literature on the reasons companies might take this approach: the business case for corporate responsibility is that it can improve corporate success through, amongst other things, improving reputation, motivating employees and reducing risk (Anderson 2005; CAMAC 2006). Equally there are sceptics of the concept who believe a company can only truly be responsible to one group and that this should be the shareholders (Friedman 1962; Jensen 2002).

Despite this ongoing debate, there has been a huge change in corporate practice in the area of corporate responsibility reporting. Professional services firm KPMG has monitored the number of companies publishing information on corporate responsibility since 1993. Using a sample made up of the 100 largest companies in each of 34 countries, reporting on corporate social responsibility went from 12 percent in 1993 to 71 percent in 2013 (KPMG 2013, p. 21). In the 250 largest global companies there was an increase in corporate social-responsibility reporting from 35 percent in 1999 to 93 percent in 2013 (KPMG 2013, p. 38). This demonstrates striking change in reporting, and yet little is known about whether it reflects equally striking changes within corporations.

At the same time, the links between corporate responsibility and corporate governance have become stronger. In 2001 Douglas Branson described the emergence of a 'new corporate social responsibility movement, different from previous efforts because of its convergence with good corporate governance (2001, p. 647). KPMG's 2011 report on the state of sustainability reporting concluded that the integration of sustainability or CSR into core business strategy and reporting was the next major development in the field. As sustainability becomes more integrated into business strategy it must also be integrated into existing corporate governance systems:

> Corporate governance is gradually becoming a framework for ensuring the public interest in business as well as structuring the procedures by which a company demonstrates its good citizenship and commitment to various constituencies.
>
> (Gill 2008, p. 455)

Corporate responsibility is not a static element of the organisation and in most countries is not mandated by law. Good practice has come about in large part because of action by various stakeholders and regulators or because companies have received bad publicity from some neglect of their corporate responsibility. This means that the practices of companies may improve or deteriorate depending on the level of volatility in their industry sector, the direction and calibre of their leadership or the degree of regulation. We still do not fully understand the causes and incentives behind companies' responsibility strategies, and thus in circumstances where action is voluntary the situation is far from stable:

> More research is needed to explore to what extent CSR efforts are initiated as a result of outside pressures, formal top down strategy setting, grass roots initiatives from employees or middle managers, or other sources, and what kinds of catalysts are most effective in creating culture and systems change.
>
> (Van Velsor 2009, p. 5)

This chapter examines the role of codes of corporate governance in this complex amalgam. Codes of corporate governance across the world are beginning to be amended to reflect this new emphasis on responsible governance. Table 7.1 demonstrates that although many codes now include provisions on corporate responsibility, they deal with it quite differently and to varying degrees. The South African code led the way in 2009 by expressly integrating issues of corporate responsibility, sustainability and ethics throughout the code and recommending integrated corporate reporting. This reflects the influence of Professor Mervyn King who not only led the development of the South African code but set up the International Integrated Reporting Council (IIRC) dedicated to promoting integrated reporting as a way of moving towards sustainable value creation. Other countries have incorporated corporate responsibility into their codes of corporate governance through provisions on codes of conduct, risk management or stakeholder engagement. Codes are not the only method of encouraging CSR, alternative methods include: changes to hard law on directors' duties; requirements on corporate reporting; or policies that encourage participation in international initiatives such as the Global Reporting Initiative (GRI).

TABLE 7.1 Corporate-governance codes and CSR

Australian Corporate Governance Principles and Recommendations (ASX Corporate Governance Council 2014)	Principle 3 Act ethically and responsibly Recommendation 3.1 A listed entity should: (a) have a code of conduct for its directors, senior executives and employees and (b) disclose that code or a summary of it. Commentary 'Acting ethically and responsibly goes well beyond mere compliance with legal obligations and involves acting with honesty, integrity and in a manner that is consistent with the reasonable expectations of investors and the broader community'. Principle 7 Risk management Recommendation 7.4 A listed entity should disclose whether it has any material exposure to economic, environmental and social sustainability risks and, if it does, how it manages or intends to manage those risks.
Denmark Recommendations on Corporate Governance (Committee on Corporate Governance 2014)	The Danish code begins in Principle 1 with a statement of stakeholder inclusiveness: 'The company's investors, employees and other stakeholders have a joint interest in stimulating the Company's growth, and in the company always being in a position to adapt to changing demands, thus allowing the company to continue to be competitive and create value. Therefore, it is essential to establish a positive interaction not merely between management and investors, but also in relation to other stakeholders'. Yet Principle 2 on tasks and responsibilities of the board of directors appears to prioritise shareholders: 'It is incumbent upon the board of directors to carefully protect the interests of the shareholders with due consideration for the other stakeholders'. Principle 2.2 on Corporate Social Responsibility recommends simply that the board adopt policies on CSR.
German Corporate Governance Code (Deutscher Corporate Governance Kodex 2015)	4.1.1 The Management Board is responsible for independently managing the enterprise in the interest of the enterprise, thus taking into account the interests of the shareholders, its employees and other stakeholders, with the objective of sustainable creation of value. 4.2.3 The compensation structure must be oriented toward sustainable growth of the enterprise.

(Continued)

Greece – Hellenic Corporate Governance Code for Listed Companies (Helenic Corporate Governance Council 2013)	1. Role and responsibilities of the board In discharging its role, the board should take into account the interests of key stakeholders such as employees, clients, creditors and the communities in which the company operates so long as this does not go against the company's interests. The responsibilities of the board should include: formulating, disseminating and implementing key values and principles of conduct governing the company's relations with its stakeholders.
Iceland Corporate Governance Guidelines 4th edition (Iceland Chamber of Commerce 2012)	2.10 Ethics and social responsibility The board should, in consultation with the employees and others which the board sees fit, determine the values and ethical norms on which the company's operation is based. By doing so, the company will not only promote a healthier economy and improved relations with stakeholders, but also reinforce its operating basis with an increased appearance of reliability and credibility, an improved sense of risk, happier employees and, in the end, improved competitiveness.
Japan's Corporate Governance Code (JPX Tokyo Stock Exchange 2015)	Companies should fully recognise that their sustainable growth and the creation of mid- to long-term corporate value are brought about as a result of the provision of resources and contributions made by a range of stakeholders, including employees, customers, business partners, creditors and local communities. As such, companies should endeavour to appropriately cooperate with these stakeholders. The board and the management should exercise their leadership in establishing a corporate culture where the rights and positions of stakeholders are respected and sound business ethics are ensured. Principle 2.1 Guided by their position concerning social responsibility, companies should undertake their businesses in order to create value for all stakeholders while increasing corporate value over the mid to long term. To this end, companies should draft and maintain business principles that will become the basis for such activities. Principle 2.3.1 With the recognition that dealing with sustainability issues is an important element of risk management, the board should take appropriate actions to this end. Given the increasing demand and interest with respect to sustainability issues in recent years, the board should consider addressing these matters positively and proactively.

The Norwegian Code of Practice for Corporate Governance (Norwegian Corporate Governance Board 2014)	1. The board of directors should define the company's basic corporate values and formulate ethical guidelines and guidelines for corporate social responsibility in accordance with these values. At the core of the concept of corporate social responsibility is the company's responsibility for the manner in which its activities affect people, society and the environment, and it typically addresses human rights, prevention of corruption, employee rights, health and safety and the working environment, and discrimination, as well as environmental issues.
Russian Code of Corporate Governance (Moscow Exchange and OECD 2014)	Corporate governance should be based on the principles of sustainable development of a company and increasing long-term returns on investments in its share capital. 291. The company should disclose the following information on its social and environmental responsibility: 1) the company's social and environmental policy; 2) a report on its sustainable development of company drawn up in accordance with internationally recognised standards; and 3) the results of a technical audit, an audit of quality control systems, and the results of certification of its quality management system in terms of its compliance with international standards.
Singapore Code of Corporate Governance (Monetary Authority of Singapore 2012)	1.1 The board's role is to: (d) identify the key stakeholder groups and recognise that their perceptions affect the company's reputation; (e) set the company's values and standards (including ethical standards), and ensure that obligations to shareholders and other stakeholders are understood and met; and (f) consider sustainability issues, e.g. environmental and social factors, as part of its strategic formulation.
King Code of Governance for South Africa (Institute of Directors Southern Africa 2009)	The South African code was the first code to recommend integrated reporting and an 'inclusive stakeholder approach' to governance. It includes elements of CSR in every principle: 'The philosophy of the Report revolves around leadership, sustainability and corporate citizenship.' 'A key challenge for leadership is to make sustainability issues mainstream. Strategy, risk, performance and sustainability have become inseparable; hence the phrase 'integrated reporting' which is used throughout this Report.' Principle 1 on Ethical leadership and corporate citizenship clearly places responsibility for CSR on the board of directors. Principle 8 on governing stakeholder relationships provides guidance on identifying and engaging with stakeholder groups.

(Continued)

Spanish Good Governance Code of Listed Companies (CNMV 2015)	Principle 24: The company should deploy an appropriate corporate social responsibility policy, as a non-delegable board power, and report transparently and in sufficient detail on its development, application and results
	Environmental awareness and understanding, a sense of community, innovation capacity and a forward vision stand alongside the core purpose of value creation as mainstays of business activity.
	Companies should accordingly take time to analyse how their business impacts on society and vice versa. In this way, taking as reference their own value chain, they can identify social issues that lend themselves to shared value creation.
Sri Lanka Code of Best Practice on Corporate Governance 2013 (Institute of Chartered Accountants and Securities and Exchange Commission 2013)	2013 edition introduced Principle G on sustainability reporting:
	G.1.7 – Sustainable reporting and disclosure should be formalised as part of the company's reporting processes and take place on a regular basis.
	• Sustainability reporting is a board responsibility, and it is designed to add value by providing a credible account of the company's economic, social and environmental impact.
	• Sustainability reporting should link sustainable issues more closely to strategy.
Thailand The Principles of Good Corporate Governance for Listed Companies 2012 (SET 2012)	Section 3 Role of stakeholders
	The board should set clear policies on fair treatment for each and every stakeholder. The rights of stakeholders that are established by law or through mutual agreements are to be respected. Any actions that can be considered in violation of stakeholders' legal rights should be prohibited. Any violation should be effectively redressed.
	The board should provide a mechanism so that stakeholders can be involved in improving the company's performance, helping to ensure the firm's sustainability. In order for stakeholders to participate effectively, all relevant information should be disclosed to them.

Defining corporate responsibility

Like corporate governance, corporate responsibility is a famously difficult concept to define (Dahlsrud 2008; Moir 2001; Whitehouse 2006). In fact, the confusion is even greater as there is no universally agreed term for the concept, let alone a definition. The Australian Parliamentary Joint Committee Report on corporate responsibility (PJC Report) commented that the terms 'corporate responsibility', 'corporate social responsibility (CSR)', 'corporate social transparency', 'triple bottom line', 'corporate sustainability' and 'social and environmental responsibility' are all used to refer to the same concept (2006, p. 4). In this chapter, the term corporate responsibility is used interchangeably with the terms corporate sustainability and CSR, to include social as well as environmental aspects of acting responsibly. The International Organization for Standardization uses a definition that is both practical and comprehensive:

> Social responsibility is the responsibility of an organisation for the impacts of its decisions and activities on society and the environment, through transparent and ethical behaviour that:
> * contributes to sustainable development, including the health and the welfare of society;
> * takes into account the expectations of stakeholders;
> * is in compliance with applicable law and consistent with international norms of behaviour; and
> * is integrated throughout the organisation and practised in its relationships.
> (ISO 26000, 2010)

In this wide interpretation corporate responsibility encompasses not only compliance with legal obligations (environmental and employment legislation, for example), but also voluntary commitment to ethical and sustainable practices that benefit both society and the long-term success of the company. Carroll (1991) provided a definition of CSR depicting a pyramid of responsibilities. He placed economic viability at the base of the pyramid as the foundation for corporate activity. This is important as some opponents of CSR suggest that it is about compromising profits to do good. This is not the understanding taken in this chapter; rather, CSR is concerned with creating profits without causing undue harm.

The next layer of Carroll's pyramid comprised the need to comply with relevant law. Even the oft-cited sceptic of CSR, Milton Friedman, agreed that companies must play within the rules of the game. Every company must comply with relevant environment, employment and occupational health and safety laws, as well as laws that protect corporate creditors and consumers. In fact many critics of CSR claim that these specific laws are the correct way to protect society and that the responsibility should remain on government to implement protective legislation if and when necessary rather than shifting the onus to corporations.

Next in Carroll's pyramid is the layer of corporate responsibility that is the subject of this chapter – voluntary activities that fall within the scope of ethical behaviour rather than compliance. Thus we are, by definition, not in the realm of hard law but that of soft law and norms – recommendations, standards and unwritten rules. Carroll defines ethical responsibilities as 'those standards, norms or expectations that reflect a concern for what consumers, employees, shareholders and the community regard as fair, just or in keeping with the respect or protection of stakeholders' moral rights' (1991, p. 41). Redmond defines CSR as 'voluntary measures undertaken by companies to integrate social, environmental and business concerns in their operations and their interaction with stakeholders' (2012, p. 320).

This concept of stakeholders is core to both the theory and practice of corporate responsibility. A commonly used definition of corporate stakeholders is all those with an interest in the company's operations (Freeman 1994; Freeman and Reed 1990). In practice, corporate behaviour is socially responsible as long as it meets stakeholders' expectations regarding appropriate and acceptable corporate behaviour' (Campbell 2007, p. 950). This means that corporate responsibility will have a unique meaning for every company and is a dynamic concept that will change depending on the expectations of society and the operations of any particular corporation:

> It is important to reemphasize that corporate sustainability is fundamentally a complex problem and there are no approaches that universally apply. Corporations are faced with differing stakeholder demands, continually shifting priorities, and a multitude of alternatives to address their sustainability challenges.
>
> (Searcy 2012, p. 250)

Lastly, it is important to mention the top of Carroll's pyramid where he placed philanthropy to describe companies going further than ethics and positively contributing to social welfare. This chapter does not include philanthropy as corporate responsibility for two reasons. First, it can be a dangerous distraction from fundamentally irresponsible business practices: in the past companies may have attempted to balance the harming effects of their operations by donating profits towards charities that mitigate the effects of such harm. Second, there is a legal argument that donating profits to charities that have no connection with a company's operations has the potential to be contrary to directors' legal duty to act in the best interests of the corporation (Klein and du Plessis 2005). This chapter takes corporate responsibility as pertaining to the way in which the core operations of an organisation are carried out, not the addition of charitable activities.

Regulating corporate responsibility

On the basis that CSR is a difficult concept to define it is not surprising that it is also a difficult concept to regulate. Indeed, if CSR is defined as voluntary behaviour, 'the very idea that law might make business responsible for corporate social responsibility is paradoxical': it cannot be possible 'for the *law* to make companies accountable for going *beyond the law*' (Parker 2007, p. 207). This has not stopped legislatures, courts and legal commentators from amending and interpreting the law to permit CSR and encourage it through reporting requirements. Indeed Martin comments that, 'the line between CSR and voluntary action and what the law requires is often rather thin: many CSR voluntary activities are underpinned by a strong legislative framework, and many follow directly from it (2005, p. 91).

Hard law – directors' duties

McConvill and Joy optimistically observed in 2003 that, 'the emerging trend is that social and environmental concerns will be incorporated into the legal framework which governs corporations (2003, p. 117). Despite much debate, this has still not occurred in most countries. In Australia, although the directors' duty to act in the best interests of the corporation has been interpreted to permit consideration of the interests of all stakeholders, there is no express legal requirement to do so, and the extent to which this is done is at the discretion of the board (PJC 2006; CAMAC 2006). The argument against expanding directors' duties to expressly include all stakeholders is that it would leave them accountable to no-one and struggling to determine priorities amidst conflicting interests (CAMAC 2006, p. 97).

Nevertheless, several years ago the United Kingdom did exactly this, and no accountability problems appear to have arisen (Keay 2007). Section 172(1) Companies Act 2006 expressly includes the interests of a wide range of stakeholders as matters that directors must have regard to:

> A director of a company must act in a way that he considers, in good faith, would be most likely to promote the success of the company for the benefit of its members as a whole, and in doing so have regard (amongst other matters) to –
> (a) the likely consequences of any decision in the long term
> (b) the interests of the company's employees
> (c) the need to foster the company's business relationships with suppliers, customers and others
> (d) the impact of the company's operations on the community and the environment
> (e) the desirability of the company maintaining a reputation for high standards of business conduct, and
> (f) the need to act fairly between the members of the company.

However there is little evidence at this stage that this restatement of directors' duties has in itself made a material difference to board decision-making in the UK (Keay 2010). Although this law better reflects the state of current norms on corporate responsibility, in a practical sense it still gives wide discretion to company directors, arguably entrenching shareholders as the priority group (Keay 2007).

Soft law – corporate governance codes

The second edition of the Australian Code of Corporate Governance made clear the important role of the board in determining a strategy for corporate responsibility in terms of balancing stakeholder interests. Corporate responsibility was squarely placed within the context of corporate governance:

> To make ethical and responsible decisions, companies should not only comply with their legal obligations, but should also consider the reasonable expectations of their stakeholders including: shareholders, employees, customers, suppliers, creditors, consumers and the broader community in which they operate. It is a matter for the board to consider and assess what is appropriate in each company's circumstances.
>
> (ASX 2007, p. 21)

The third edition uses different wording but still stresses the importance of ethical and responsible decision-making, particularly in maintaining corporate reputation (ASX 2014, p. 19). However, the only formal recommendation is for companies to establish a code of conduct articulating the company's responsibilities to its stakeholders. In fact, it is suggested that this code of conduct covers both ethical practices within the company and responsibilities to external stakeholders. This is in contrast to the first edition of the Australian code, which dealt with these issues separately. The corporate governance code contains no mention of actually engaging with stakeholders – it describes a very one-sided process of making statements about the company's view of stakeholder expectations and related company policies rather than developing these in conjunction with stakeholders. The commentary refers to the importance of governance structures and processes for ensuring implementation of policies that support corporate responsibility but without giving guidance on what these structures and processes might look like.

One advantage of CSR, now expressly recognised in the third edition of the Australian code, is to improve risk management. There was consultation in 2006 on whether to introduce into the ASX code a recommendation regarding corporate responsibility reporting. It was suggested it could comprise a recommendation that companies describe the nature of their non-financial material business risks and how they are managed. This was rejected for many reasons, in particular, respondents to the consultation feared that it would require commercially confidential information to be disclosed and/or put companies at risk of litigation. It was argued that the changing nature of risk would mean that any disclosures would only be accurate for a short time. As a result the second edition of the code was amended only to make it clear that a risk management system should cover all material business risks, both financial and non-financial. Disclosure was limited to a statement confirming that such a system was in place. The commentary was amended to explain that:

> Failure to consider the reasonable expectations of stakeholders can threaten a company's reputation and the success of its business operations. Effective risk management involves considering factors which bear upon the company's continued good standing with its stakeholders.
>
> (ASX 2007 p. 33)

Nevertheless, the issue raised its head again in relation to the third edition of the ASX code, and this time a recommendation on CSR risk reporting was added, perhaps reflecting changing attitudes and increasing acceptance of CSR. Recommendation 7.4 now suggests that a company should 'disclose whether it has any material exposure to economic, environmental and social sustainability risks and, if it does, how it manages or intends to manage those risks' (ASX 2014, p. 30). The inclusion of the term 'material exposure' was a result of similar concerns to those expressed in 2006. It limits reporting to substantial risks that ought to be disclosed to investors for many reasons.

International initiatives

Corporate responsibility has become an international issue, and much of the impetus in its development has come from international organisations rather than national policy. There are many international organisations that provide reporting frameworks or standards that are guiding the way in which companies report (Gobbels 2006). This chapter discusses four well-known initiatives, the Global Reporting Initiative, the UN Global Compact, the Carbon Disclosure Project and the London Benchmarking Group. Are these frameworks simply being used as window dressing or are they motivating real change? Only in-depth case-study research can really answer this question, but it is interesting to examine which frameworks, from a constantly burgeoning range of options, are voluntarily being adopted and how they may be influencing corporate behaviour.

The Global Reporting Initiative is a non-profit organisation that promotes economic, environmental and social sustainability by providing organisational reporting guidance. The GRI's Sustainability Reporting Framework has become the primary international standard for sustainability reporting, widely used around the world (Szejnwald Brown et al. 2009). This framework provides guidelines for reporting on the strategy and profile of the organisation as well as its efforts towards economic, environmental and social sustainability. There are sector-specific guidelines for major industries that deal with the particular issues faced by that industry. Of relevance to corporate governance and outlined in Table 7.2 are the guidelines within 'strategy and profile', which recommend disclosure surrounding the governance of sustainability and stakeholder engagement. When this research was carried out G3.1 was the relevant version of the Guidelines – a new version, G4, has since been published, but the provisions on governance have not been significantly altered.

Another highly influential initiative, the UN Global Compact, comprises 10 broad principles in the areas of human rights, labour, the environment and anti-corruption, which companies can voluntarily commit to uphold. It is expected that companies will provide an annual 'communication on progress' (COP) to demonstrate their implementation of the principles. The Carbon Disclosure Project and London Benchmarking Group are more like the GRI in their format: they provide a detailed framework for reporting; the aim is to offer a methodology for measuring and disclosing information so it can then be meaningfully compared and benchmarked across different companies. The Carbon Disclosure Project provides methods for measuring not only greenhouse gas emissions but also water management and climate-change strategies. The London Benchmarking Group develops methodologies that enable benchmarking of the value of community investment.

TABLE 7.2 GRI guidelines regarding governance of CSR

Guideline 4.5 Linkage between compensation for members of the highest governance body, senior managers, and executives (including departure arrangements) and the organisation's performance (including social and environmental performance)

Guideline 4.9 Procedures of the highest governance body for overseeing the organisation's identification and management of economic, environmental, and social performance, including relevant risks and opportunities, and adherence or compliance with internationally agreed standards, codes of conduct, and principles. Include frequency with which the highest governance body assesses sustainability performance.

Guideline 4.12 Externally developed economic, environmental, and social charters, principles or other initiatives to which the organisation subscribes. If applicable: date of adoption; countries/operations where applied; range of stakeholders involved in the development and governance of these; differentiate between non-binding, voluntary and obligatory compliance.

Guideline 4.14 List of stakeholder groups engaged by the organisation.

Guideline 4.15 Basis for identification and selection of stakeholders with whom to engage.

Guideline 4.16 Approaches to stakeholder engagement, including frequency of engagement by type and by stakeholder group.

Guideline 4.17 Key topics and concerns that have been raised through stakeholder engagement, and how the organisation has responded to those key topics and concerns, including through its reporting.

Methodology

This chapter explores how corporate governance processes and structures are being used in large Australian companies to develop, lead and implement corporate responsibility strategies. It presents an empirical analysis of the governance of corporate responsibility in 50 large listed companies based on each company's disclosures in 2012 annual and sustainability reports. This evidence, together with interview data from 2006, is used to discuss the effectiveness of the Australian corporate governance code in this area and the influence of international soft law on corporate behaviour.

The data collected was reviewed against a set of objective criteria using a form of content analysis. Similar methodologies have been used to examine, for example, the implementation of the United Nations Global Compact in Swiss companies (Baumann and Scherer 2010); the embeddedness of corporate citizenship (Kolk 2008; Morgan et al. 2009); and the uptake of environmental reporting (Jose and Lee 2007). The criteria were developed based on both the literature and the content of existing regulation and are grouped into four categories:

1. **Communication:** this section analyses voluntary commitment to corporate responsibility reporting frameworks as well as attitudes towards mandatory CSR reporting and integrated reporting.
2. **Engagement:** this section discusses corporate practice in identifying stakeholders as well as methods for engaging with them.
3. **Leadership:** this sections looks for evidence of strategic leadership of CSR including board or executive committees accountable for corporate responsibility.
4. **Implementation:** this section reviews evidence of systems and policies for implementation of corporate responsibility, particularly integration into remuneration systems

The findings provide insights into the influence of soft law on corporate behaviour, including the interaction of international and national policies.

Communication: reporting frameworks for CSR

Voluntary reporting

The research sample confirmed the use of the Global Reporting Initiative (GRI) as the primary standard for sustainability reporting, at least in large companies. Of the 50 companies, 31 used GRI indicators in their reporting. Of these, 28 provided a GRI index, a reference table that enables the reader to see which guidelines the company has disclosed against and where to find those disclosures. These indexes make it possible for an interested reader to find comparable information across different companies. Of the 50 companies in the sample, 15 stated that they reported at an A level, 8 companies at B level and 5 at C level. Three companies did not specify their GRI application level, whereas 21 had used external assurance to confirm their application level. It must be emphasised that GRI A, B or C levels refer only to the extent of reporting (the number of guidelines disclosed against) and do not reflect an assessment of the quality or accuracy of the reporting.

In another Australian survey in 2012, this time of the top 200 companies, the Australian Council for Superannuation Investors (ACSI) found that 38 companies structured their sustainability reporting to the GRI, meaning that they used a GRI index and declared an application level (ACSI 2012, p. 5). They found a strong correlation between company size and use of the GRI, with 52 percent of the ASX 50 structuring their reporting in accordance with the GRI as compared to only 5 percent of the ASX 101–200 (ACSI 2012, p. 12). Interviews in 2006 confirmed that preparation of a CSR report requires a certain level of resources:

> This year we have aimed to meet the international standard. It is a company-wide approach – you can't prepare such a thing without the support of all the divisions – they've all bought into it. They are autonomous divisions but they have all supported the report despite being very busy and it being a lot of effort – there is so much data to verify – it's a big job.
>
> *(Company secretary, ASX 100)*

> The major banks do their big glossy CSR brochures but there's no way we'd do one of those. We'll just do investor presentations and use our website.
>
> *(Company secretary, ASX 300)*

The GRI recommends that companies disclose their involvement in 'externally developed economic, environmental and social charters, principles or other initiatives' and that their disclosures 'differentiate between non-binding, voluntary initiatives and those with which the organization has an obligation to comply' (Guideline 4.12). Of the 28 companies in the sample producing a GRI Index, 24 stated that they reported against guideline 4.12. Importantly, this requires companies to distinguish between compliance with voluntary and mandatory initiatives. In reviewing sustainability reports, several companies did not make this clear. For example, many companies mentioned Australian government initiatives such as the Energy Efficiency Opportunities scheme, the National Greenhouse and Energy Reporting system and the National Pollutant Inventory. These initiatives have been implemented by law, meaning that companies falling within their remit must comply or face potential penalties. There were a handful of statements where companies mentioned these initiatives in a way that could potentially mislead the reader into believing that their involvement was voluntary.

The research recorded voluntary commitment by companies to three other well-established initiatives: the United Nations Global Compact, the Carbon Disclosure Project and the London Benchmarking Group. A positive finding

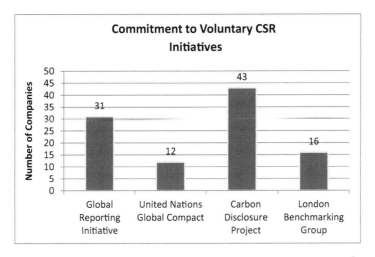

FIGURE 7.1 Commitment to CSR reporting initiatives 2012.

was that 43 out of 50 companies stated they were voluntary members of the Carbon Disclosure Project, which means that they produce and publish a report on their greenhouse gas emissions every year. On the social side, only 16 of the 50 companies stated that they used the London Benchmarking Group framework to measure community contributions. Twelve of 50 companies had signed up to the UN Global Compact (Figure 7.1).

Mandatory reporting

Views on mandatory CSR reporting have changed significantly over the last decade. Many interviewees in 2006 had a strong view that corporate responsibility ought to remain voluntary. Reasons for this included the fact that certain industries were already heavily regulated through environmental, planning or occupational health and safety regulation but also that mandatory reporting would lead to a focus on compliance rather than more creative solutions. The most common reason against mandatory reporting is the difficulty in prescribing what ought to be reported when CSR means such different things for different companies:

> The issues are so specific case by case for each company it is almost impossible to prescribe rules.
>
> *(Company secretary, ASX 300)*

> Because companies are so diverse I think we'd struggle with mandatory reporting. However, you clearly have to address the issue when there is such public interest.
>
> *(Company secretary, ASX 100)*

The other difficulty is that one size doesn't fit all e.g. Westpac's sustainability report looks nothing like ours – even across the same industry they are all very different. To mandate it to fit all would be really difficult.

(Company secretary, ASX 100)

Nevertheless, 10 years later, many countries are in the process of introducing mandatory reporting. In December 2014, the European Union 'Directive on disclosure of non-financial and diversity information by certain large companies' came into force. This will require companies with over 500 employees (around 6000 entities in total) to report on environmental, social and employee-related, human rights, anti-corruption and bribery matters. They are encouraged to use international initiatives such as the GRI and ISO standards as a framework for reporting. EU nations have two years to implement the directive so it is expected that the first company reports will be published in 2018. However, some countries have already implemented legislation. In Denmark the Danish *Financial Statements Act* was amended in 2008 to require mandatory CSR reporting for all listed companies. A review of the corporate response in 2009 annual reports found that the legal requirement was more often seen as a positive initiative than a source of irritation (Danish Commerce and Companies Agency 2010). In Sweden, legislation came into force in 2007 requiring state-owned companies (SOCs) to report on CSR. Similar legislation, applying to SOCs, has been enacted in the Netherlands, China and Spain. The Spanish 'Sustainable Economy Law' was approved in February 2011 and came into force in 2012 requiring SOCs with over 1000 employees to produce an annual CSR report. Does this mean soft regulation is a transitional phase in law-making, or does it just formalise what was already occurring? It may be that hard law will cement the incentive to report and soft law will provide the detail on how to report. It will be interesting to examine whether this legislation causes any changes in corporate behaviour or just standardises the information already being produced.

Integrated reporting

Despite a range of different approaches to sustainability across the companies reviewed in this research, there was a clear trend towards increased 'mainstreaming' of sustainability and signs of its integration into core business strategy. Reflecting this increased integration, 36 out of 50 companies had integrated sustainability information within their annual report, and 27 had a substantial stand-alone sustainability report. Only one company (News Corporation Ltd) had no formal reporting on sustainability although there was a section of the company's website dedicated to the company's 'global energy initiative'.

These findings support the predictions of KPMG in 2011 that integrated reporting would be the next step in the development of corporate reporting. In their 2008 survey KPMG found that only 4 percent of the 250 largest global companies had experimented with some form of integrated reporting, whereas in 2011 the percentage had risen to 26 percent. The findings also support KPMG's view that, although companies are attempting to integrate their reporting, in the majority of cases this involves a dedicated section in the annual report rather than truly combined performance reporting, suggesting that integrated reporting is still in an 'experimental stage' (2011, p. 24). In classifying reports as 'integrated' this research followed KPMG's approach of taking a broad view of integrated reporting: classing a report as integrated if it included sustainability information. As the KPMG report (2011) comments, many companies only go as far as including a dedicated section on sustainability, and it is less common to find companies that have taken the extra step of weaving corporate responsibility information throughout the directors' report.

The status of integrated reporting as the next phase of reporting is confirmed by the establishment in 2010 of the International Integrated Reporting Committee (IIRC), which is leading the development of a globally accepted integrated reporting framework. The Committee states that:

> An integrated report is a concise communication about how an organization's strategy, governance, performance and prospects lead to the creation of value over the short, medium and long term.
>
> (IIRC 2015)

The prototype integrated reporting framework encourages companies to report in relation to a broad range of 'capitals' or resources used and created by the organisation. These include the traditional focus: financial capital, but also manufactured capital, human capital, intellectual capital, natural capital and relationship (or social) capital. The IIRC sees the integrated report as a concise document that may be supplemented by separate sustainability reports and financial statements.

The companies reviewed for this research revealed a broad range of approaches towards CSR reporting. For example, Commonwealth Bank Australia and Westpac Banking Corporation published both an integrated report and a stand-alone sustainability report. National Australia Bank, Telstra, Orica and Oil Search, in addition to publishing an integrated report, produced several stand-alone sustainability reports, providing additional information on particular aspects of sustainability – people, community environment etc. Rio Tinto's main sustainability report was integrated, and it had produced several individual reports for specific sites and projects.

Thus the traditional annual report still exists, as do the comprehensive stand-alone sustainability reports that became popular 10 years ago. All companies now have websites, some of which simply provide electronic copies of the published reports; others present information that may summarise or supplement what is in the formal publication. Some companies had two corporate websites, one consumer-focused and one shareholder-focused: potentially confusing for a stakeholder interested in sustainability issues, especially if sustainability is dealt with differently on the two websites.

In 2008, Kolk concluded that it was unclear how information on sustainability governance might best be reported. Certainly, companies are still experimenting with different communication approaches, each of which has its advantages and disadvantages. International guidance is being progressed on this issue, and some countries are leading the way with their own guidance and legal requirements on CSR reporting.

Engagement: interaction with stakeholders

As mentioned above, one of the criticisms of dealing with corporate responsibility via a code of conduct (as recommended by the Australian corporate governance code) is that there is often a lack of stakeholder engagement in developing these internal codes. Codes often follow a standard format and reflect no insight into the practical challenges faced by the company and the actual concerns of its stakeholders (Painter-Morland 2006). In contrast the GRI guidelines refer to actual engagement, its frequency and outcomes. Some interviewees in 2006 commented on the increasing importance of dealing with stakeholder expectations:

> The social aspect is an issue for all mining companies and is often raised by NGOs. China has become much more environmentally conscious in the last few years. When we meet with officials environmental issues are always discussed. It's only been in the last 3–4 years.
>
> *(Company secretary, ASX 300)*

> There is real peer pressure to have CSR from the rest of the globe. Society takes it seriously – global warming etc.
>
> *(Company secretary, ASX 100)*

Before any company can engage with stakeholders it must first define and identify who is included in this term. A broad definition of stakeholder includes any group or individual that can affect or is affected by the corporation (Freeman 1994). This is commonly thought to include shareholders, employees, customers, suppliers, government, local communities and those representing the environment, meaning a broad range of engagement methods will be necessary:

> Given the varied set of organisational stakeholders, engagement practices may exist in many areas of organisational activity including public relations, customer service, supplier relations, management accounting and human resource management.
>
> (Greenwood 2007, p. 318)

Like corporate responsibility, academic understandings of stakeholder engagement tend to vary depending on the context or background from which research stems. Greenwood lists at least 20 different perspectives found in the literature, including: risk management, knowledge appropriation, human resource management, legitimisation, participation and trust-building (2007, p. 319). Her point is that engagement in itself does not amount to responsibility unless the corporation actually acts on what it finds and 'balances the interests of legitimate stakeholders in a manner in keeping with justifiable moral principles' (2007, p. 322).

Of the 50 companies reviewed in this research, 43 identified their stakeholders and, of these, 32 explained the methods used to engage with stakeholders. Reporting on stakeholder engagement ranged from a brief sentence, for example, 'we... will continue to engage with stakeholders, improve our performance and drive for a sustainable future', to detailed tables clearly describing the use of engagement methods such as: customer focus groups, investor briefings and input into government policy-making. A wide range of stakeholders were identified including: the investment community, shareholders, customers, media, business partners, employees, contractors, local and indigenous communities, industry associations, suppliers, governments, regulators, NGOs, community-based organisations and labour unions. Engagement methods described included: letters, email, websites, webcasts, internal employee groups, annual general meetings, bi-annual investor briefings, meetings with key industry groups, meetings with government representatives and initiatives with non-government organisations.

There was a correlation between those companies claiming to report to a high level against the GRI and the amount of information provided on stakeholder engagement. Companies claiming to report to application level A+ all set out clearly and comprehensively the methods of stakeholder engagement used and the topics discussed. Of the 28 companies in the sample using the GRI framework, 22 reported against all of the GRI guidelines on stakeholder engagement (4.14 to 4.17), and five companies reported against some of these guidelines.

This marks a change from interviewees' responses in 2006, which tended to suggest minimal stakeholder engagement. In answer to the question, 'Does the corporation have a policy promoting or encouraging stakeholders' participation in corporate governance and does the company provide sufficient information to enable them to do so?', the most common answer was that there was no specific policy, and engagement only occurred where necessary for smooth business operations:

> We engage to the extent we need to in order to get on with our stakeholders and ensure and enhance the viability of the business. We are smart enough to realise that and engage with whoever we need to whether that means politicians, unions or our neighbours.
>
> *(Company secretary, ASX 100)*

Several participants were of the opinion that you would never choose to engage:

> No, why would we want them to tell us how to run our business!
>
> *(Company secretary, ASX 300)*

This raises one of the limitations of this research, which is that voluntary report-ing can reveal a company's policy to engage rather than describing actual en-gagement and whether it occurs on a regular basis. Using in-depth case studies as a methodology, Baumann and Scherer found that 'external stakeholders are not integrated on a regular but on a case-by-case basis and most of the time interac-tion takes place in a situation of crisis' (2010, p. 30). This supports the 1997 model of stakeholder salience put forth by Mitchell et al., which argues that stakeholder theory must account for power and urgency as well as legitimacy. It also sup-ports Greenwood's theory that stakeholder engagement and management do not equate to corporate responsibility, rather are a process that may or may not lead to corporate responsibility (2007).

In terms of regulatory effectiveness, it seems that the Australian Corporate Governance Code is out-of-date in recommending only one-sided statements of approaches to stakeholders rather than suggesting engagement with stakeholders and disclosure of the methods, frequency and outcomes of engagement as per the GRI guidelines. Other countries have recently updated their corporate governance codes to improve stakeholder engagement. Japan's code was amended in 2015 to adopt a much clearer focus on sustainability in general with a new subtitle: 'Seeking Sustain-able Corporate Growth and Increased Corporate Value over the Mid to Long-term'.

Leadership: strategy and committees

Like any other aspect of corporate governance, implementing sustainability strat-egies requires clear leadership as well as structures and processes that ensure plans are properly developed, monitored and implemented. Academic research on the topic of leadership of sustainability, as opposed to leadership in general, is only in its early stages: 'studies are only beginning to surface which identify real leader-ship practices, systems, and processes that organisations have used to effectively face the challenges posed by moving towards more socially responsible business operations on a global scale' (Van Velsor 2009). Werther and Chandler outline a strategic approach to sustainability as involving four components:

- a sustainability perspective is incorporated into the strategic planning process;
- any actions taken on sustainability are directly related to core operations;
- stakeholder perspectives about social and environmental issues are incorpo-rated; and
- the focus of activities is medium to long term, not short term.

(2011, p. 40)

Of the companies sampled, there were several that appeared to be going through a strategic change process in relation to sustainability, explicitly stating that they had a new sustainability strategy or method of reporting for 2011. Reports demon-strated an awareness of the expectation that sustainability ought to be managed more formally. However, the type of information in the published material on governance of sustainability varied greatly both in quality and quantity. Some companies focused on the business case for sustainability and the strategic business drivers: the *why* of CSR. Others focused on the company's chosen priority areas, or a unifying code of conduct: the *what* of CSR. Relatively few companies discussed organisational structures such as board or management committees: the *how* of CSR. Only the more progressive companies appeared to be putting in place procedures and frameworks to ensure sustainability is embedded across their organisation. Kolk's research conducted in 2004 found these sorts of structures and systems just starting to emerge in some of the world's largest companies, particularly those in Japan and Europe. A decade later there is still a need for more research to better guide companies as to what it means to provide good governance and leadership for corporate responsibility: how to develop CSR strategies and monitor progress.

The board's role in CSR

Leadership is essential if sustainability is to be truly integrated into core business strategy, and this is true both at board level and below. Boards must shape and govern corporate responsibility and ensure robust management systems are in place to integrate it into the operations of the firm (Morgan et al. 2009). The approach taken by a company has to be guided from the top with clear strategic goals, policy framework and priorities as well as accountability for outcomes. Morgan et al. found 'that while corporate Boards are assuming more responsibility for oversight of conduct and taking account of specific social and environmental issues, citizenship is not yet fully embedded into Boards or the operating structures and systems of most firms' (2009, p. 40).

This is not because boards see CSR as outside of their role. To the contrary, interviews confirmed that the ability to balance the interests of different stakeholders when decision-making is a fundamental part of the role of the board and always has been. It seems that directors do not find the theoretical conflict between shareholders and other stakeholders to be anything other than an occasional fact of life. Directors had a common-sense view of their legal duty to act in the best interests of the corporation: they were aware that for a firm to be successful and create good returns for its investors, employees must be motivated, communities supportive and customers loyal. Interviewees in 2006 expressed a view that, although the ultimate aim of a corporation remains to be profitable, this has to involve taking into account and balancing other stakeholder interests:

> Business has to work in society in the same way as an individual has to work in society – it's a balance. So we work with the community and with our workforce.
>
> *(Company secretary, ASX 300)*

> It's about getting a track record of doing a good job so that you can get a licence to operate – its enlightened self-interest.
>
> *(Company secretary, ASX 100)*

Most company officers had a pragmatic view, bearing in mind that economic success has to underpin other considerations:

> At the end of the day if it's non-value-adding it's hard to justify. Listed companies are measured by their financial performance. If you are not performing well financially no-one is going to say: 'never mind because you are a great corporate citizen'. You wouldn't last long. It's all about balance.
>
> *(Company secretary, ASX 300)*

Marshall and Ramsay (2012) conducted an extensive study of directors' perceptions of their legal duties under Australian law. They also found a strong belief amongst directors that their legal duties were broad enough to allow them to take the interests of a wide range of stakeholders into account (2012, p. 304). The increasing inclusion of corporate responsibility in corporate governance codes will consolidate this role of the board.

Board committees

A committee dedicated to sustainability can provide a framework to facilitate the flow of sustainability-related information into strategic planning at board and executive levels, ensuring that engagement processes (with both internal and external stakeholders) are relevant in the context of wider business strategy. Bryan Horrigan points to the need for research on 'the design and testing of boardroom decision-making frameworks that integrate CSR' (2010, p. 373).

Of the ASX 50 companies reviewed, 22 disclosed that they had a board committee responsible for sustainability, six had allocated this responsibility to a senior executive committee, three reported they had a dedicated network of managers; this left 19 with no formal sustainability committee, even though many of these did have other structures and processes in place for managing their sustainability strategies (see Figure 7.2).

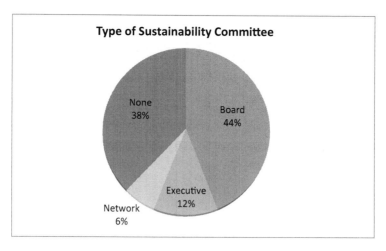

FIGURE 7.2 Sustainability leadership committees.

The names of the dedicated board committees varied – 12 included the word sustainability in their title; 11 were called health, safety and environment committees or similar; and three had corporate responsibility in the title. These labels were not mutually exclusive, for example, AGL Energy's 'Safety, Sustainability and CSR Committee' would fall into all of these categories. The decision as to whether a company had a true sustainability committee was not always easy to make. For example, on the borderline was IAG and its 'nomination, remuneration and sustainability committee', which perhaps covered rather too many other important functions. Another committee difficult to place was Dexus Property's 'risk management and sustainability' committee, which despite having sustainability in the title, appeared from its charter to have a role much like any other risk committee. Categorisation was based on the committee titles to avoid making potentially subjective judgments about the real role of committees using the limited information in published reports.

Indeed, existence of a committee is only one indicator of the use of governance mechanisms to lead sustainability. As a comparison, ANZ specifically stated that its nomination committee had responsibility for sustainability without putting this word in the title; Westpac had recently disbanded its sustainability committee to give responsibility to the full board; and Westfield gave a detailed description of reporting lines for the individuals responsible for Australian sustainability strategy without actually having a committee. A full understanding of how companies lead, monitor and implement their strategies requires more in-depth qualitative analysis: an area ripe for case-study research.

This research was limited to a review of the title and role description of the committee provided in annual reporting. Companies' descriptions of the role of their CSR committees, where provided, demonstrated a wide spectrum of functions covered by these committees. For seven companies, it was clear from the role description of the committee that it was primarily a compliance committee and perhaps not concerned with overall sustainability strategy. This suggests that these companies are still in the compliance phase of sustainability, put forth by Dunphy et al. (2014), where the board role is primarily monitoring rather than strategy-setting. Compliance with health and safety legislation has long been a priority in the mining and oil and gas industries, particularly at board level as directors can be personally responsible. As one interviewee in 2006 commented:

> With OHS, there is responsibility for directors if there are deaths on site. The regulation means it's a very serious issue. We've not reported well in the past, very light, but we are thinking what we might do in future and how we might be able to pull stats out of the business.
>
> *(Company secretary, ASX 100)*

Thus, health and safety committees are not a new phenomenon but are perhaps being re-branded to include a broader range of issues. Yuan et al. (2011) include this 'relabelling' phenomenon as one of their seven patterns of CSR integration.

They recognise that in some cases this can represent a convenient way to put forward a more positive image of the firm without any real changes in substance (2011, p. 84). Moving up the spectrum there were four similar health, safety and environment committees where broader sustainability issues had been expressly added on to their compliance mandate. This was sometimes only evident because more information had been given about the actions of the committee during the year. Lastly, seven companies were considered to be at the top of the scale in terms of having a board committee with a focus on overall sustainability strategy and broad policy issues, even if compliance also featured in their list of responsibilities. These companies might be said to have reached the strategic proactivity stage of sustainability (Dunphy et al. 2014). This is a significant development considering that in 2007 Kakabadse and Kakabadse in interviews with 42 board members (albeit from only four companies) found that 'one strongly held perspective of UK and US participants is that CSR has no place in boardroom discussions' (2007, p. 196). This was in contrast to French and German board directors who considered CSR crucial as a strategy for stakeholder engagement (Kakabadse & Kakabadse 2007, p. 196).

Interestingly, all of the six companies in the sample with executive (rather than board) committees dedicated to sustainability would also fall at the top of the spectrum. These companies were ANZ, NAB, Telstra, Brambles, Macquarie and Amcor, and their executive committees were described in terms of having a strategy-focus, some explained reporting lines and coordinated implementation processes for sustainability across the organisation – these appeared as the most advanced sustainability leadership bodies. Further research exploring company motivations in setting up committees would be valuable, particularly why some decided to have a committee at management rather than board level and the consequences this may have in terms of stakeholder representation.

Companies describing a committee or network for sustainability below senior executive level also appeared advanced in their thinking. These committees comprise representatives from different business units or locations who meet regularly to improve awareness and ensure consistency in the implementation of sustainability strategies across a large organisation. Case-study research would be valuable to assess whether these committees represent a bottom-up process of sustainability strategy-development or are simply concerned with implementation of specific initiatives.

Implementation: remuneration incentives

Implementation of top-led CSR strategies is another area where there is a lack of both academic theory and practical guidance (Lindgreen et al. 2008, p. 252). As Maon et al. comment, 'a framework has yet to be offered that integrates the development and implementation of CSR into the organization's strategy, structure and culture' (2009, p. 73).

Specifically, practitioners lack guidance on various CSR implementation issues including architecture; management; building and maintenance; repositioning; communication; and performance measures.

(Lindgreen et al. 2008)

Several interviewees in 2006 commented on the importance of active enforcement by company leaders of policies on business ethics and responsibility:

> The board sets the tone just by the way it operates – through the messages management get from the board regarding its tolerance for sailing close to the breeze. There was a wonderful example a couple of years ago.... He was a very talented person and had done it for the right motives – the manager here was wringing his hands over it but the CEO had no hesitation in immediately sacking him. It sent a very powerful message. You can say all you like in codes but that got round in milliseconds. He may have been a good performer but he did the wrong thing.
>
> *(Company secretary, ASX 100)*

One of the reasons for the lack of guidance on CSR implementation is that it can have a very different practical meaning for every company. Consequently, this chapter focuses on generic processes and structures governing the development and implementation of corporate responsibility rather than specific environmental or social goals. The implication is that by integrating corporate responsibility into existing corporate governance systems, companies have a mechanism to develop, implement, monitor and improve their corporate responsibility strategies whatever they may be.

Companies' disclosures were reviewed for information on how they implement their sustainability strategies. There was wide variation in the amount and type of information provided. Some companies offered significant detail on the policies, standards and management systems used to implement sustainability practices across the company. Others referred to the existence of such policies, for example, 'health and safety documents', without giving detail of their content. Some appeared to focus more on the human-resources aspects of implementation, for example, the development of business unit leaders for sustainability and employee training. These disclosures illustrate the broad range of issues that can fall within the concept of sustainability and the near impossibility of trying to provide generic guidance for the practical implementation of sustainability.

Remuneration incentives

An alternative is to examine the incentives in place for implementation of sustainability strategy by executives. For this research each company's remuneration report was reviewed to find out if executive remuneration was tied to non-financial performance indicators. Berrone and Gomez Meja note that 'the academic community has largely neglected the link between social issues and managerial pay' (2009). This is still the case despite widespread belief that short term remuneration schemes contributed to the 2008 global financial crisis, an issue discussed more in Chapter 8. GRI Guideline 4.5 suggests that companies should disclose the linkage between senior executive's remuneration and the organisation's performance and expressly states that this should include social and environmental performance. Of the 28 companies in the research sample publishing a GRI index, 24 stated that they had reported against this guideline.

Overall, a significant 94 percent of the sample, or 47 of the 50 companies, stated that they incorporated non-financial performance in their remuneration schemes, usually in the short-term incentive (STI) plan. However, it was often unclear as to what the non-financial indicators were and the proportion of remuneration dependent on them. It became clear that non-financial indicators do not equate to sustainability indicators, rather they include many operational metrics as well as some relating to corporate responsibility. Possibly the percentage of total remuneration dependent on these factors was only a very small component of total remuneration and therefore questionable as a significant motivator for employees. Even so, this was a notable finding and clearly something that warrants further research.

Across the 47 companies who stated that they linked non-financial performance to executive remuneration there was a wide range in the level of detail on how this was done. For example, QBE Insurance states, 'Our remuneration framework is designed to drive the achievement and outperformance of financial and non-financial targets', without giving further explanation. Oilsearch explains that short-term incentive plan hurdles are based on:

> Corporate performance against operational metrics which include: safety; production; costs; increases in hydrocarbon reserves under development; and Transformational metrics which include: acquisition of new hydrocarbon resources and progress towards commercialisation of 3C gas reserves.
>
> (Oilsearch)

Here there is no explanation of how the single mention of safety is balanced against the multiple mentions of an array of potentially conflicting production-focused metrics or how much of short-term incentive is dependent upon it. It is important to note that non-financial indicators do not necessarily equate to corporate sustainability indicators and can include measures such as production volumes. As Fortescue metals points out in relation to their short-term incentive scheme, 'Of the performance objectives listed above, Cost per tonne shipped and Relative TSR would be considered 'financial' and tonnes shipped, safety and target percentage of reserves mined would be considered 'non-financial' objectives.'

Thirty two companies, that is, 64 percent, gave specific information on the weighting of non-financial performance indicators and the amount of remuneration at stake. This ranged from a possible 60 percent of STI at AGL to 10 percent at Iluka (plus potential sustainability-related individual objectives). It was common for the percentage to vary depending on each individual's role and capacity to influence relevant non-financial measures. Sometimes non-financial indicators made up an unspecified proportion of the 'individual objectives' for each executive. This lack of detail, and the potential conflict between financial and non-financial KPIs, was also noted in Adams and Frost's study:

> Occupational, health and safety targets are now built into the employee share plan based on the organisation meeting specific targets. Specific aspects of social and environmental performance are also built into the performance evaluation of the relevant managers, although the impact may be limited since profit remains the predominant determinant of the bonus.
>
> (2008, p. 297)

Nevertheless, linking sustainability performance with remuneration is gaining attention as a way to monitor and encourage implementation on the basis that executive bonus packages tend to direct attention. Longitudinal research into this phenomenon would be interesting as it seems likely that this is a relatively new development, and companies are still grappling with how to measure non-financial performance. Morgan et al. in their study of 25 Fortune 500 companies across five industry sectors found 'brief to no disclosure' on 'employee compensation linked to corporate responsibility goals and targets' across all sectors, commenting:

> ... there is scant evidence in this sample that firms are linking citizenship into their performance appraisal and compensation systems. Interestingly, many feel that this is the missing component of the citizenship integration puzzle. Over 60 percent of respondents of an Ethical Corporation Magazine (2003) survey, for example, believe that management compensation linked to citizenship performance is among the top three strategies to more effective management of corporate citizenship.
>
> (2009, p. 45)

In their interviews conducted in 2003–2004 Adams and Frost found companies just starting to use balanced scorecards in assessing executive remuneration – one British company had, '... moved away from assessing managers' performance against financial KPIs and adopted a companywide balanced scorecard that has 16 measures on it, three of the four quadrants of which relate to non-financial issues. Performance against these measures is linked to their remuneration' (2008, p. 295). This research finds many companies using this balanced scorecard approach, particularly in service industries.

In terms of the type of non-financial indicators used to measure sustainability performance, companies were assessed in terms of their inclusion of five areas: safety, employee engagement, customer satisfaction, environment and community. Of these, the three most common areas of corporate sustainability to be linked to executive remuneration were occupational health and safety, employee satisfaction and customer service, with environment and community being less common (see Figure 7.3). There were of course other sustainability issues linked

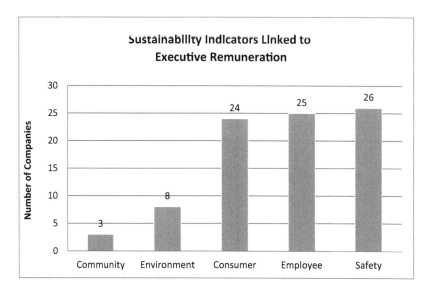

FIGURE 7.3 Sustainability performance indicators linked to executive remuneration.

to remuneration, for example, Sonic Healthcare focused on culture, risk management and external reputation.

Twenty six companies included occupational health and safety as a non-financial performance indicator. Unsurprisingly, this was often a focus for mining or industrial companies. For example, Rio Tinto explained that:

> Health and safety key performance indicators (measured in relation to all injury frequency rate (AIFR), Significant Potential Incidents (SPI) and Semi Quantitative Risk Assessment (SQRA)), comprise 17.5 per cent of the short-term incentive plan for executives. The extent of the impact of a fatality on the STIP score for all executives is based on an assessment by the Committee of the impact of leadership, individual behaviour and systems in the incident. For some executives, where relevant, an additional proportion of their individual objectives under the STIP are linked to safety objectives.
>
> *(Rio Tinto)*

Westpac explained that 10 percent of STI was linked to safety measured in terms of the Lost Time Injury Frequency Rate (LTIFR). The company stated that 'the health and safety of our employees continues to be a priority for us and our LTIFR improved by 25 percent this year, outperforming our target'. AGL's remuneration report went into impressive detail and demonstrates the detailed measuring and target-setting that is required to include these issues in remuneration schemes:

> 99 percent of all specific safety action plans for 2011/12 were completed. However in terms of lagging indicators the Lost Time Injury Frequency Rate for 2011/12 was 4.2 compared to 2.1 for 2010/11 and the Total Injury Frequency Rate (TIFR) for 2011/12 was 6.6 compared to 5.0 for 2010/11.

These results were not in line with our safety targets of 100 percent completion of our safety action plans and TIFR target of 4.0. Short-term incentive plan payments were adjusted downwards accordingly.

(Westpac)

Clearly it is a positive thing for a company to want to make the workplace safer; however, it is easy to be sceptical about corporate motives. First, there are strict penalties for breach of occupational health and safety laws and, as one interviewee mentioned, there are also cost implications:

OH&S is the first topic on the board papers each month. We use measures – lost time, injuries - and report all that to the board – it affects the workcover premium etc.

(Company secretary, ASX 100)

Almost as common as OHS was linking remuneration to customer service: 24 companies gauged customer satisfaction and incorporated it in remuneration schemes. For example, a performance indicator at Suncorp was to 'improve external confidence in the Suncorp Group and achievement of target customer satisfaction'. ANZ explained that their aim in this category was 'to achieve top quartile customer satisfaction scores in each business based on external surveys'.

There were also 25 companies describing a link between employee satisfaction and executive remuneration. The most common measure used was an employee-engagement survey; however, some companies went further. For example, Stockland set and disclosed numerical targets for reducing employee-initiated turnover; increasing employee engagement; and increasing women in management roles. It then disclosed its progress in relation to each target. Since the introduction of gender diversity onto the corporate governance agenda, discussed in Chapter 6, it is expected that more companies will tie their gender targets to remuneration hurdles.

Only eight companies used environmental impact as a performance indicator, and it was often difficult to see how this was measured; for example, Woolworths stated that STI was based on the vague and broad measure of: 'Enhancing Woolworths' public image and reputation in community involvement, government relations, environmental sustainability and regulatory compliance'. Iluka was more precise, referring to 'level two and above environmental incidents' as presumably impacting negatively on remuneration. Only three of the 50 companies linked executive remuneration to community issues. In all cases this was a weak link with community matters included within a bundle of other indicators.

Clearly more guidance is required on how these disclosures should be framed and the level of detail required. A statement confirming linkage between a performance measure and remuneration is not very helpful unless the nature and extent of that link are explained. These findings highlight an important area for further research: to identify the extent to which sustainability performance influences total remuneration. Such research would assist boards, shareholders and stakeholders in the development of more meaningful incentive and disclosure systems.

Discussion and conclusions

The introduction to this chapter briefly refers to the conflicting theories of the purpose of the corporation. One view is that the corporation is a private entity, operating for the financial benefit of its shareholders. The opposing view places wider responsibilities on the corporation to create long-term value for all of its stakeholders. In practice there appears to be a developing acceptance amongst large corporations that efforts towards improved corporate sustainability are not only expected but are of value to the business. One interviewee commented in 2006 that, 'there is a lot of evidence that the move to sustainability rather than compliance, has been value-added'. It could be suggested that these findings are evidence of a managerial shift away from a strict shareholder primacy understanding of the corporation towards a more stakeholder-orientated view. It seems that companies are making efforts to move towards a stakeholder approach despite prevailing market pressures to focus heavily on short-term share price. Although institutional investors are becoming more alert to what they term environment social and governance (ESG) issues, this too is a relatively new phenomenon that was just emerging as an issue for financial sector companies in 2006:

> We recently looked at investment decisions and said we would develop guidelines for the managers on social and environmental issues. It has not been a burning issue but has been elevated. The action list will remain before the committee until something gets done. Clearly you want guidelines for the manager or else they will be looking purely at IRR (investment rate of return).
>
> *(Company secretary, small financial company)*

Corporate responsibility is an area where the direct influence of the Australian Corporate Governance Code on corporate behaviour has been weak. This is partly by design: the ASX chose not to incorporate corporate responsibility reporting into its mandate after consultation in 2006 and has included it only as an element of risk management in 2014. Although the code refers to the key concepts behind corporate responsibility it does so in a rather indirect and outmoded manner by including them within the principles on ethical conduct and risk management. As discussed above, most large Australian companies publish detailed reports on CSR or sustainability, but these are rarely placed under the heading of a code of conduct, nor are they deemed merely a form of reputational risk management – they are stand-alone reports dedicated to a topic that has grown considerably bigger.

It is a shame that the second edition of the ASX Principles took away corporate responsibility as a separate principle and parcelled it into the general code of conduct. This was in contrast to what was happening in other parts of the world. Painter-Morland notes that:

> The second South African King Report on Corporate Governance (King II), promulgated in March 2002, set itself apart from many other governance regulations in succeeding to bridge the gap between CSR and good governance.
>
> (2006, p. 355)

The third King report on corporate governance published in 2009 went further with a focus on leadership, sustainability and corporate citizenship. It is certainly time for the Australian approach to corporate responsibility to be updated. Nearly a decade has gone by since the PJC report concluded that it was too early to recommend the GRI as a standard for Australian companies (2006, p. xvi). Despite this, in the absence of domestic guidance it is this kind of international soft law that has filled the gap. Australian institutions have been remarkably passive on the issue of CSR with law reform consistently rejected despite legal changes overseas. Nevertheless, large Australian corporations have developed strategies surrounding sustainability and corporate responsibility, and most provide comprehensive reporting. This is an area where behaviour has voluntarily developed much further than anything suggested in the ASX corporate governance code due to a mix of changing stakeholder expectations and international initiatives.

Of course, a degree of caution must remain when basing conclusions on voluntary reporting. As described by Yuan et al. (2011) some CSR activities may only comprise relabelling of existing activities or the addition of peripheral practices. Quite rightly there remains scepticism about corporate motivations surrounding corporate responsibility and whether reporting actually translates to positive action on the part of companies:

> This ability to implement policies founded upon a concept that remains ambiguous raises a number of questions regarding the definition employed by those who profess a commitment to CSR, why they have chosen to implement CSR policies, how they develop those policies and their value in terms of reducing the adverse impact of corporate activity.
>
> (Whitehouse 2006, p. 280)

What is clear however is that CSR has been institutionalised creating norms and expectations of behaviour that assist to encourage corporate action. Full corporate accountability for sustainability may require tougher regulation to ensure both good and bad information is revealed, or at least a statement by the chief executive officer that disclosure is 'true and fair' akin to that required for financial reporting. Certainly, this is an area where guidance and recommendations can lead to more consistent and comparable disclosures supported by governance structures that facilitate genuine integration into corporate strategy.

Summary of chapter 7

The research presented in this chapter provides a snapshot of some of the practices being employed in large Australian companies to govern and manage their corporate responsibility strategies. This information can be used to better understand the state of play of corporate responsibility and can inform the debate on whether stronger regulation would be of value in this area. The research provides empirical evidence of developing norms in the area of corporate sustainability and the influence of codes of corporate governance as well as international soft law on corporate behaviour. It contributes to corporate governance theory by providing evidence that supports a shift towards a stakeholder or 'social entity conception' of the corporation (Blair 2004). By putting in place governance structures and processes for CSR, companies are better able to take stakeholders' interests into account in their strategy development and to monitor and report on progress towards greater corporate sustainability.

References

Adams, CA & Frost, GR 2008, 'Integrating sustainability reporting into management practices', *Accounting Forum,* vol. 32, pp. 288–302.

Anderson, H 2005, 'Corporate social responsibility: some critical questions for Australia', *University of Tasmania Law Review,* vol. 24, no. 2, pp. 143–72.

Baumann, D & Scherer, AG 2010, 'MNEs and the UN global compact: an empirical analysis of the organizational implementation of corporate citizenship', Institute of Organisation and Administrative Science, University of Zurich, IOU Working Paper No. 114.

Berrone, P & Gomez-Mejía, LR 2009, 'Environmental performance and executive compensation: an integrated agency-institutional perspective', *Academy of Management Journal,* vol. 52, no. 1, pp. 103–26.

Blair, MM 2004, 'Ownership and control: rethinking corporate governance for the twenty-first century', in T Clarke (ed.), *Theories of Corporate Governance: the philosophical foundations of corporate governance,* New York: Routledge.

Branson, D 2001, 'Corporate governance "reform" and the new corporate social responsibility', *University of Pittsburgh Law Review,* vol. 62, pp. 605–47.

CAMAC (Corporations and Markets Advisory Committee) 2006, *The Social Responsibility of Corporations,* Australian Government, December 2006.

Campbell, JL 2007 'Why would corporations behave in socially responsible ways? An institutional theory of corporate social responsibility', *Academy of Management Review,* vol. 32, no. 3, pp. 946–67.

Carroll, AB 1999, 'Corporate social responsibility – evolution of a definitional construction', *Business and Society,* vol. 38, no. 3, pp. 268–95.

Dahlsrud, A 2008, 'How corporate social responsibility is defined: an analysis of 37 definitions', *Corporate Social Responsibility and Environmental Management,* vol. 15, pp. 1–13.

Danish Commerce and Companies Agency 2010, *Corporate Social Responsibility and Reporting in Denmark: impact of the legal requirement for reporting on CSR in the Danish Financial Statements Act.*

Dunphy, D, Griffiths, A & Benn, S 2014, *Organizational Change for Corporate Sustainability*, 3rd ed., Oxford and New York: Routledge.

Freeman, RE 1994 'The politics of stakeholder theory: some future directions', *Business Ethics Quarterly*, vol. 4, pp. 409–22.

Freeman, RE & Reed, WM 1990, 'Corporate governance: a stakeholder interpretation', *Journal of Behavioural Economics*, vol. 19, no. 4, pp. 337–60.

Friedman, M 1962, *Capitalism and Freedom*, Chicago: University of Chicago Press.

Gill, AG 2008, 'Corporate governance as social responsibility: a research agenda', *Berkley Journal of International Law*, vol. 26, pp. 452–78.

Gobbels, M 2006, 'Standards for corporate social responsibility', in J Jonker and M de Witte (eds.), *The Challenge of Organizing and Implementing Corporate Social Responsibility*, New York: Palgrave Macmillan.

Gray, R, Kouhy, R & Lavers, DS 1995, 'Constructing a research database of social and environmental reporting by UK companies', *Accounting, Auditing and Accountability Journal*, vol. 8, pp. 78–101.

Greenwood, M 2007 'Stakeholder engagement: beyond the myth of corporate responsibility', *Journal of Business Ethics*, vol. 74, pp. 315–27.

Horrigan, B 2010, *Corporate Social Responsibility in the 21st Century: debates, models and practices across government, law and business*, Cheltenham, UK: Edward Elgar Publishing.

Jensen, MC 2002, 'Value maximization, stakeholder theory, and the corporate objective function', *Business Ethics Quarterly*, vol. 12, no. 2, pp. 235–56.

Jose, A & Lee, S 2007, 'Environmental reporting of global corporations; a content analysis based on website disclosures', *Journal of Business Ethics*, vol. 72, pp. 307–21.

Kakabadse, A & Kakabadse, N (eds.) 2007, *CSR in Practice: delving deep*, New York: Palgrave Macmilllan.

Keay, A 2007, 'Tackling the issue of the corporate objective: an analysis of the United Kingdom's "Enlightened shareholder value approach"', *Sydney Law Review*, vol. 29, p. 577.

Keay, A 2010 'Moving towards stakeholderism? Consituency statutes, enlightened shareholder value, and all that: much ado about little?', Working paper.

King, M 2009, *King Report on Governance for South Africa 2009*, Institute of Directors Southern Africa.

Klein, E & du Plessis, JJ 2005, 'Corporate donations, the best interest of the company and the proper purpose doctrine', *University of New South Wales Law Journal*, vol. 28, no. 1, pp. 69–97.

Kolk, A 2008, 'Sustainability, accountability and corporate governance: exploring multinationals' reporting practices', *Business Strategy and the Environment*, vol. 18, pp. 1–15.

KPMG 2011, *International Survey of Corporate Responsibility Reporting.*

KPMG 2013, *The KPMG Survey of Corporate Responsibility Reporting.*

Lindgreen, A, Swaen, V & Maon, F 2008, 'Introduction: corporate social responsibility Implementation' *Journal of Business Ethics*, vol. 85, pp. 251–56.

Maon, F, Lindgreen A & Swaen, V 2009 'Designing and implementing corporate social responsibility: an integrative framework grounded in theory and practice', *Journal of Business Ethics*, vol. 87, pp. 71–89.

Marshall, S & Ramsay, I 2012, 'Stakeholders and directors' duties: law theory and evidence', *University of New South Wales Law Journal*, vol. 35, pp. 291–316.

Martin, F 2005, 'Corporate social responsibility and public policy', in R Mullerat (ed.), *Corporate Social Responsibility: the corporate governance of the 21st century*, Netherlands: International Bar Association, pp. 77–95.

McConvill, J & Joy, M 2003, 'The interaction of directors duties and sustainable development in Australia: setting off on the uncharted road', *Melbourne University Law Review*, vol. 27, pp. 116–38.

Mitchell, RK, Agle, BR & Wood, DJ 1997, 'Toward a theory of stakeholder identification and salience: defining the principle of who and what really counts', *Academy of Management Review*, vol. 22, no. 4, pp. 853–86.

Moir, L 2001 'What do we mean by corporate social responsibility?', *Corporate Governance*, vol. 1, no. 2, pp. 16–22.

Morgan, G, Ryu, K & Mirvis, P 2009, 'Leading corporate citizenship: governance, structure, systems', *Corporate Governance*, vol. 9, no. 1, pp. 39–49.

Parker, C 2007 'Meta-regulation - legal accountability for corporate social responsibility', in D McBarnet, A Voiculescu & T Campbell (eds.), *The New Corporate Accountability: corporate social responsibility and the law*, Cambridge: Cambridge University Press.

Painter-Morland, M 2006, 'Triple bottom-line reporting as social grammar: integrating corporate social responsibility and corporate codes of conduct', *Business Ethics: A European Review*, vol. 15, no. 4, pp. 352–64.

PJC, Parliamentary Joint Committee on Corporations and Financial Services, 2006, *Corporate Responsibility: Managing risk and creating value*, June 2006.

Redmond, P 2012, 'Directors' duties and corporate social responsiveness', *University of New South Wales Law Journal*, vol. 35, pp. 317–40.

Searcy, C 2012, 'Corporate sustainability performance measurement systems: a review and research agenda', *Journal of Business Ethics*, vol. 107, no. 3, pp. 239–53.

Szejnwald Brown, H, de Jong, M & Lessidrenska, T 2009, 'The rise of the global reporting initiative (GRI) as a case of institutional entrepreneurship', *Environmental Politics*, vol. 18, no. 2, pp. 182–200.

Taneja, SS, Taneja, PK & Gupta, RK 2011, 'Researches in corporate social responsibility: a review of shifting focus, paradigms and methodologies', *Journal of Business Ethics*, vol. 101, pp. 343–64.

Van Velsor E 2009, 'Introduction: leadership and corporate social responsibility', *Corporate Governance*, vol. 9, no. 1, pp. 3–6.

Werther WB & Chandler, D 2011, *Strategic Corporate Social Responsibility: stakeholders in a global environment*, 2nd ed, Thousand Oaks: SAGE Publications.

Whitehouse, 2006 'Corporate social responsibility: views from the frontline', *Journal of Business Ethics*, vol. 63, pp. 279–96.

Yuan, W, Bao, Y & Verbeke, A 2011, 'Integrating CSR initiatives in business: an organizing framework', *Journal of Business Ethics*, vol. 101, pp. 75–92.

8

EXECUTIVE REMUNERATION

Introduction

Another very topical issue within the realm of corporate governance is the role
of the board in determining executive remuneration. A chief executive officer
(CEO) of a large corporation in the United States will earn approximately 200
times that of the average worker. Other countries have less tolerance for income
inequality, but still the difference is significant. What is surprising is that despite
being in the media spotlight for the last decade or more and despite the introduction of regulation designed to better link pay to performance, executive pay
continues to rise much faster than the pay of the average employee as well as
much faster than the stock market (BIS 2011). In the UK, FTSE 100 CEOs were
paid about 25 times the average worker in 1980, but the multiple in 2015 was
130 times (Farrell 2015). In Australia, the average cash remuneration of CEOs in
the top 50 listed companies ballooned from 18 times average full-time earnings
in 1990 to a multiple of 63 times in 2005 (Shields 2005). Indeed, it is said that
this differential was caused rather than mitigated by the 'pay-for-performance'
movement because it can be accounted for by the growth of incentive-based
remuneration, not base salary (Productivity Commission 2009).

Executive remuneration became a point of public interest after many of the
major corporate collapses in 2001, with public outrage at the fact that executives
were able to walk away with huge bonuses while employees and investors lost all
their savings. In particular the scandals drew attention to dubious perks and termination payments (Hill 2006). However, the regulatory reforms that emerged
in the mid-2000s did nothing to prevent remuneration schemes from again being
identified as problematic by inquiries into the global financial crisis in 2008.
Although bosses may have walked away with less outrageous termination payments, the structure of remuneration schemes was said to have incentivised the
risk-taking that caused the crisis in the first place (Kirkpatrick 2009). The role

of remuneration in incentivising short-term strategies and share-price manipulation, although identified in 2001, had not been remedied at all. If anything, the situation appeared to be worse: not only were pay schemes unfair, but they had become dangerous for both corporate and economic longevity.

The questions at the heart of the debate over executive pay are numerous and complex. Reflecting the agency theory of corporate governance more generally, there is seen to be an inherent conflict of interest between rent-seeking managers and profit-seeking shareholders. The board's role is to mediate between the two parties to find a pay structure that assures optimal performance from the executive team without overly reducing the funds left for shareholders. The 'managerial entrenchment' view of executive remuneration presumes that without board intervention, powerful managers will try to extract overly generous pay arrangements unconnected to performance (Cambini et al. 2015). Although evidence suggests this rent-extraction theory proves true in the United States, the relationship is weaker in Australia with labour demand explaining a certain proportion of CEO compensation (Chalmers et al. 2006).

To complicate matters further, in the early 1990s the purpose of executive remuneration was subtly redefined – rather than the board simply finding a fair value, it was thought that remuneration could be used as a tool to align the interests of executives with those of shareholders. Cambini et al. (2015) describe this as the efficiency view of executive remuneration whereby it is used as an incentive mechanism that alters managerial behaviour in a manner that maximises shareholder wealth. As Jennifer Hill neatly states, 'Executive remuneration, which had traditionally been treated as a corporate governance problem, was now viewed as a governance solution in its own right' (2006, p. 10). This was the beginning of complex remuneration schemes, involving share ownership and options, which spawned an industry of consultants and arguably created an upward spiral of executive remuneration way out of proportion to individual effort.

In September 2015, the UK's Investment Association initiated a review of executive pay, led by influential corporate leaders including chair, Helena Morrissey. Rumours were that it would consider completely scrapping long-term share incentives in favour of a single variable annual bonus figure (Kleinman 2015). However the final report simply recommended more flexibility, recognising that existing long-term incentive schemes were not universally effective or appropriate (Executive Remuneration Working Group 2016).

There are various regulatory strategies for dealing with the issue of executive remuneration and different methods for implementing them. Codes of corporate governance comprise just one string of the bow – usually focusing on the board's role in setting remuneration policy. Most countries also deal with executive remuneration through hard law, which is used to mandate corporate reporting and prohibit certain practices. Table 8.1 provides some examples of

TABLE 8.1 Code provisions on executive remuneration internationally

Code	Provision
Australian Corporate Governance Principles and Recommendations (ASX Corporate Governance Council 2014)	A listed entity should have a formal and transparent process for developing its remuneration policy and for fixing the remuneration packages of directors and senior executives. No individual director or senior executive should be involved in deciding his or her own remuneration. Recommendation 8.1 The board of a listed entity should: (a) have a remuneration committee which: (1) has at least three members, a majority of whom are independent directors; and (2) is chaired by an independent director. Recommendation 8.2 A listed entity should separately disclose its policies and practices regarding the remuneration of non-executive directors and the remuneration of executive directors and other senior executives.
The 2009 Belgian Code on Corporate Governance (Corporate Governance Committee 2009	The introduction to the 2009 edition states: … most attention, however, is likely to go to the recommendations that are made concerning executive remuneration. The Code advocates complete transparency about remuneration and severance pay towards shareholders and the outside world. The Committee hopes to have achieved a major breakthrough in this area. 5.4 The board should set up a remuneration committee following the provisions set out in Appendix E (non-executives only and at least a majority independent). 7.1 Levels of remuneration should be sufficient to attract, retain and motivate directors and executive managers who have the profile determined by the board. 7.3 The company should disclose in its remuneration report: a description of its internal procedure for developing (i) a remuneration policy for non-executive directors and executive managers and (ii) for setting the level of remuneration for non-executive directors and executive managers.

(Continued)

Code	Provision
Denmark Recommendations on Corporate Governance (Committee on Corporate Governance 2014)	3.4.7. The committee recommends that the board of directors establish a remuneration committee.... to recommend the remuneration policy (including the general guidelines for incentive-based remuneration) to the board of directors and the executive board for approval by the board of directors prior to approval by the general meeting. Principle 4 Competitive remuneration is a prerequisite for attracting and retaining competent members of the management of the company (the board of directors and the executive board). The company should have a remuneration policy, according to which the total remuneration package, i.e. the fixed and variable components and other remuneration components, as well as other significant employment terms, should be reasonable and reflect the governing body members' independent performance, responsibilities and value creation for the company. The variable component of the remuneration (the incentive pay scheme) should be based on actual achievements over a period of time with a view to long-term value creation so as not to promote short-term and risky behaviour.
French Corporate governance code of listed corporations (afep-MEDEF, 2013)	18.1. The committee in charge of compensation should not include any executive directors, and should have a majority of independent directors. It should be chaired by an independent director. It is advised that an employee director be a member of this committee. 23.1. Boards of Directors and Supervisory Boards are responsible for determining the compensation of executive directors, based on proposals made by the compensation committee.
Japan's Corporate Governance Code (JPX Tokyo Stock Exchange 2015)	4. Companies may choose one of three main forms of organizational structure under the Companies Act (Revised in 2014): Company with *Kansayaku* Board, Company with Three Committees (Nomination, Audit and Remuneration) or Company with Supervisory Committee. 4.2 remuneration of the management should include incentives such that it reflects mid– to long-term business results and potential risks, as well as promotes healthy entrepreneurship. 3.1 Full Disclosure should include: Board policies and procedures in determining the remuneration of the senior management and directors

Singapore Code of Corporate Governance (Monetary Authority of Singapore 2012)	7 There should be a formal and transparent procedure for developing policy on executive remuneration and for fixing the remuneration packages of individual directors. No director should be involved in deciding his own remuneration. 7.1 The Board should establish a Remuneration Committee ("**RC**") with written terms of reference which clearly set out its authority and duties. The RC should comprise at least three directors, the majority of whom, including the RC Chairman, should be independent. All of the members of the RC should be non-executive directors. This is to minimise the risk of any potential conflict of interest. 8 The level and structure of remuneration should be aligned with the long-term interest and risk policies of the company, and should be appropriate to attract, retain and motivate (a) the directors to provide good stewardship of the company, and (b) key management personnel to successfully manage the company. However, companies should avoid paying more than is necessary for this purpose.
King Code of Governance for South Africa (Institute of Directors Southern Africa 2009)	Sustainability also means that management pay schemes must not create incentives to maximise relatively short-term results at the expense of longer-term performance. 2.23.6. Companies should establish risk, nomination and remuneration committees. 2.23.7. Committees, other than the risk committee, should comprise a majority of nonexecutive directors of which the majority should be independent. 2.25. Companies should remunerate directors and executives fairly and responsibly 2.26. Companies should disclose the remuneration of each individual director and certain senior executives: 2.26.2. the salaries of the three most highly-paid employees who are not directors 2.27. Shareholders should approve the company's remuneration policy: 2.27.1 Shareholders should pass a non-binding advisory vote on the company's yearly remuneration policy.
UK Corporate Governance Code (Financial Reporting Council 2014)	Principle D.1 Executive directors' remuneration should be designed to promote the long-term success of the company. Performance-related elements should be transparent, stretching and rigorously applied. Principle D.2 There should be a formal and transparent procedure for developing policy on executive remuneration and for fixing the remuneration packages of individual directors. No director should be involved in deciding his or her own remuneration. D.2.1 The board should establish a remuneration committee of at least three, or in the case of smaller companies, two, independent non-executive directors.

provisions from codes of corporate governance across the globe that deal with executive remuneration. Most set broad principles regarding fair remuneration and transparency whilst leaving the details of disclosure requirements to hard law or accounting standards. Their main feature is to recommend board structures and procedures for overseeing remuneration policy such as a remuneration committee made up of independent directors.

Methodology

This chapter explores the role of codes of corporate governance in regulating executive remuneration. Regulation on executive remuneration tends to deal with four issues:

1 disclosure of information on remuneration;
2 remuneration practices and policies;
3 the role of the board in determining remuneration policy; and
4 shareholder engagement and approval of remuneration.

This chapter will review each of these issues in turn drawing on evidence from interviews with company officers in Australia as well as corporate reports. These interviews were conducted in 2006 with over 60 companies, and their corporate governance statements in annual reports were reviewed prior to each interview. The sample was self-selected, meaning that the interviewees volunteered to participate after receiving a letter mailed to a wide variety of listed companies of all sizes. As discussed in Chapter 4 this means the findings cannot be widely generalised; rather they provide a case-study that can be compared to findings elsewhere.

Disclosure of remuneration

Many countries require disclosure of the remuneration of top executives as well as corporate policy on remuneration. Usually this does not restrict or reduce in any way the amounts paid but allows investors to make their own decisions on whether remuneration payments are justified. An Australian inquiry into executive remuneration referred to disclosure as having twin objectives: 'minimising conflicts of interest and providing information relevant to company risks and prospects' (Productivity Commission 2009, p. 265).

Regulatory provisions requiring disclosure are often found in hard law yet are supplemented by soft-law provisions in codes of corporate governance. The Austrian code of corporate governance helpfully summarises both the mandatory legal provisions on executive remuneration and the comply-or-explain provisions. Sometimes, for example in Canada, the soft regulation simply extends the legal regime suggesting rather than mandating more extensive disclosure.

In Australia disclosure requirements for executive pay have been reformed several times. Prior to 1998, pay only had to be disclosed in terms of 'bands' without naming any individuals. In 1998, requirements were strengthened to require information on the actual remuneration packages of directors and the five highest paid executives. In 2004 there was an attempt to harmonise with accounting standards, and the pay of 'key management personnel' was required to be disclosed in a dedicated 'remuneration report' within the company's annual report. Information on the link between pay and performance was also required to be disclosed as well as details of bonus schemes, options and termination payments. These reporting requirements were set out in the *Corporations Act 2001* and *Corporations Regulations 2001*, hard law rather than soft regulation.

Interviews in 2006 revealed a view that disclosure requirements were becoming too lengthy and complex. As a consequence, the remuneration report was extremely expensive to produce yet difficult to understand:

> Our concern is that it's gone too far and the information is too technical. You need a degree in HR to understand it.
>
> *(Company secretary, ASX 300)*

> Remuneration reports are a good example of regulation with a worthy policy objective but that are very hard to understand. Option valuations for example, that's voodoo economics.
>
> *(Company secretary, small listed company)*

Compliance costs both in terms of consultants' fees and the time spent by directors on the remuneration report were seen as out of proportion:

> This year we have spent hours on the directors' retirement fund – its only 30,000 a year – we spent days on it which would have been much better spent on growth strategies for example.
>
> *(Company secretary, ASX 100)*

These concerns were also highlighted by the Productivity Commission's 2009 report, which described remuneration reports as impenetrable and 'not particularly illuminating for investors' (2009, p. 247). A further concern raised by the report was the fact that the statutory requirements, based on accounting costs to the company, were resulting in disclosure of figures that did not always reflect the actual pay realised by executives.

Although disclosure of remuneration is not intended to limit executive pay, some interviewees felt that it had the opposite effect: pushing up salaries due to cross-industry comparison. This ratcheting of pay has also been recognised in other countries as an effect of peer-comparison (Bebchuk and Fried 2005; Ferrarini and Moloney 2004). The 2014 edition of the UK code expressly advises companies to be wary of comparisons with other companies for this reason:

> The remuneration committee should judge where to position their company relative to other companies. But they should use such comparisons with caution, in view of the risk of an upward ratchet of remuneration levels with no corresponding improvement in corporate and individual performance, and should avoid paying more than is necessary.
>
> (FRC 2014, p. 20)

Australian interviewees felt strongly that head-hunters would try to entice away any executives seen to be receiving less than market rates. On the other hand there was some embarrassment in making large payments public for the first time:

> It's an issue when you have friends out there who can just look up your salary on the web.
>
> *(Company secretary, ASX 300)*

> There has been lots of discussion because it's very sensitive – for the factory floor to see what their manager earns is difficult.
>
> *(Company secretary, small listed company)*

> If you have wider responsibility across the group and are paid a lot it can sound outrageously high.
>
> *(Company secretary, ASX 300)*

A common justification for large executive payments was the need to recruit from an international pool and compete against international salary levels. It was felt that if pay did not keep pace with other countries vital executives might consider leaving:

> In the hot areas – finance and development – people are getting offers from all over the world with higher salaries and tax breaks – we have a serious retention issue.
>
> *(Company secretary, ASX 100)*

A UK report notes that this global market for talent is frequently cited as a reason for high levels of pay, but the evidence is mixed (Gregory-Smith and Main 2011). An alternative argument is that globalisation should have increased the number of potential candidates for director-level positions thereby depressing pay. In reality it may be that the international mobility of CEOs is limited whereas within-country competition can be high (Gregory-Smith and Main 2011).

Remuneration practice

Pay and performance

A history of remuneration practices would show that although different schemes and mechanisms have gone in and out of favour, methods have become increasingly complex over time. In fact, prior to the mid-1990s most executive remuneration was very simple: usually a base salary plus some benefits and allowances. Twenty years later most schemes involve a fixed base salary and then a variety of incentive payments that are 'at risk', dependent on performance hurdles being met, many related to company rather than individual performance. The whole concept of pay-for-performance is relatively new and designed to align the interests of managers with those of shareholders. Indeed, of the 60 Australian remuneration reports reviewed in 2006, 23 stressed that remuneration was aimed at aligning the interests of senior executives with those of security holders by using a measure of shareholder value (usually TSR or total shareholder return) as a performance criteria. In a classic example of legal boilerplate (discussed further in Chapter 9) five companies made the following statement:

> The framework aligns executive reward with achievement of strategy objectives and the creation of value for shareholders.
>
> *(Oxiana, Transfield, SAI, Portland, Commander)*

Importantly, the focus on shareholder value at this time was reflective of a strong belief in shareholder primacy and economic theories of the firm. Pay-for-performance schemes tend to involve the granting of share options or bonus payments, usually linked to the financial performance of the company over the next one to five years. Financial economists in the 1990s argued that shareholders should endorse these potentially much-larger executive pay packages on the basis they would provide high-powered incentives for effective management (Jensen and Murphy 1990). However, after the collapse of Enron and Worldcom these practices were highly criticised. Many share schemes failed to prevent executives from selling their shares or hedging the value of their options, thereby decoupling the link between their remuneration and the company's performance. Termination and retirement payments came under the spotlight both for their size and the fact they were payable even when executives were forced to depart due to poor performance. For example in the US, Franklin Raines, who was forced to retire as CEO of Fannie Mae in late 2004, was entitled to receive an annual pension of approximately $1.4 million thereafter (Jensen and Fried 2005).

Regulation has attempted to deal with these issues but usually in a retrospective way when practices have already gone out of favour. Interviewees explained that most Australian companies had already wound up retirement schemes long before the law changed to make them subject to shareholder approval. Section 200B(1) of the *Corporations Act* came into force in November 2009 and, subject to certain exceptions, it made retirement benefits in excess of annual base salary illegal unless approved by shareholders. Prior to this, termination payments in Australia were permitted within the much larger threshold of seven times total remuneration. In the same way, when it was revealed that options hedging had become commonplace, firms were quick to expressly ban it. The *Corporations Act* was formally amended in June 2007 to require disclosure of board policy on hedging, yet all interviewees in 2006 already claimed it was strictly disallowed. The concern about detailed and specific regulation of this sort is not only that it arrives too late but that it simply pushes the money into other aspects of overall remuneration.

In the United States, the *Sarbanes Oxley Act* did not address executive compensation directly but did contain provisions that would allow the Securities Exchange Commission (SEC) to freeze certain payments, for example executives' golden parachutes, in the event of fraud. However, this provision has been largely ignored, used only twice in the six years following the Act's implementation (Cherry and Wong 2009, p. 7). In 2006, the option backdating scandal demonstrated ongoing attempts to circumvent the concept of pay-for-performance. By adjusting the date of grant of stock options to a date when the share price was low, companies could ensure that options were a 'sure thing' rather than linked to both performance and risk. The response to this widespread practice was the introduction of SEC regulation requiring detailed disclosure of executive compensation packages including options and bonuses.

Another regulatory idea to prevent 'reward for failure' is the concept of 'clawback' of executive remuneration. Cherry and Wong explain how clawback provisions can refer to a variety of legal mechanisms whereby benefits, conferred under a claim of right, are later recoverable in order to prevent unfairness (2009, p. 3). In the US, legislation attempting to retrospectively clawback bonuses from the executives of failed firms post-GFC was not hugely successful. Interviewees in 2006 also referred to the difficulties surrounding retrospective changes:

> We design our programs to be responsive to the market at the time although you can't undo the sins of the past. There is an element of history and build up in the contracts which you can't just wipe. That's why the consultants are now saying fixed, short and long is maybe not the right way to go. We don't want the reward for failure thing.
>
> *(Company secretary, ASX 100)*

However, awareness of these issues has led to voluntary inclusion of clawback provisions in executive contracts going forward, possibly due to the threat of potential regulation in this area. Rules made by the SEC in 2015 under the *Dodd Frank Act* now make it a requirement for all listed companies to adopt clawback policies that would recover incentive-based compensation in circumstances where the company is required to materially restate its financial statements.

Several other countries have made steps towards mandatory clawback provisions. In Australia a consultation paper was released by the Treasury in December 2010, and draft legislation was put forward in December 2012 that would permit clawback in the event that a company's financial statements were found to be materially misstated. Unfortunately, the legislation lapsed due to a change of government in 2013 but may still be revived. In the UK a clawback provision was included in the corporate governance code in 2014 that applies to companies on a comply-or-explain basis. It states that performance-related remuneration schemes for executive directors should include both clawback and malus provisions. Clawback refers to recovery of awards *after* they have been paid whereas malus provisions permit companies to adjust bonuses *before* they are paid out. Grant Thornton (2014) reported that 75 percent of companies in the FTSE 350 disclosed the existence of a clawback policy in 2014 as compared to only 21 percent in 2011. The 2015 edition of the OECD principles confirms and cements this emerging norm:

> The introduction of malus and claw-back provisions is considered good practice. They grant the company to right to withhold and recover compensation from executives in cases of managerial fraud and other circumstances, such as when the company is required to restate its financial statements due to material noncompliance with financial reporting requirements.
>
> (OECD 2015, p. 32)

Remunerating for the long-term

An issue touched on in other chapters is the huge influence that remuneration schemes can have on executive decision-making when dealing with a conflict between short-term profit and long-term sustainability. Indeed, this conflict is possibly the most important and difficult issue facing economies, regulators and corporations this century. One of the main hurdles for corporate social responsibility and sustainability is the market pressure to maintain short-term share price. If this pressure is reflected in and reinforced by executive remuneration schemes there is little hope of truly long-term strategies being adopted. Rewards for short-term results are said to encourage manipulation of the share price rather than sustainable growth.

Of 60 companies in the research sample, 49 said they had a long-term incentive scheme. The companies that said they did not were usually on the smaller side, some commenting that it was too difficult to determine performance hurdles that could realistically be achieved. In some industries linking pay to firm performance was seen as inappropriate because the key drivers of firm performance were outside of managers' control, such as the weather or commodity prices:

> Our performance depends on the [commodity] price and there is nothing anyone can do about it. Performance measures such as Total Shareholder Return (TSR) may work for the steady companies but not for us. When the price drops we need to retain people.
>
> *(Director, ASX 300)*

For other small companies it was regulatory uncertainty around the rules for remuneration schemes that had discouraged them from putting resources into setting up long-term incentive schemes. They had viewed the emergence and downfall of complex option or loan schemes in larger companies and were reluctant to follow current trends for fear of further regulatory change. Even in the large firms, interviews confirmed the very complex nature of designing long-term incentives. Many company secretaries mentioned the long discussions that they had been through with remuneration consultants. Problems raised included options going 'under water', questions over appropriate vesting periods and the difficulties of benchmarking with other companies in a small market. For some, there was definitely a feeling that the complexity of these schemes was a potential danger or had failed to provide the desired incentives:

> Yes – it's a very complicated system. The size of the overall package is fine but the structure is very complicated – somehow the more successful the company is the less you get as a long-term incentive so I'm not sure that it works as an incentive. There is always scope to work the system to advantage.
>
> *(Company secretary, ASX 300)*

> We got some remuneration consultants in initially but we prefer simple approaches. This whole area hasn't worked for us at all. The LTIs have not lived up to expectations.
>
> *(Company secretary, small listed company)*

Even if remuneration schemes can be designed to incorporate genuine long-term incentives, interviewees felt the institutional forces focusing on short-term shareholder value were hard to ignore:

> Short-term growth is very difficult to manage in conjunction with long-term growth. For example, buying land dilutes our EPS (earnings per share) but means we have a large land bank for the future. The institutional focus on EPS growth has overshadowed this.
>
> *(Company secretary, ASX 300)*

As mentioned above, of the remuneration reports reviewed in 2006, the large majority mentioned measures of shareholder value (usually TSR) as the main performance hurdle. Only three companies referred to inclusion of non-financial performance hurdles in their long-term incentive scheme. However, it must be noted that this was based on a review of the corporate governance statement rather than on detailed analysis of the remuneration report. Nevertheless, it contrasts with the findings of Chapter 7, that in 2012, 94 percent of the largest companies in Australia reported inclusion of non-financial indicators in their performance hurdles for executives. It may reflect differences in the two samples (large versus smaller companies), or it may indicate changing practices over time.

Remuneration and risk

As discussed in Chapter 2, after the global financial crisis the focus of remuneration reform internationally was to ensure that remuneration policies linked pay to risk and encouraged prudent risk management. It was believed that short-term bonuses had promoted excessive risk-taking in the financial sector – one of the causes of the crisis. The introduction to the Financial Stability Forum's *Principles for Sound Compensation Practices* (FSF Principles) explained that:

> High short term profits led to generous bonus payments to employees without adequate regard to the longer-term risks they imposed on their firms. These perverse incentives amplified the excessive risk-taking that severely threatened the global financial system....

> (FSF, 2009, p. 1)

The FSF Principles, published in April 2009, were a G-20 initiated effort to rectify this situation. They were intended to be implemented only by large financial institutions but have had much wider impact, finding their way into corporate governance codes and other non-sector-specific regulation. The Principles have three main components: (1) they place responsibility for compensation practices clearly upon the board of directors; (2) they stress that compensation must be aligned with all types of risk; and (3) they encourage effective disclosure by firms and supervision by national regulators. In September 2009 the FSF (renamed Financial Stability Board, FSB) published Implementation Standards to provide further practical guidance around the Principles and speed up the change process. They explained that the allocation of variable compensation must be aligned with the risks assumed in the conduct of business as well as the likelihood of potential future revenues. At the 2011 G-20 summit it was agreed that the FSB would undertake an ongoing monitoring and reporting process regarding the implementation of the Principles. Annual progress reports have been published detailing the extent of implementation of each principle in each of the 24 nations that agreed to implement them. Most jurisdictions report effective implementation including identification of major risk-takers (MRTs) and alignment of compensation to include both ex-ante and ex-post adjustment (FSB 2014).

The main change to existing practice was the bringing together of compensation systems and risk-management systems, which were previously seen as unrelated in many companies. Only one interviewee in 2006 referred to links between the two, possibly because of a strategic focus for that particular year rather than regular inclusion in remuneration policy:

> We've included risk management as part of executive performance assessment and remuneration. The STI is determined, 70 percent on profit and 30 percent split between personal performance and team objectives. This year the team objective is risk management, it's not been nutted out for 2008 but I expect risk will be in there again.

> *(Company secretary, ASX 300)*

Exactly how these two systems ought to be integrated is complex. In 2006 interviewees were struggling with improving risk management in general let alone linking it to remuneration. First, risks are not static, and second, only some of them can be linked directly to executive behaviour:

> There is an appreciation that risks are fluid. We have various offices in different parts of the world and as they expand and the business develops the risks are constantly in flux.
>
> *(Company secretary, small listed company)*

> The formal [risk management] process is new to us – we had advice on it from Ernst and Young but some of their suggestions were too difficult – involving probabilities etc. So we went back to them for some more practical suggestions – it's an evolving process.
>
> *(Company secretary, ASX 300)*

In the 2014 edition of the Australian code, risk committees were formally recommended for the first time, yet in 2006 some interviewees explained that it was more effective to deal with different categories of risk separately:

> We don't have a risk committee. We think we've identified the key areas of risk within safety, health, environment and the relevant committees and board deal with them without parcelling them all together. The risks are too diverse to do that – they don't all have to be covered in one place.
>
> *(Company secretary, ASX 100)*

This again demonstrates a need for flexibility in corporate governance guidelines. It seems that some businesses find it useful to allocate responsibility for risk management to a committee, but others do not. Indeed, some interviewees felt strongly that risk should remain a matter for the full board because it is so vital to overall strategy. Other companies explained that their audit and risk committees met at separate times to deal with the two topics as separate matters (one meeting as an audit committee and another as a risk committee). Risk reviews outside of the finance sector were closely related to renewal of insurance policies or liability for occupational health and safety.

Commentary to the FSF Principles touched on theoretical treatment of how to motivate different categories of employees. The motivational problems caused by option-based executive compensation had been researched prior to the crisis with increasing agreement amongst researchers on the risk-inducing effects of such schemes (Chen et al. 2006; John et al. 2000). In their summary of research in the area, Geletkanycz and Sanders confirm that 'research uniformly supports the idea that executive pay impacts decision-making, and in the case of option-based pay, risk taking especially' (2011, p. 520). They draw on upper-echelons theory to explain how executive compensation works in tandem with executive personal attributes to shape strategic choices and firm performance:

> In as much as individual executives differ in their backgrounds, profiles, motivations, etc., we would expect to see significant differences across managers in the effects of pay on risk taking and other strategic behaviors.
>
> *(Geletkanycz and Sanders 2011, p. 520)*

Here we see the need for human assessment of personality and likely behavioural traits when determining remuneration. As with other corporate governance mechanisms, there is a need for a level of flexibility and tailoring of systems to the circumstances involved. Who better to perform this task than a group of independent yet experienced individuals who know the executive team well, in other words, the board of directors.

The board's role

One of the core responsibilities of a board of directors is to appoint and set the remuneration of the CEO and usually many of the other senior executives. However, the relationships between board functions (monitoring, strategic input etc.) and executive remuneration are not well understood (Kumar and Zattoni 2016). Is the board's role to monitor and keep a check on pay or to use it as a strategy to enhance performance? Common practice, recommended by most codes of corporate governance, is to delegate the task of setting executive remuneration to a board sub-committee. Directors will also seek advice from specialist consultants, lawyers and tax agents. Remuneration can be one method through which the board provides 'tone from the top', setting the culture of the organisation and expectations regarding appropriate behaviour. Interviewees emphasised the importance of this role of the board:

> … its about leadership and rewarding appropriate behaviour and not rewarding inappropriate behaviour – which does happen, like when a deal gets done by cutting corners etc and the person is given a big bonus. Culture is very important.
>
> *(Director, ASX 100)*

Reforms since the global financial crisis have focused on improving the independence of remuneration committees, thereby reducing the inherent conflict of interest between managers and shareholders. Clearly it is not a good idea for executive directors to be permitted on remuneration committees and involved in deciding their own pay: they will be tempted to make decisions that favour personal interests rather than those of shareholders. In Australia the corporate governance code was amended in 2010 to recommend a remuneration committee comprised of at least three non-executive directors including an independent chair and majority of independent members. Also the *Corporations Act* was amended in 2011 to prohibit executives from voting their shares in relation to the remuneration report and any related resolutions. These are measures designed to reduce the likelihood of 'managerial entrenchment' whereby top managers are able to 'capture' the board and influence their own salary package regardless of firm performance (Cambini et al. 2015).

Bebchuk and Fried (2004) argue that when remuneration schemes permit excessive reward this is not due to honest mistake or omission, rather it is the result of managerial influence over the design of pay arrangements, permitted by the overall structure of corporate governance systems. They argue that even independent directors are faced with social and psychological incentives that encourage them to allow remuneration practices that are not in shareholders' interests. Indeed, Gregory-Smith found no relationship between remuneration committee independence and CEO pay in his study of UK boards (2011). These incentives to over-pay are partly unconscious: because directors have been executives themselves they will have beliefs, friendships and loyalties that make it difficult to resist executive-serving compensation arrangements (Bebchuk and Fried, 2005). If this is the case, boards are no match for clever executives who will continue to find creative methods to add to their pay packets. There were a few interviewees in 2006 who agreed with this concept:

> The boards don't have the fortitude to withstand tough negotiations on salary packages – they get tied in to attract people. Although boards are getting more aware now. If you disclose at the time you can't be criticised at the end. So it's good to make it public from the start.
>
> *(Company secretary, ASX 100)*

In fact, there generally appeared to be a stronger concern amongst interviewees about losing key executives than about over-compensating executives. The answer to this lack of control at board level is perhaps to give shareholders more power over the issue, an idea put forward by Bebchuk and Fried in 2005 and since embraced by policy-makers.

Shareholder engagement

The most recent regulatory reforms attempt to provide shareholders with more than just knowledge of remuneration decisions by permitting them to vote on remuneration reports. The theory is that the combination of increased disclosure together with new voting powers may improve direct monitoring by shareholders (Ferrarini and Moloney 2004). The UK introduced a 'say on pay' vote for shareholders in 2002; Australia followed suit in 2005; and after a certain amount of international encouragement, the US introduced a similar provision via the *Dodd Frank Act* in 2010. Many European countries have also introduced say-on-pay laws, which vary in terms of the circumstances triggering a vote and the consequences of a negative vote (Stathopoulous and Voulgaris 2016). In many countries, the vote is non-binding; it enables shareholders to signal their support or disapproval of the remuneration policy of a company but does not prevent the remuneration policy from being implemented. The reasoning is that, although companies are not legally required to respond to a substantial vote against their remuneration policy, most organisations will be sensitive to shareholder opinion and will make changes. Also, the vote is seen to improve engagement between companies and shareholders prior to the AGM as companies attempt to gather support and pre-empt any problems by explaining their policies.

Nevertheless, following examples of companies receiving consecutive 'no' votes at their AGMs and appearing to be resistant to change, many countries have strengthened their laws. In most Scandinavian countries the vote is binding on companies and, in 2013, the United Kingdom amended its legislation to make votes binding – remuneration policies cannot be changed without shareholder approval. Also in 2013, a high-profile referendum in Switzerland resulted in increased powers for shareholders both in terms of remuneration and election of directors.

Australia has also implemented innovative changes to its say-on-pay legislation to give considerable power to shareholders. This was following lengthy consideration of the 'non-binding' nature of the vote by Australia's Productivity Commission in 2009. The Commission proposed a 'two strike' mechanism whereby two consecutive 'no' votes (each above 25 percent) would trigger a resolution putting the entire board of directors up for re-election. The government supported this proposal, and legislation was passed, which took effect from 1 July 2011. It provides a wonderful example of Braithwaite's concept of responsive regulation (mentioned in Chapter 3) where a hierarchy of increasingly stringent sanctions can be used to influence behaviour based on the response of the target (Braithwaite 2011). Although there has not yet been a case of a board spill, the regulation has certainly generated media and investor attention towards remuneration reports. In the 2015 AGM season approximately 9 percent of ASX 200 companies received a vote of more than 25 percent against their remuneration report (Featherstone 2015).

Opinions on the effectiveness of say-on-pay provisions vary. It is thought that even if the regulation does not rein in absolute pay it has forced boards to better explain their remuneration strategy to institutional investors and provide a clearer annual remuneration report. However, recent research on the 'two strike' mechanism shows that it does have the potential to curb excessive pay (Faghani et al. 2015). Australian companies that received a 'first strike' were found to have reduced one or more components of CEO pay and/or increased the proportion of performance-related pay (Faghani et al. 2015). Research in the UK found that pay increases had radically slowed in the two years following regulatory change (BIS 2015, p. 8).

Certainly, it seems companies are taking action in response to shareholder concerns, but they do not always feel that this is justified. The corporate community has criticised the 'two strike' mechanism on the basis that dissenting votes are used to punish companies suffering from challenging market conditions rather than being based on an objective assessment of executive remuneration (Thomas and van der Elst 2015). There may be an element of truth in this: recent research suggests that shareholders are more likely to express dissent in circumstances where the firm is performing poorly (Krause et al. 2014).

Discussion and conclusions

Although executive remuneration is a recurring feature of codes of corporate governance, it is a topic also regulated by a complex mix of hard law. Some of these laws set out rules regarding methods of remuneration, but a large proportion dictate reporting requirements. In general, although these laws make disclosure mandatory there is still a degree of discretion in the nature of disclosures provided. Thus the way in which they are drafted results in a similar effect to a comply-or-explain code. For example in the UK there is a legal requirement for companies to make a statement in their remuneration report regarding how workforce pay is taken into consideration when setting executive pay. As long as a company makes a statement of some sort it will be in compliance with the legislation, yet research has shown that there is considerable variety in the quality of these statements (BIS 2015). Some companies simply make a statement that relevant information has been considered, while others provide an explanation of exactly what this information comprises and how it has been used (BIS 2015, p. 28). This variety in the extent and scope of disclosure is a common finding in studies of disclosure-based regulation worthy of further research (Spira and Page 2010). We do not know what motivates companies to go further than the minimum level of disclosure and whether it brings benefits. It may be an example of an 'action-cycle' as described by Weil et al. (2006) whereby the information is first embedded into the decision-making behaviour of information-users (investors), which in turn causes changes in the behaviour of information-disclosers (companies).

The influence of codes of corporate governance in the overall regulation of executive remuneration is hard to separate from these other forms of harder regulation. In some ways the early code provisions paved the way for increased legislation after they failed to have a significant impact on pay levels. Research in the UK suggested that the Cadbury code was unsuccessful at making executive pay more sensitive to firm performance (Girma et al. 2007). Indeed, since code provisions were introduced there have been at least two economic downturns where corporate collapses have revealed seemingly excessive pay in circumstances of firm failure.

Nevertheless, the findings of this research suggest that codes have not been entirely useless. They were not really intended to significantly adjust pay levels; instead their aim was to provide structures and processes to permit improved board control over managerial pay as well as increased transparency. In this sense codes can be seen to be successful: in 2012 all ASX 100 companies had a remuneration committee and, of those, approximately 98 percent were comprised of a majority of independent directors and an independent chair (Grant Thornton 2012). A similar story is seen in other jurisdictions showing that code provisions on remuneration committees have helped boards to gain a level of power over executives that may not have been so easily achieved in the past. Interviewees explained that code provisions give directors 'something to point at' when trying to ensure their separation from management, particularly in smaller firms. Although this power may not have significantly reduced executive pay there is certainly no evidence that it has made matters worse (Conyon and Peck 2012). Code provisions also make directors more accountable for executive pay, and there are some suggestions that engagement between board and investors over remuneration is steadily increasing. In the UK, 93 percent of chairmen provided a personal introduction to the remuneration report in 2014, whereas only 50 percent did this in 2012. Overall, code provisions on board remuneration committees are an important piece in the executive remuneration puzzle. As seen in previous chapters the effects of corporate governance codes are subtle and slow, supported by other external forces. Certainly since the global financial crisis, board-remuneration committees have had a host of mechanisms to aid them in their task. With increasing shareholder involvement in remuneration policy their role will remain vital both as monitors and boundary spanners.

Summary of chapter 8

This chapter reviews the role of corporate governance codes in regulating executive remuneration. It explores the four ways in which executive remuneration is regulated: (1) through requiring disclosure in corporate reports; (2) by recommending or prohibiting particular remuneration practices; (3) ensuring board oversight of remuneration policy; and (4) permitting and encouraging shareholder engagement. Together these regulatory strategies have certainly made executive remuneration more transparent even if they have not yet significantly slowed the excessive growth in CEO pay. The role of the board in setting executive pay is important both in terms of its monitoring function and its institutional role in maintaining corporate legitimacy. Codes of corporate governance can help the board to overcome power asymmetries through stressing the need for a separation between board and management, vital when it comes to determining remuneration policy.

References

ACSI, 'CEO pay in ASX 200 companies: 13th Annual ACSI Survey of Chief Executive Remuneration', September 2014.

Australian Government, *Executive Remuneration in Australia*, Productivity Commission Inquiry Report, No. 49, 19 December 2009.

Bebchuk, L & Fried, J 2004, *Pay without Performance: the unfulfilled promise of executive compensation*, Cambridge: Harvard University Press.

BIS, 2015, *How Companies and Shareholders Have Responded to New Requirements on the Reporting and Governance of Directors' Remuneration*, Department for Business Innovation and Skills, BIS Research Paper Number 208, March 2015.

Braithwaite, J 2011, 'The essence of responsive regulation', *University of British Columbia Law Review*, vol. 44, p. 475.

Cambini, C, Rondi, L & De Masi, S 2015, 'Incentive compensation in energy firms: does regulation matter?', *Corporate Governance: An International Review*, vol. 23, no. 4, pp. 378–95.

Chalmers, K, Koh, P & Stapledon, G, 2006, 'The determinants of CEO compensation: rent extraction or labour demand', *The British Accounting Review*, vol. 38, pp. 259–75.

Cheffins, BR 2001, 'The metamorphosis of 'Germany Inc.' – the case of executive pay', *American Journal of Comparative Law*, vol. 49 pp. 525–28.

Chen, CR, Steiner, TL & Whyte, A 2006, 'Does stock option based executive compensation induce risk-taking? An analysis of the banking industry', *Journal of Banking and Finance*, vol. 30, pp. 915–45.

Cherry, MA & Wong, J 2009, 'Clawbacks: prospective contract measures in an era of excessive executive compensation and Ponzi schemes', *Minnesota Law Review*, vol. 94.

Clarke, T & Branson, D 2012 (eds.), *The SAGE Handbook of Corporate Governance*, London: SAGE.

Conyon, MJ & Murphy, KJ 2000, 'The prince and the pauper? CEO pay in the US and the UK', *Economic Journal of Finance*, vol. 110, p. 640.

Dittmann, I & Maug, E 2007, 'Optimal structure of executive pay', *The Journal of Finance*, vol. 62, no. 1, pp. 303–43.

Executive Remuneration Working Group, Final Report, July 2016.

Faghani, M, Monem, R & Ng, C 2015, ''Say on pay' regulation and chief executive officer pay: evidence from Australia', *Corporate Ownership and Control*, vol. 12, no. 3, pp. 28–39.

Farrell, S 2015, 'Boris Johnson swings his axe at 'gigantic sequoias' of FTSE 100' citing figures from the High Pay Centre, highpaycentre.org', Wednesday 7 October, the Guardian.

Featherstone T, *Two Strikes round one*, Morningstar, 17 December 2015.

Fels, A 2010, 'Executive remuneration in Australia', *Australian Accounting Review*, vol. 20, no. 1, pp. 76–82.

Ferrarini, G & Moloney, N 2004, 'Executive remuneration and corporate governance in the EU: convergence, divergence, and reform perspectives', *European Company and Financial Law Review*, vol. 3, pp. 251–339.

Filatotchev, I & Allcock, D 2010, 'Corporate governance and executive remuneration: a contingency framework', *Academy of Management Perspectives*, vol. 24, no. 1, pp. 20–33.

Geletkanycz, MA & Sanders, WG 2012, 'New directions on compensation and upper echelons', *Corporate Governance: An International Review*, vol. 20, no. 6, pp. 519–25.

Girma, S, Thompson, S & Wright PW 2007, 'Corporate governance reforms and executive compensation determination: evidence from the UK', *The Manchester School*, vol. 75, no. 1, pp. 65–81.

Grant Thornton, 2014, *Corporate Governance Review 2014: plotting a new course to improved governance*, Grant Thornton, UK.

Gregory-Smith, I 2012, 'Chief executive pay and remuneration committee independence', *Oxford Bulletin of Economics and Statistics*, vol. 74, no. 4, pp. 510–31.

Gregory-Smith, I & Main, B 2011, 'The executive labour market at work', University of Edinburgh Business School, Research Paper, September 2011.

Hill, J 2006, 'Regulating executive remuneration: international developments in the post-scandal era', *Journal of Corporate & Securities Law*.

Jensen, MC & Murphy, KJ 1990, 'CEO incentives – it's not how much you pay, but how', *Harvard Business Review*, May–June, pp. 21–23.

John, K, Saunders, A & Senbet, LW, 2000, 'A theory of bank regulation and management compensation', *Review of Financial Studies,* vol. 13, pp. 95–125.

Kirkpatrick, G 2009, Corporate Governance Lessons from the Financial Crisis, OECD.

Kleinman M, 2015, 'FTSE 100 bosses and executive pay review has share awards in its sights' City A.M., 10 September 2015.

Krause, R, Whitler, K & Semadeni, M 2014, 'Power to the principals! An experimental look at shareholder say-on-pay voting', *Academy of Management Journal,* vol. 57, pp. 94–115.

Kumar, P & Zattoni, A 2016, 'Executive compensation, board functioning and corporate governance', *Corporate Governance: An International Review,* vol. 24, no. 1, pp. 2–4.

Murray, W 2009, 'The role of company boards; are they to blame for excessive executive remuneration', *Australian Journal of Corporate Law,* vol. 23, pp. 178–94.

Romano, R & Bhagat, S 2009, 'Reforming executive compensation: focusing and committing to the Long-term', *Yale Journal on Regulation,* vol. 26, no. 2, pp. 359–72.

Sheehan, KM 2012, *The Regulation of Executive Compensation: greed, accountability and say on pay,* Cheltenham: Edward Elgar.

Stathopoulos, K & Voulgaris, G 2015, 'The importance of shareholder activism: the case of say-on-pay', *Corporate Governance: An International Review,* vol. 24, no. 3, pp. 359–70.

Thomas, RS 2003, 'Should directors reduce executive pay?', *Hastings Law Journal,* vol. 54, p. 437.

Thomas, RS & Van der Elst, C, 2015, 'Say on pay around the world', *Washington University Law Review,* vol. 92, no. 3, pp. 653–731.

The High Pay Commission, *Cheques with Balances: why tackling high pay is in the national interest.* Final report of the High Pay Commission.

9

CONCLUSIONS

Introduction

This book presents research that aims to contribute to both practical and academic understanding of corporate governance and its regulation, particularly the use of comply-or-explain codes of corporate governance. The previous four chapters have presented research into four areas of corporate governance: board evaluation; gender diversity; corporate responsibility and executive remuneration, each of which is regulated in whole or in part by comply-or-explain code provisions. This chapter aims to synthesise this research and compare it against some of the theories presented in Chapter 3. It reviews what the empirical evidence tells us about both the role of the board and the effect of soft regulation on board and organisational behaviour. In doing so the aim is to bring the theory and practice of corporate governance regulation closer together in circumstances where the gap has been widening (Aguilera and Cuervo-Cazzuro 2009).

The book draws on at least two areas of theory that are important in understanding the practical effectiveness of corporate governance regulation. The first is theory around the role of the board. If the objective of corporate governance regulation is to assist or increase the likelihood of the board fulfilling its role, it is important to have an understanding of what that role ought to involve. Management and legal scholars have put forward many, quite different theories about the role of the board. The only thing that emerges as clear is that it is a multi-faceted role, contingent on company circumstances. It can involve monitoring, advising, strategising, networking, reputation-building and boundary-setting as well as ensuring the organisation is accountable to its shareholders and wider stakeholders. This book presents evidence of the practical role of the board in large, listed companies and discusses its implications for both academic theory and regulatory policy.

The second area of theory comprises the ideas behind contemporary regulatory mechanisms. All regulation has the aim of restricting and/or encouraging certain behaviours. Regulatory theories help us understand how different types of regulation impact on behaviour and how regulation can be designed to maximise effectiveness. Corporate governance is regulated by a wide variety of mechanisms ranging from strict command-and-control legislation (backed by financial or criminal sanctions) to voluntary, self-imposed standards. This book presents evidence of the corporate response to specific recommendations of the Australian corporate governance code and in doing so throws light on the processes through which this kind of comply-or-explain regulation can influence and change behaviour. It provides evidence to test and build on some of the theories of soft regulation including responsive regulation, management-based regulation and meta-regulation (Baldwin et al. 2012).

The modern role of the board

The research findings can be compared against the multiple theories surrounding the role of the board of directors. As introduced in Chapter 3, these theories include, amongst others, agency theory, stewardship theory, stakeholder theory, resource-dependency theory and institutional theory. Many academics are coming to the conclusion that none of these theories can independently provide a full explanation of the role of the board and that there is a need for theoretical pluralism (van Eees et al. 2009; Lynall et al. 2003). The research findings presented here support such a conclusion suggesting that the role of the board is not only complex and multi-faceted but is dynamic, changes over time and is dependent on industry and market context. Broad economic theories that explain overall corporate purpose can be relevant to the role of the board as can detailed psychological theories about board dynamics. The research findings confirm the importance of the three levels of theory introduced in Chapter 3 but turn them upside down (see Figure 9.1) to represent the fact that it is board behaviour that is the leading factor in the fulfilment of both board roles and corporate purpose. The way the board interacts with management determines the information it receives and the level of strategic and advisory input management will accept. Board behaviour, conditioned by the institutional environment, also plays a role in determining the operating style of the board and the purpose of the corporation. It is up to the discretion of directors how to balance stakeholder interests, and to some extent it will be the board's personality as a group that determines how much influence external factors, such as short-term market pressures, will have upon their decision-making.

The evidence presented in this book suggests that the modern role of the corporate board is a collaborative one with dialogue the key to board effectiveness. This evidence supports and develops theories that see the board of directors as having a co-ordinating role and acting as a trustee for the corporation as a whole

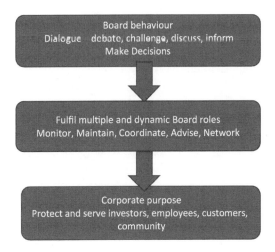

FIGURE 9.1 Levels of board theory.

and not just its shareholders (Blair and Stout 2001a; Lan and Heracleous 2010). Key findings regarding the role of the board are as follows:

- **The role of the board is changeable** depending on company size, maturity, ownership and industry. This confirms the need for flexibility in corporate governance regulation to enable companies to take a contingency approach to designing and updating their corporate governance structures and systems.
- **An effective board has a collaborative relationship** with management rather than acting primarily as a monitor or police force. It is the process of dialogue that enables the board to fulfil its multiple roles. This suggests recent reforms focused on independent monitoring and agency theory may be too narrow in their objectives.
- **An effective board builds trust** – between directors, between board and management and between company and stakeholders. This suggests that emerging theories of corporate governance based on social capital and relationships of trust may be of more assistance in developing future corporate governance regulation than agency theory.
- **The board is a co-ordinating body** – theories that put forward a role for the board in balancing the interests of all stakeholders appear to reflect modern reality more accurately than theories of strict shareholder primacy. Contemporary boards are taking more of a role in corporate responsibility strategy, although directors have always had to balance the interests of all stakeholders in the long-term interests of the company. Directors do not necessarily see this as corporate responsibility but as common sense in a world where there are heightened expectations regarding corporate behaviour, ever faster communication networks and diminishing natural resources.

The book assists the development of a behavioural theory of boards of directors as called for by van Ees et al. (2009). Their review paper challenges the dominant agency theory view of the board as a monitoring body by developing an alternative theoretical perspective: that of the board as a value-adding body, its main purpose to enable co-operation among the many stakeholders in a firm. Van Ees et al. explain that building a behavioural theory of boards requires accurate and precise description of what boards actually do in practice. This book has attempted to draw together descriptive evidence as well as theoretical understanding of board roles to assess the effectiveness of corporate governance regulation.

Changing role: flexible regulation

Lynall et al. point out that the changing role of the board over time means 'that it is not a question of *if* existing theories are helpful to our understanding of board and firm performance but a question of *when* each is helpful' (2003, p. 416). Roche's interviews with Canadian directors resulted in similar conclusions: he considered that regulatory emphasis on the monitoring function at the expense of the board's other functions was not likely to improve board effectiveness particularly at certain stages of an organisation's life cycle (2009, p. 174). As a consequence, corporate governance regulation should not be based solely on agency theory and an assumption that boards should be independent monitors, nor should it be based on resource dependency theory and only consider the skills and networks of directors. The changeable nature of the role of the board confirms the need for flexibility in corporate governance regulation and warns against regulation that prescribes board composition or board process. Chapter 5 demonstrates the need for flexibility in the process and timing of board-performance evaluations so that the process can be designed to take into account board longevity, and evaluations can be conducted when most needed.

Perhaps more importantly, it is not simply that corporate governance codes based on only one theory may be inappropriate but that they may impede successful transition from one stage of life to another. On the other hand, 'the right mix of governance functions may help the firm to overcome its strategic thresholds' (Filatotchev et al. 2006, p. 275). Filatotchev et al. concluded that corporate governance codes 'may focus on wealth protection issues in mature companies to the detriment of wealth creation in early stage companies and those companies needing to reinvent themselves' (2006, p. 273). Chapter 8 shows how the area of remuneration policy has recently been dominated by zealous risk management, which, although important for large systemic financial institutions, may not be so positive for small start-ups where it can hinder entrepreneurialism and innovation.

Chapters 5 and 6 demonstrate that although independence and diversity on boards are both important, there will be times and circumstances where other skills and director attributes are of more value to overall board effectiveness. This is noted in other studies with Filatotchev et al. commenting that 'in line with results from qualitative research, the number of external directors may matter less than the expertise of those directors' (2006, p. 273). Overall it seems that Lynall et al. (2003) are correct that the appropriate corporate governance structure (and the theory behind it) will differ as firm circumstances differ. The consequence of this for regulatory policy is that regulation ought to remain flexible, retaining the voluntary nature of any particular board composition or structure.

The collaborative role of the board

Chapters 5 and 7 also suggest that the contemporary role of the board in practice is not primarily as a monitor in the sense of a policing body to prevent management's misbehaving. Indeed, as recent corporate collapses demonstrate, if managers are intent on misbehaving it is very difficult for any board to prevent this, just as a police force cannot prevent all intentional crime. Although the presence of an active board will act as a deterrent to misbehaviour, the research finds that the board also plays a positive collaborative role involving guiding and advising management. The research supports an emerging view of the board of directors as active leaders rather than retrospective monitors. Charan et al. (2014) similarly suggests that the modern role of the board is to set strategy and manage risk in concert with the executives rather than standing guard and policing executive behaviour. They suggest that this new board role has emerged as a result of factors such as increased regulation, shareholder pressures and governance reforms that, although designed to strengthen board oversight, have also encouraged more active board leadership (Charan et al. 2014, p. 4). Although their book is primarily a practical guide for directors, its underlying premise, based on interviews with company leaders, is that the role of the board is changing, and governance models need to be redefined.

The concept of the board and management as a creative partnership is not a new one. When the American Law Institute, in 1983, proposed that all boards ought to have a majority of independent directors and set up audit, remuneration and nomination committees, this was strongly criticised as assigning a formal monitoring role that would impede or preclude their evolving role as a constructive participant (Brundy 1983). History shows that the role of the board has swung from a responsibility to manage the corporation in the 1940s and '50s, to a more passive role in overseeing management in the 1970s and '80s (Branson 2006; Gordon 2007). When this passive role was seen to have gone too far, reforms in the 1990s tried to strengthen the monitoring role. However this was not enough. After Enron and Worldcom there was effectively a call for boards to go back to a more active managing role. Yet, as Branson comments, modern corporations are much larger and more complex than they were in the 1950s, and there will be inherent limits in the ability of directors to actively manage in such situations (2006, p. 111). This is why the findings of Roberts et al. (2005) that place constructive dialogue at the heart of board effectiveness are so important. The modern board is highly reliant on management for information and therefore cannot monitor or advise without first creating an environment of open discussion and information sharing.

Chapter 5 finds that a positive relationship between board and management is fundamental to an effective, value-adding board. Indeed, a common outcome of the board-evaluation process is a desire to re-focus the board on strategy and reduce the time spent on compliance. Anderson et al. conducted an interview-based study of directors in Australia, Canada, New Zealand and the United States that similarly found 'a fundamental shift in the positioning of the board toward becoming a strategic partner to management' (2007, p. 780). This is an important finding as it supports stewardship theory rather than agency theory. It has implications for the design of corporate governance regulation, which in recent years has been strongly influenced by agency theory and a need for directors to monitor. If agency theory does not accurately explain the way boards function in practice, regulation should not be based on an agency theory view of the role of the board. Indeed, agency theory's portrayal of managers as self-interested maximisers and the board as the shareholders' force of private detectives is something to be avoided if the ultimate objective is a well-functioning firm. Monitoring behaviour on the part of non-executive directors implies a lack of trust whereas collaborative behaviour builds and strengthens trust.

Dialogue as the key to an effective board

The 2005 paper by Roberts et al. describes a study with similar objectives to this research: empirical work designed to better understand board effectiveness; work that was used to inform the reform of corporate governance regulation in the UK. Roberts et al. conducted 40 in-depth interviews with company directors as part of the UK government's Higgs review of the role of non-executive directors in corporate governance. They came to the belief that, although board structure and composition can condition or set the scene for an effective board, actual board effectiveness is determined by the behavioural dynamics of a board (2005, p. S11). Lorsch also conducted interview-based research and came to the conclusion that a board 'can execute its role successfully only if it develops and maintains a sound relationship with management' (2011, p. 186). This conclusion was based on 45 interviews with experienced directors of large complex organisations where one of the main hurdles to effective board functioning is making sure directors receive adequate information.

Chapter 5 confirms that cultural and behavioural dynamics are at the heart of board effectiveness. It finds that the characteristics of effective boards revolve around communication, debate and transparency rather than monitoring or specific skills. Chapter 6 refers to the positive impact that female directors can have on board dynamics and quality of decision-making. The research supports the conclusion by Roberts et al. that the lived experience of directors is not reflected in the theoretical division between agency (control) and stewardship (collaboration). Much of the academic literature posits an inherent conflict between these two roles whereas in practice, in a well-performing board, this conflict is not evident (Dallas 2003; Sundaramurthy and Lewis 2003). Roberts et al. suggest that this is because the same board processes or behaviours (challenging, questioning, discussing, informing, debating) are used to fulfil both roles: they enable independent directors to provide valuable input based on experience and also enable them to draw out information to maintain their own confidence in the conduct of management. Roberts et al. describe these behaviours as processes of accountability: 'rather than an awkward switching between control and collaboration, skilful accountability combines elements of both' (2005, p. S18).

Chapter 5 confirms that communication and collaboration are vital to board effectiveness. Importantly, there was no evidence of conflict between board roles, supporting the idea that the same board processes are behind different board functions. Directors do not have to switch between monitoring and advising, rather both roles are fulfilled through a bilateral process of communication. Arguably, the term 'accountability' fails to effectively reflect the two-way nature of these vital board processes, perhaps because (as Roberts et al. admit) we have been conditioned to think of accountability as drawing information out of a company in order to monitor rather than provide positive input (2005, p. S21). The term 'dialogue' is perhaps more appropriate and fits with the description of these processes as 'creating the conditions for dialogue' or a 'culture of openness' (Roberts et al. 2005, p. S19). It seems that processes fostering such an environment are the key to an effective board as depicted in Figure 9.2. Future research needs to explore these dialogue processes in more depth, testing the hypothesis that they are crucial to both the board's monitoring and performance roles.

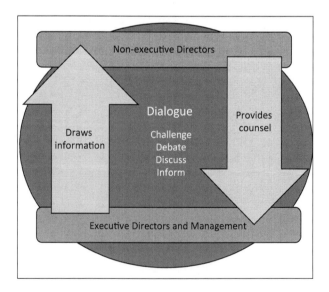

FIGURE 9.2 Dialogue as the key to board effectiveness.

The consequences of the centrality of dialogue for corporate governance regulation are subtle. The directors interviewed by Lorsch felt that board effectiveness, 'has little to do with regulators and laws and everything to do with what transpires within individual boards' (2011, p. 185). Based on a review of board research Huse (2005) also concludes that the crux of board effectiveness may be found in the board's decision-making culture. He refers to a Norwegian study that found openness and generosity, preparedness and involvement, creativity and criticality as important factors in board effectiveness (2005, p. S73). Chapter 5 shows that regulation can influence what transpires within individual boards. Indeed, Lorsch's conclusion that boards must define their own roles with precision and decide how to perform those roles supports regulation that encourages board-performance evaluation. If regulation can encourage or even force boards to go through this review process it may indirectly improve a host of other board processes.

Trust and the board

Roberts et al. (2005) explain that the outcome of dialogue processes working effectively is the building of a relationship of trust. Here their work links to Blair and Stout's important work on trust and trustworthiness (2001b). Blair and Stout (2001b) argue that effective co-operation between corporate participants is not facilitated by external constraints in law or contract but by internal constraints determined by social context. For example, it is not just the likelihood of receiving a bonus or promotion that determines a manager's actions but whether he or she feels obliged to co-operate with colleagues due to a sense of group identity. Chapter 8 confirms the importance of understanding the interaction between regulatory policy (for example around long-term incentive schemes) and human behaviour. This again shows the interplay between soft regulation (regarding remuneration policy) and norms (corporate culture). If a toxic culture is ingrained in an organisation then soft regulation will likely struggle to take effect (Gunningham and Sinclair 2009). Academic research into trust crosses many disciplinary boundaries but 'the majority of organizational scholars connect trust with highly positive effects on performance' (Lane 1998, p. 19). As with other aspects of corporate governance the effects of trust can be viewed both through an economic lens in terms of reducing agency costs (less need for monitoring) or through a behavioural or sociological lens as confirmation of common values and norms.

Scholars have explored the relationship between trust and law, concluding that legal regulation can contribute to the development and strengthening of trust (Lane 1998, p. 26). Blair and Stout conclude that 'without taking account of trust, we cannot fully comprehend or explain the substantive structure of corporate law, how it channels behavior or where its limits lie' (2001b, p. 1808). They suggest that a trust-building environment can be the crucial determinant of whether people shift from purely self-interested to other-regarding modes of behaviour. In other words, it can be culture that determines whether managers act as agents or stewards rather than the other way around. Chapters 7 and 8 demonstrate the role of remuneration systems in building culture through sending messages about the behaviours that are valued within the firm.

Schoorman et al. (2007) have explored organisational trust including the relationship between trust and control systems. They raise the point that if control systems are too strong, they can inhibit the development of trust. Chapter 5 provides evidence of the importance of trust in board effectiveness and its consequences for processes of board evaluation and director selection. The reluctance to conduct individual director evaluations and to search outside known networks for new directors is connected to concerns about negative effects upon trust and group dynamics.

The research findings support the idea of trust-building processes as being at the core of good corporate governance. What this means for regulation is that it should aim to encourage environments that foster trust and be wary of inhibiting trust development. Certainly the persistence of the old-boys network revealed by Chapters 5 and 6 can be seen as evidence of the need for trust amongst board members. Maintaining this trust, whilst also accessing the benefits of diversity, is a challenge that regulation needs to address. There is certainly an argument that use of flexible soft regulation to promote gender diversity rather than hard quotas is more likely to foster trust. Further research into the effects of corporate governance regulation on trust could yield valuable results in terms of board performance.

Trust is relevant to both internal corporate governance and external relationships. Chapter 7 shows that directors understand the need to gain the trust of external stakeholders – it is one of the reasons behind voluntary CSR reporting. Ntim et al. (2012) explore corporate governance disclosures in South Africa separating them into shareholder and stakeholder disclosures. They find that disclosures aimed at stakeholders can improve firm legitimacy and facilitate access to critical resources: an example of regulation that sets up trust-building processes.

However, the development of trust and legitimacy in personal relationships with external stakeholders is arguably more important than anything published in an annual report. Chapter 5 suggests that this kind of personal trust based on director reputations seems to trump the broader, impersonal trust arising from reliance on structures and systems such as corporate governance regulation. Fund managers still base their investment decisions on director profiles and their trust in those individuals rather than on annual report disclosures (Pye 2001, p. 42). This has implications for director selection and appointment because building a reputation takes time and is a hurdle that can be difficult to overcome. Research on female directors has shown that they often have contact with boards in their professional fields that builds the relationship of trust necessary for future appointment as a director (Klettner et al. 2016). Researchers have called for more investigation into how trust, both in and among the constituencies comprising the corporation, can be increased, including the possible impact of board gender diversity (Perrault 2015; MacLeod Hemingway 2007).

The mediating role of the board

Chapter 7 supports a theory of the board as a mediating or co-ordinating body that balances the needs of all stakeholders in order to maintain the productive coalition that is the firm (Blair and Stout 2001a). Thus it supports a stakeholder theory understanding of the role of the board. It confirms Marshall and Ramsay's empirical findings that this is how directors view their role (2012). Horrigan argues quite rightly that the shareholder versus stakeholder debate is distracting us from the more complex balancing task that corporate governance requires:

> To govern a corporation in a way which promotes sustainable corporate vi-ability and value in response to the risks, challenges, and opportunities gen-erated by financial concerns, politico-regulatory dynamics, socioeconomic factors and environmental interests is to govern in a way which frames those responsibilities beyond a simple dichotomy between shareholder and stake-holder interests. It responds to internal and external organisational pressures and dynamics which structure and influence corporate behaviour.
>
> (2002, p. 525)

For the most part, directors do not pursue a strict shareholder primacy approach when making decisions but take a common sense view that takes into account other vital stakeholders – employees, customers and local communities. Chapter 5 pro-vides examples of effective boards that are able to balance the interests of different stakeholders due to their independence. Here we see that although independence is thought to be necessary for the board's monitoring role it can also facilitate the board's mediating role. Chapter 7 finds that novel board structures and processes are being developed to formalise procedures for engaging with stakeholders and for incorporating their concerns into firm strategy. Although stakeholder engage-ment in a formal sense is a relatively recent development, interview evidence from 2006 shows that it has been a common sense approach to improving product quality or ease of access to resources for many years.

Comply-or-explain regulation

A second contribution of this book is to the literature on modern forms of reg-ulation. The trend away from traditional command-and-control laws to more flexible forms of regulation has been noted in many domains, but, as yet, we do not fully understand how these new forms of regulation work, their limits or effectiveness in different conditions (Coglianese and Lazer 2003; Aalders and Wilthagen 1997). As introduced in Chapter 3, there is not yet an agreed termi-nology for this kind of regulation with studies in the United States using the term 'new governance' or 'management-based regulation' and Australian schol-ars naming similar systems as 'responsive,' 'smart' or 'meta-regulation' amongst many other terms (Lobel 2004; Coglianese and Lazer 2003; Braithwaite 2011;

Gunningham and Grabosky 1998). This chapter will use the term 'soft regulation' on the basis it seems to be the broadest term encompassing most forms of contemporary regulation falling between command-and-control regulation and self-regulation (Lobel 2004). Baldwin et al. comment that 'these freshly developing agendas of regulation have not always gelled into highly coherent packages of policy or theory' (2012, p. 10).

The findings of this book contribute to some of the theories behind soft regulation by using the Australian corporate governance code as a case-study. As demonstrated in Figure 9.3, by comparing theory with practice, the book aims to contribute to three aspects of regulatory theory:

1 When to use soft regulation – the sorts of issues that it may be most effective at solving
2 Why it works – how it causes behavioural change
3 How to make it effective – incentives for voluntary action and their limits

The research presented in this book requires us to think of regulation in a new way. It builds on theories of norm-building through responsive regulation, which purposely permits flexibility in the manner of adoption, encouraging innovative solutions to complex problems (Majumdar and Marcus 2001). This kind of regulation, if backed up by the possibility of harder rules or sanctions and supported by institutional forces, can be effective at instigating behavioural and cultural change rather than superficial compliance. Key findings regarding soft regulation in the area of corporate governance are as follows:

- Soft regulation is suited as a means of regulating **complex situations** where variation in the nature of the targets means prescriptive regulation is unlikely to be effective. It can be used to encourage deeper social or **cultural change** rather than compliance-oriented behaviour.

FIGURE 9.3 Use of soft regulation.

- **Norm development** – Social norms and soft regulation work in parallel to reinforce and develop emerging practices.
- **Innovative solutions** – Soft regulation can trigger innovative and effective problem-solving by engaging targets in a responsive and flexible manner so that they use their knowledge to find a tailored solution.
- **Progress reporting** – Recommended practices can be internalised into organisational practice through processes of self-review and self-set objectives encouraged by public disclosure.
- **Balancing freedom and control** – Soft regulation will only be successful if there are **incentives** (positive or negative) that steer the targets towards the overall outcome desired by the regulator. These incentives may be built into a meta-regulatory framework directly through escalating sanctions for non-compliance or indirectly by tapping into other institutional forces such as investment markets or reputational concerns. An understanding of the interplay between soft regulation and institutional forces is essential to effective regulatory design.

Complex problems and cultural reform

First, the research findings support the general theory behind soft regulation, which is that it may provide a solution to problems that are too complex, dynamic or unpredictable for traditional hard-law approaches (Hess 2008, p. 450). Corporate governance as a whole can be said to fall into this bracket because of the variable and dynamic nature of corporate operations and financial markets. Chapters 6 and 7 show how soft law goes 'further than law' to influence behaviour in the grey area of business ethics and social responsibility. It can delve into areas where prescriptive regulation would be inappropriate because of variation in the nature of companies and their operations.

The research supports Ford and Hess's conclusion that new governance techniques have the potential to encourage 'a more meaningful process of corporate cultural reform than more traditional enforcement techniques' (2011, p. 513). These techniques can be used to tackle complicated social problems related to corporate behaviour such as lack of women in leadership and wider issues of corporate responsibility. As Hess states, 'the challenge the law faces is to... support internal change initiatives that may be unique to any particular corporation' (2008, p. 452). These could be operational changes to improve corporate governance and risk management or cultural change to improve gender diversity, occupational health and safety or environmental performance.

Chapter 6 presents evidence suggesting that the Australian Corporate Governance Code has been successful in triggering change management processes. The recent amendments regarding gender diversity include many of the steps that organisational scholars include in change-management theory: analysis of the need for change (measuring women across the workforce); strong leadership; and implementation and institutionalisation of success through formal policies, systems and structures (Todnem 2005). These code provisions have re-sulted in policies and procedures that, if implemented properly, could have a sig-nificant positive effect on women in the workforce at all levels of the organisation (Klettner et al. 2016). Chapter 5 shows that the Australian code has also helped to bring about acceptance and development of board-evaluation processes: another example of positive cultural change brought about by soft regulation. Chapter 7 shows how soft regulation has institutionalised CSR and its reporting, moving it from the margins to the mainstream. Lastly, Chapter 8 shows the complexities inherent in determining executive remuneration and understanding the effect of a chosen policy on different individuals and in different market circumstances. If designed with care, remuneration schemes have the potential to control risk and improve organisational culture.

Norm development

The research in this book shows that successful soft regulation both builds on and develops social norms. Regulation has an important role in initiating discourse around social norms thereby developing and refining those norms. As Fasterling comments 'the potential of compliance disclosure regimes lies in their capacity to trigger a communicative process' (2012, p. 27). Even if corporate governance codes are not always effective in terms of disciplining certain behaviours they still have value in triggering dialogue and norm development (Fasterling 2012).

A strong theme across all chapters is that corporate governance codes tend to formalise what large companies are already doing in the way of governance rather than presenting anything entirely new. For example, CSR and diversity commit-tees had begun to emerge prior to any regulatory changes as had the process of board evaluation. Voluntary behaviour is driven by both internal value and ex-ternal expectations and soft law reflects rather than dictates emerging behavioural norms. It may help to spread these practices from large listed companies to small and/or private entities, further entrenching norms of behaviour. The effects of soft law are gradual and subtle – incremental change rather than a sudden turn-around. As Chapter 6 discusses, the Norwegian gender quota for boards demonstrates that more dramatic change can be achieved using hard law with its deadlines and sanc-tions but that this kind of change may be more superficial. The same can be seen more generally across corporate governance and CSR with compliance-type reporting often missing the fundamental problems in favour of ticking boxes.

Thus norms and soft regulation work in parallel, each reinforcing the other. This was seen clearly in Chapter 6 where the emerging international norm of including women on corporate boards is being encouraged by the ASX code as well as a wealth of other initiatives set up by governments and not-for-profits. Chapter 7 confirms that, despite there being very little regulatory guidance in Australia with regard to corporate responsibility, most large listed Australian companies are voluntarily developing strategies towards becoming more sus-tainable. It presents evidence that companies are formalising these strategies by embedding them within existing corporate governance systems. The link between norms, soft regulation and theories of organisational isomorphism becomes apparent through the uptake of CSR reporting (DiMaggio and Powell 1983). Kingsford Smith claims that the normative force of soft regulation can be seen from the fact that many companies follow its standards, believing it to have no legal effect but acknowledging in their public documents that they accept its obligations (2012, p. 403). Supporting the theory of Aguilera et al., the research shows that by building on emerging norms, soft regulation can encourage corporations to be 'agents of social change' (2007, p. 836).

It is in the area of CSR and remuneration policy that the influence of international initiatives can be seen most clearly. Chapter 7 shows that the GRI guidelines are having a strong effect on the behaviour of Australian corporations and are filling the gaps left by Australian law. Here is evidence supporting Bryan Horrigan's observation that 'non-binding CSR standards can have a normative effect on corporate activity' (2010, p. 28). Some of the reform agendas arising as a consequence of the global financial crisis have had a more direct effect on Australian regulation. Chapter 8 discusses the impact of G20 initiatives and the Financial Stability Board's *Principles for Sound Compensation Practices* on Australian regulation.

This international influence has been permitted by the huge technological advances that have been made over the last two decades enabling expansion of communication networks and markets. Laws in Norway have had a snowball effect around the world in terms of gender diversity on boards (Machold et al. 2013). Norway's quota for women on boards has undoubtedly influenced the response of Australian companies to the 2010 diversity recommendations. This quota and the fact that many other European countries have followed suit provide a clear demonstration that hard law approaches can be used when softer options fail to have the desired effect. The United States' more prescriptive approach to corporate governance regulation also influences Australian behaviour. This demonstration of what is seen as more onerous regulation makes the Australian approach appear reasonable and encourages engagement (Klettner et al. 2010, p. 174).

Thus international developments work both to develop norms of behaviour and condition regulatory responses. Civil society expects our companies to meet emerging global norms, for example with regard to human rights, child labour, environmental protection and gender equality. Corporations will watch carefully any regulatory developments overseas and try to avoid strict regulation by voluntarily taking steps in that direction (von Nessen 2003).

Innovative, effective, tailored solutions

The findings of this book support theories of soft regulation that predict that by delegating problem-solving to the targets of regulation, effective solutions can be found. The idea is that because targets have greater knowledge about their operations than the regulator, they are more likely to be able to find the most cost-effective solution (Coglianese and Mendelson 2010). They may also perceive their own rules as more reasonable than those imposed by outsiders and therefore be more likely to comply with them. Coglianese and Mendelson describe the theoretical rationale for new governance regulation as a process of shifting discretion about how to regulate, from the regulator to the target. This mechanism is designed to encourage organisations to manage themselves in a way that aligns with public goals whilst permitting them flexibility in how to do this (Coglianese and Lazer 2003). This book confirms the benefits of soft regulation in the field of corporate governance: first, companies are best placed to understand and implement cost-effective governance structures; second, they see comply-or-explain corporate governance regulation as reasonable and, in most circumstances, of value to the corporation. The research also acknowledges the limitations of soft regulation: confirming the need for some sort of hierarchy whereby companies know that if they do not engage, there is a risk of more stringent requirements from regulators or other consequences emanating from civil society.

Chapter 5 demonstrates that by permitting flexibility through the comply-or-explain mechanism, the Australian corporate governance code enables companies to tailor their board composition to the needs of the company. Chapter 6 demonstrates that by giving companies the scope to set their own organisation-specific gender targets, the ASX recommendations have permitted innovative change towards the overall policy objective of increasing gender diversity. Firms are setting up training programs as well as reviewing pay equity and leave policies in order to better understand, and one hopes mitigate, the barriers to female career progression. Chapter 7 demonstrates increasing integration of CSR into corporate operations such that each company focuses on the areas where it has potentially harmful impact. Some companies are putting in place better programs for health and safety at work whereas others are improving customer service or environmental performance. Chapters 7 and 8 show how the power of remuneration incentives can be tailored to encourage sustainability rather than short-termism. Majumdar and Marcus have pointed out that 'when those who implement requirements play an active role in their design, the results are better', partly because of their greater knowledge of the target company but also because of a feeling of ownership (2001, p. 171). Through encouraging design of tailored solutions by managers within companies the ASX recommendations tap into local expertise and foster creative solutions to wider social and environmental problems.

Based on the evidence presented in this book, the term 'management-based regulation' may be the most appropriate in describing how corporate governance codes actually change behaviour. They permit internalisation of corporate governance practices in a customised fashion. Indeed, Kingsford Smith places behavioural change as the most compelling reason for corporate governance guidelines – the fact that they 'might help good governance practices to be internalised in the corporation's everyday operations' (2012, p. 399). This is exactly what this book suggests can happen, particularly if recommendations are designed accurately with this objective in mind.

Self-review and progress reporting

Code recommendations that encourage self-review and assessment can be some of the most effective at causing behavioural change. Chapter 6 on diversity shows that the need to measure diversity, set targets and then report on progress against them has triggered innovative programs and initiatives that permeate the whole organisation. The FSB remuneration principles also place the onus on companies to identify their 'major risk takers' and put in place plans to manage them.

Coglianese and Lazer (2003) analyse the types of situations where a regulator ought to regulate both the planning of a policy and its implementation. They conclude that a need to regulate both stages is the most likely scenario but also the most demanding for the regulator. This book confirms the importance of regulatory involvement in both planning and implementation and suggests that to be effective, corporate governance regulation should expressly aim to set up processes of monitoring and review such that practices are not established and forgotten but regularly reviewed, updated and maintained. However, in contrast to Coglianese and Lazer's view, this review of corporate governance codes shows that this objective can be achieved through well-designed disclosure-based regulation and does not have to involve demanding inspection regimes on the part of the regulator. Chapter 6 demonstrates that regulation designed to incorporate public-progress reporting, in this case progress towards diversity targets, may be enough. Chapter 7 shows that CSR reporting is following the same strategy by encouraging measurable targets and reporting on progress towards them. For example the Global Compact requires companies to report annually on progress towards their sustainability goals. The same conclusion was reached in Chapter 5 – if board-performance evaluation is to be effective there must be some disclosure confirming the fact that outcomes were followed up and implemented. This amounts to a form of responsive regulation where disclosure is not only for the benefit of investors and stakeholders but is designed to satisfy the regulator that further action is unnecessary. Knowledge of the need to satisfy the regulator may be enough to encourage systems and processes that ensure implementation. For example, Chapters 7 and 8 both demonstrate the beginnings of a practice of tying the achievement of CSR or diversity goals to executive remuneration.

The two purposes of disclosure

Chapter 3 introduced the three main purposes of corporate governance disclosures: (1) securing corporate accountability to stakeholders; (2) enabling better investment decisions and smooth-running capital markets; (3) indirectly encouraging behavioural change (Spira and Page 2010). Although disclosure of corporate information is primarily for the benefit of external interested parties, it can also affect behaviour within a firm. Spira and Page point out that 'the knowledge that disclosure is required may have an earlier and equally important effect on management behavior' (2010, p. 411). Coglianese and Lazer (2003) accept that some forms of disclosure-based regulation have behavioural change as a purpose and therefore fall within the category of management-based regulation. As they state, 'the gathering of information is, after all, a necessary step in any management or planning process' (2003, p. 695). This is demonstrated by Chapter 6, which shows that the process of extracting and measuring gender metrics for disclosure can provide benefits to a company internally. As Spira and Page comment:

> There are two principal motives for requiring companies to disclose information about their risk management and internal control: either regulators want the company to improve its risk management and internal control, or they want the company to give more information to financial markets, or both.
>
> (2010, p. 415)

This book reviews code recommendations that combine these different purposes in that they are aimed at improving internal corporate governance as well as improving flow of information to external stakeholders. In fact, most of the recommendations of the Australian Corporate Governance Code have two objectives – they suggest changes to internal corporate governance practices and suggest disclosure of these practices. Chapter 5 demonstrates this dual purpose in relation to board-performance evaluation. Although the wording of the code focuses on disclosure of the process used to evaluate board performance, the real value of the recommendation has been to encourage and entrench the norm of regular performance evaluation into corporate practice. In their 2012 review Boardroom Partners concluded that the Australian code ought to be clearer on the distinction between 'doing and disclosing', a suggestion that was taken account of in the 2014 edition of the Principles.

It seems that the Australian corporate governance code has been effective at causing organisational change but less successful at enabling better investment decisions. This may not matter. Instead of seeing information disclosure as reading material for investors we perhaps ought to view it as a process that initiates internal change:

> Studies of disclosure tend to focus on the readily observable—the content of the disclosures themselves—rather than the behavioural effects in corporate policies and processes which disclosure is intended to secure but which are far more difficult to assess.
>
> (Spira and Page 2010, p. 411)

Kingsford Smith (2012) cites similar advantages for soft regulation in general: it can set specific standards, has an educative role and can be internalised in organisational practice. This book confirms all of these advantages: the Australian corporate governance code, particularly its recommendations that encourage on-going processes rather than one-off structures, can have a strong and positive effect on behaviour within corporations.

The challenge of incentive: balancing freedom and control

The primary problem for soft regulation is one of incentive. Although targets may have the information to craft solutions to regulatory problems, they may not always have the incentive to spend time and money doing so. The challenge is to ensure that targets use the discretion afforded them in ways that are consistent with public regulatory goals rather than their own private interests (Coglianese and Mendelson 2010). If regulation is voluntary, with no sanctions for non-compliance, there have to be other incentives at work to encourage behavioural change.

By advocating the benefits of good corporate governance – improved efficiency, reputation, performance, investment – codes of good governance have tried to find a win-win situation where companies choose to implement the recommendations in order to provide performance benefits to their investors and wider stakeholders (corporate objective) and at the same time, are run better, reducing the likelihood of collapse and economic damage (public regulatory objective). What can be seen from drawing together the different chapters of this book is that the end-result in terms of corporate behaviour is influenced by many things, only one of which is the introduction of corporate governance recommendations. Others include market pressures, social norms and institutional expectations.

Further research will be required to understand if the cultural changes and associated increases in gender diversity observed in Chapter 6 are limited only to companies with a 'natural interest' in diversity or high social visibility (Aalders and Wilthagen 1997). Chapter 7 shows that the development and dissemination of international standards of corporate responsibility reporting have helped to fuel what will hopefully amount to meaningful cultural change towards long-term sustainability and more ethical corporate cultures. Of course this apparent progress may amount only to 'enlightened self-interest' where the extent of responsibility is limited to situations where social objectives overlap with corporate objectives (Vogel 2005). For example, companies may only act responsibly if they perceive a financial risk in being irresponsible, perhaps loss of customers due to a tainted reputation. This kind of reputational risk may only apply to large retailers with an established brand and not to smaller companies in a supply chain that have less need for a public profile.

Where the 'business case' for corporate responsibility is weak there is an argument that stronger regulation may be necessary. Indeed, Hess (2008) is very sceptical at the ability of purely voluntary corporate social reporting to create meaningful improvement in corporate sustainability, suggesting that what companies say can be decoupled from what they actually do. Every time a corporate scandal arises, this scepticism is validated. Hess suggests making basic reporting mandatory thereby forcing all firms to report on standardised indicators rather than relying on a business case. This would prevent strategic disclosure of only positive information but would not prevent firms from voluntarily disclosing over and above the minimum standard. This seems to be the route in which we may be heading with Europe's new Directive on non-financial reporting, yet it runs the risk of encouraging box-ticking rather than intelligent engagement.

Braithwaite's theory of responsive regulation and regulatory pyramids provides a commonly used solution to finding the balance between flexibility and control. Only if targets fail to reach a certain level of compliance or performance will stricter regulatory sanctions be imposed. The theory of responsive regulation stresses the importance of regulation that is perceived as legitimate and fair (Braithwaite 2011). Seidl et al. (2013) refer to the responsive nature of codes of corporate governance in their discussion of how codes can be reviewed to amend or strengthen controversial recommendations. Every time the Australian code has been amended there has been a public consultation process around the proposed changes to ensure a balanced and fair outcome that takes into account the concerns of all stakeholders. This type of participatory process has also been termed 'restorative justice', whereby all stakeholders investigate and come to an understanding of the reasons behind past injustice or harm and agree on a set of reforms to prevent recurrence and instigate repair (Braithwaite 2011).

Of course the potential for strengthened or more stringent requirements can be seen as a regulatory sanction. Certainly, this research finds that the threat of stronger regulation is an effective incentive to comply with existing requirements. Awareness of the stringent requirements of the United States SOX Act has tended to make companies view the Australian code in a favourable light. In the same way, awareness of the introduction of quotas for women on boards in Europe has encouraged compliance with the more flexible requirements of the ASX code. What we see are changing norms and expectations at an international level that impact on behaviour at a national level.

Aguilera and Cuervo-Cazzuro (2009) point out that the effectiveness of a corporate governance code is likely to depend on the nature of the issuer of the code (government, stock exchange or investor association etc.) as this will affect both code content and enforceability. Similarly Kingsford Smith comments that it is the fact that corporate governance regulation operates in connection with state law (the meta-regulatory nature of the overall system) that gives it strength. It is the degree to which soft regulation operates in the shadow of the state or in tandem with state law that mitigates some of its usual drawbacks (Kingsford Smith 2012, p. 380). In other words it is the multi-level, meta-regulatory nature of the system that makes it effective: the ability to escalate matters through a hierarchy of increasingly stringent regulation as shown most clearly by the 'two strike' rule for remuneration reports.

Understanding institutional forces

The effectiveness of soft regulation lies in understanding the institutional forces at play and making sure that they provide the right incentives and do not work against the regulatory objectives. This is a difficult task. Indeed, Julia Black describes the relationship between regulatory rules and market behaviour as 'a complex dance in which market behaviour and regulatory action shadow, anticipate, and react to each others' moves in turn' (2010, p. 166). This book discusses the fact that the market forces that the designers of corporate governance codes had hoped to tap into have not always interacted with the regulation exactly as expected. First, investors do not engage as actively as expected, yet a need for legitimacy (in whose eyes we are not sure) seems to encourage uniform compliance.

As Kingsford Smith comments, 'although the ASX Principles could be a powerful corporate governance mechanism, the hurdle is investor cost of identifying company underperformance and mounting any action' (2012, p. 397). MacNeil and Li (2006) provide evidence of a 'comply or perform' reality where shareholders are not concerned about how their companies are governed provided that they are performing well financially. As introduced in Chapter 4, Keay (2014) also notes lack of investor engagement around corporate governance disclosures, and on this basis he claims that corporate governance codes are not effective. Spira and Page's (2010) research again found that investors do not find corporate governance statements useful in making investment decisions. The value of such statements is seen only as an audit report or checklist where absence of a disclosure would be noted. In fact, it may be that investors see disclosures only as a starting point for discussion rather than the sum of information to be disclosed, in which case there is little incentive for companies to provide high-quality detailed corporate governance information. Perhaps the main value of disclosure is in the thinking and board discussion that precedes the making of any public statement. Spira and Page suggest that it may not matter that statements tend towards boilerplate because 'the form and content of the disclosure may be less important than the internal process by which the disclosure is produced' (2010, p. 429). To keep the process active, regulation needs to encourage reporting of progress or change rather than static structures or processes.

Second, several scholars argue that the flexibility provided by codes of corporate governance is not used by companies in practice due to institutional pressures to conform. Hooghiemstra and van Ees examined the corporate response to the Dutch comply-or-explain corporate governance code. They found that companies tended to comply with the code or confine themselves to accepted arguments to explain non-compliance. (Hooghiemstra and van Ees 2011, p. 480).

Research has provided evidence of this pressure to comply but suggests this was a temporary phenomenon, triggered in part by ratings agencies, which lessened over time as the corporate community became more familiar with the comply-or-explain concept (Klettner et al. 2010). In the framework of meta-regulation, although the regulator intended to confer discretion on corporations this was taken away by other external forces. The ASX Corporate Governance Council took steps to educate both companies and investors on the option of non-adoption of the code recommendations after its own survey revealed this early pressure to conform. In South Africa, following similar problems, the third edition of the corporate governance code introduced an 'apply-or-explain' mechanism instead of comply-or-explain. This book demonstrates that Australian companies have developed corporate governance structures specific to their organisation, for example, in the area of board sub-committees. Over time the market's understanding of the regulation appears to have become more sophisticated, thereby permitting companies to be more unique in their application of code principles.

Hooghiemstra and van Ees might disagree with this last proposition. They argue that the increased use of the option of 'explaining' rather than 'complying' only demonstrates a process whereby non-conforming explanations also become standardised. They use institutional theory to explain that external pressures – expectations of compliance and a need to maintain legitimacy – are enough to motivate high levels of code adoption. Over time, certain 'explanations' also become accepted and therefore legitimate, meaning these deviations from compliance become more common but also more uniform – a standardisation of non-standard corporate governance practices. Further research would have to be carried out to explore whether the findings of this book support Hooghiemstra and van Ees' conclusion, for example, whether the non-recommended committees revealed in Chapters 6 and 7 adhere to some form of uniformity; however, it seems more likely that the pressure to conform has genuinely lessened.

Institutional isomorphism or standardisation in response to disclosure-based regulation can also be seen in the use of 'boilerplate' disclosures. 'Boilerplate' is a term used in a legal context to mean standard terms and conditions that can be inserted without change into a wide variety of documents. Certainly this research found examples of boilerplate disclosures, also identified by Spira and Page, 'we observe that the format and content of such disclosures may converge into a standardised boilerplate' (2010, p. 411). In the UK the Financial Reporting Council described its 2010 changes to the Corporate Governance Code as fighting the 'fungus of boilerplate'. The UK code now asks Chairmen to include a personal discussion of risk-management procedures in annual reports rather than resorting to standard statements. Spira and Page point out that:

> While the use of 'boilerplate' has generally been deplored, there has been little analysis of why it occurs and whether it is an inevitable result of the 'disclosure as regulation' process.
>
> (2010, p. 417)

One method that appears to help reduce boilerplate and produce engaging disclosure is to design corporate governance codes to include forward-looking provisions that monitor implementation, for example the diversity recommendations that require reports on companies' progress towards achieving targets. This forces companies to look ahead and sets up a process of review that keeps implementation plans alive and moving.

Final points

The aim of this book was to explore the effectiveness of corporate governance codes, not through compliance levels, but by assessing whether and how they can encourage positive changes in corporate behaviour. This is where the research differentiates itself by taking an inter-disciplinary approach. It does not take a purely legal view of compliance but incorporates management theories on the role of the board of directors and how regulation might improve fulfilment of this role. It examines qualitative evidence of the changes being put in place within corporations and the role of information disclosure in encouraging such changes. It reveals the influence of codes of corporate governance in improving board performance, increasing gender diversity, integrating sustainability and monitoring executive pay. Good corporate governance has both economic and public interest benefits – it improves firm performance and efficiency and acts to protect our superannuation investments and our interests as employees and customers of corporations.

As explained in Chapter 2, one aim of corporate governance regulation is to create the internal structures and processes necessary for good corporate governance, thereby reducing the risk of corporate failure. Another aim is to improve information flow out of the company to improve transparency and investor confidence. The findings of this research suggest that the Australian corporate governance code has been successful at improving companies' internal corporate governance structures even though investor engagement with information disclosure has not functioned entirely in the way intended. Weil et al. (2006) explain how policies based on information disclosure are only effective when information becomes embedded in the decision-making action cycle. This is not always easy to achieve because information users tend to make decisions based on 'satisficing' behaviour, that is, they seek out enough information to make satisfactory rather than optimal decisions (Weil et al. 2006).

In terms of regulatory theory the research finds that modern forms of layered meta-regulation, whereby voluntary action is supported by potentially stricter measures, can be remarkably effective. Understanding the interplay between soft regulation and its institutional environment is not always easy yet is essential to effective policy-making. Voluntary regulation relies on tapping into this institutional environment to provide incentives for desired behaviour. In the case of corporate governance codes, emerging norms of practice and wider stakeholder expectations provide a strong influence. Codes tend to build on and reinforce emerging norms of behaviour and entrench them into corporate culture through a slow process of change management.

Regulation that incorporates a level of flexibility is appropriate in complex situations where uniformly applied prescriptive regulation could have negative effects. Both corporate governance and CSR mean different things to different companies depending on their stage of life-cycle, organisational structure and industry. Forcing companies to set up specific governance committees or report on a list of environmental measures would, for many companies, amount to an expensive compliance exercise with no improvement to the running of the company or its responsibility. On the other hand tailored implementation of corporate governance regulation can not only reduce risk but enhance board and wider organisational performance.

The book concludes that codes of corporate governance should maintain their flexibility but should be clearer on how recommended structures and processes are envisioned to lead to better governance. Chapters 5 to 8 demonstrate that at the heart of most corporate governance recommendations is an assumption that if the recommendation is carried out it will assist the board in fulfilling a certain role. Indeed, the UK Corporate Governance Code clearly states that its function is to help boards discharge their duties in the best interests of their companies (FRC 2012). However, the connection between each recommendation and improved board function is not always clearly explained or empirically tested in terms of the circumstances necessary for it to be effective. It is important for company officers to understand the reasoning behind each recommendation and go through a process of assessing whether this reasoning holds true for their corporations.

This could be enabled by linking recommended corporate governance practices more clearly to the theoretical board roles of monitoring, advising, setting culture or accessing resources. For example, empirical evidence is mounting regarding the kinds of circumstances where independent board members add value to decision-making and contexts where other board characteristics are more important (Matolsky et al. 2004). This sort of discussion should be included in commentary to code provisions, much like the discussion of the reduced efficiency gains of committees for small boards. As Hooghiemstra and van Ees (2011) point out, most codes do not indicate legitimate arguments for deviation, which may be one of the reasons companies tend to take the easier route of adoption. Equally, where the aim of regulation is information disclosure, there needs to be clarity around the purpose of disclosure and what is expected – is it to allow investors to understand the workings of the company, to check that there are minimum structures in place, or to initiate internal change? On the basis that enforcement by the investment market may be limited, regulators can encourage implementation by requesting regular progress reporting.

The findings regarding the collaborative role of the board have practical implications for corporate governance regulation as they suggest that recent regulatory emphasis on strengthening the board's monitoring role should be treated with caution. Excessive control can be self-defeating, fostering the exact behaviours that it aims to stamp out. An important finding of this research is that regulatory content should aim to encourage processes of open dialogue and the development of trust among board members, management and external stakeholders. Designing regulation to achieve this is more difficult than regulation aimed at more specific and measurable objectives such as increased independence or financial skills, yet the research reveals several examples of how it might work. These include disclosure systems that include progress reporting; board evaluation processes; and remuneration policies that foster collaboration.

The role of the board at any particular time is influenced by the company's individual circumstances but also by common external contingencies including the regulatory environment. Corporate governance structures and processes can be imposed/suggested by outside influences (exogenous) or arise by choice or need internally (endogenous). If enhanced board performance is the ultimate objective of corporate governance regulation, policy-makers need to understand the endogenous factors and design regulation to build upon these rather than interfere with them. An effective corporate governance code ought to assist boards in fulfilling their multi-faceted and dynamic roles at the heads of the corporations by encouraging effective board processes and developing trust.

Future research

There is a pressing need for more research into how the role of the board is dependent on contingencies such as company size, industry and maturity. Research that explores how boardroom discussions or decisions relate to the board's different roles of monitoring, strategising, networking, co-ordinating and normalising would be of great value, especially if they could be related to different stages of the corporate life-cycle. Also more research is needed to test the theory that modern boards are adopting a more collaborative, mediating role than they may have in the past. It is a difficult area to research as actual board decisions and the factors that influence them will usually be confidential. However, directors can be asked about decision-making in a more general sense as Marshall and Ramsay (2012) did in their study. Case-studies of companies might also improve understanding of the practicalities of integrating corporate responsibility into governance systems This type of research should assist in developing practical guidelines for boards on how best to fulfil this balancing role when decision-making.

Research building on the work of Roberts et al. (2005) would also be very valuable, exploring information flow in and out of the boardroom and the role of dialogue in fulfilling board roles. Indeed, in the age of the Internet and constantly advancing communication technologies, it may be that board meeting agendas and minutes are no longer the mainstay of information flow. We may need to explore dialogue and accountability in the context of modern technology. On the other hand, this book suggests that active, challenging, old-fashioned debate and discussion are the keys to board effectiveness. Behavioural research exploring the impact of power and personality on these processes would be helpful in better understanding board effectiveness. Lastly, the role of trust in both internal and external governance relationships is an area fertile for further study. We know that trust improves performance but do not fully understand the factors that foster or inhibit trust and how they are affected by regulation.

Case-study research testing the effectiveness of soft regulation is essential for improving regulatory design and understanding the mechanisms through which behavioural change occurs. This does not mean taking specific companies as case-studies as traditionally done in management research, nor court cases in a legal sense. It means taking a piece of regulation as the subject of the case and exploring its effect in context (Weil et al. 2006). With regard to corporate governance further research is required to assess the behavioural response of companies to code recommendations. We need to ask governance professionals why it is that they respond the way they do and the value that they see in specific structures or practices. Research that focuses on the narrow objectives of a specific recommendation can throw light on the detailed mechanisms of how regulation has practical impact. Equally, the broader picture is important: placing corporate governance regulation in the context of wider legal, political and social trends.

An interesting area for future research is to explore the limits of voluntary regulation. Lynall et al. (2003) demonstrate that path dependence on boards means that patterns of board composition tend to persist even when fundamental change is needed. They suggest further research is needed into how change can be precipitated through the institutional environment including through regulatory, cognitive and normative change. The way in which norms and culture interact with soft regulation appears to be vital in determining regulatory effectiveness: they can support the aims of regulation or completely defeat them. Soft corporate governance and CSR regulation is successful in areas of mutual benefit to corporations and society, for example, where cost savings can be found in more efficient and environmentally friendly manufacturing processes or where non-executive board members are a source of cheap professional advice. If regulation needs to go further than this, to force companies into actions that do not bring them obvious benefits, harder forms of law may still be necessary.

Summary of chapter 9

This final chapter draws together the research findings to come to conclusions on both the nature of the role of the board and the ways in which corporate governance codes can facilitate effective board function and organisational change. It finds that effective boards work with management in a collaborative manner involving constant dialogue that enables directors to both extract the information needed for monitoring and have positive input into strategy. Corporate governance systems are also starting to incorporate processes for communication with a wide range of stakeholders. This reflects the role of the board as a mediator, balancing stakeholder concerns and making decisions that serve the long-term interests of the company as a whole. Importantly these communication processes also build relationships of trust vital for effective corporate governance. The complex and changeable nature of the role of the board confirms the need for flexible regulation. The comply-or-explain mechanism works well at encouraging the adoption of effective governance procedures whilst leaving scope for adaptation to individual circumstances. By building on existing or emerging norms of practice, code provisions support a slow process of cultural change supported by external expectations. The process of public disclosure acts as an enforcement mechanism irrespective of market behaviour although external engagement certainly helps to set up a cycle of accountability and action.

References

Aalders, M & Wilthagen, T 1997, 'Moving beyond command-and-control: reflexivity in the regulation of occupational safety and health and the environment', *Law & Policy,* pp. 415–43.

Aguilera, RV & Cuervo-Cazurra, A 2009, 'Codes of good governance', *Corporate Governance: An International Review,* vol. 17, no. 3, pp. 376–87.

Aguilera, RV, Rupp, DE, Williams, CA & Ganapathi, 2007, 'Putting the S back in corporate social responsibility: a multilevel theory of social change in organisations', *Academy of Management Review,* vol. 32, no. 3, pp. 836–63.

Anderson, DW, Melanson, SJ & Maly, J 2007, 'The evolution of corporate governance: power redistribution brings boards to life', *Corporate Governance: An International Review,* vol. 15, no. 5, pp. 780–97.

Baldwin, R, Cave, M & Lodge, M 2012, *Understanding Regulation,* 2nd ed, Oxford: Oxford University Press.

Black, J 2010, 'Financial markets', in P Cane & H M Kritzer (eds.), *The Oxford Handbook of Empirical Legal Research,* Oxford: Oxford University Press.

Blair, MM & Stout, LA 1999, 'A team production theory of corporate law', *Virginia Law Review,* vol. 85, no. 2, pp. 248–328.

Blair, MM & Stout, LA 2001a, 'Corporate accountability: director accountability and the mediating role of the corporate board', *Washington University Law Quarterly,* vol. 79, pp. 403–47.

Blair, MM & Stout, LA 2001b, 'Trust, trustworthiness and the behavioural foundations of corporate law', *University of Pennsylvania Law Review,* vol. 149, pp. 1735–1810.

Braithwaite, J 2011, 'The essence of responsive regulation', *University of British Columbia Law Review,* vol. 44, p. 475.

Branson, D 2006, 'Too many bells? Too many whistles? Corporate governance in the post-Enron, post-Worldcom era', *University of South Carolina Law Review,* vol. 58, pp. 65–113.

Brundy, 1983, 'The role of the board of directors: the ALI and its critics', *University of Miami Law Review,* vol. 37, pp. 223–42.

Charan, R, Carey, D & Useem, M 2014, *Boards that Lead,* Boston: Harvard Business Review Press.

Clarke, RC 2005, 'Corporate governance changes in the wake of the Sarbanes Oxley Act: a morality tale for policymakers too', *Georgia State University Law Review,* vol. 22, pp. 251–312.

Coglianese, C & Lazer, D 2003, 'Management-based regulation: prescribing private management to achieve public goals', *Law & Society Review,* vol. 37, no. 4, pp. 691–730.

Coglianese, C & Mendelson, E 2010, 'Meta-regulation and self-regulation', in R Baldwin, M Cave & M Lodge (eds.), *The Oxford Handbook of Regulation,* Oxford: Oxford University Press.

Daily, CM, Dalton, DR & Cannella Jr, AA 2003, 'Corporate governance: decades of dialogue and data', *Academy of Management Review*, vol. 28, no. 3, p. 371.

Dallas, LL 2003, 'The multiple roles of corporate boards of directors', *San Diego Law Review*, p. 781.

DiMaggio, PJ & Powell, WW 1983, 'The iron cage revisited: institutional isomorphism and collective rationality in organizational fields', *American Sociological Review*, vol. 48, no. 2, pp. 147–60.

Fasterling, B 2012, 'Development of norms through compliance disclosure', *Journal of Business Ethics,* vol. 106, pp. 73–87.

Filatotchev, I, Toms, S & Wright M 2006, 'The firm's strategic dynamics and corporate governance life-cycle', *International Journal of Managerial Finance*, vol. 2, no. 4, p. 256.

Ford, C & Hess, D 2011, 'Corporate monitorships and new governance regulation: in theory, in practice and in context', *Law & Policy*, vol. 33, no. 4, pp. 509–41.

Gordon, JN 2007, 'The rise of independent directors in the United States, 1950–2005: of shareholder value and stock market prices', *Stanford Law Review*, vol. 59, pp. 1465–1568.

Gunningham, N & Grabosky, P 1998, *Smart Regulation,* Oxford: Clarendon Press.

Gunningham, N & Sinclair D 2009, 'Organizational trust and the limits of management-based regulation', *Law & Society Review*, vol. 43, no. 4, pp. 865–900.

Hess, D 2008, 'The three pillars of corporate social reporting as new governance regulation: disclosure, dialogue and development', *Business Ethics Quarterly*, vol. 18, no. 4, pp. 447–82.

Hooghiemstra R & van Ees, H 2011, 'Uniformity as response to soft law: evidence from compliance and non-compliance with the Dutch corporate governance code', *Regulation & Governance*, vol. 5, pp. 480–98.

Horrigan, B 2002, 'Fault lines in the intersection between corporate governance and social responsibility', *University of New South Wales Law Journal*, vol. 25, no. 2, pp. 515–55.

Horrigan, B 2010, *Corporate Social Responsibility in the 21st Century: debates, models and practices across government law and business*, Cheltenham: Edward Elgar Publishing.

Huse, M 2005, 'Accountability and creating accountability: a framework for exploring behavioural perspectives of corporate governance', *British Journal of Management*, vol. 16, pp. S65–S79.

Keay, A 2014, 'Comply or explain: in need of greater regulatory oversight', *Legal Studies*, vol. 34, no. 2, pp. 279–304.

Kingsford Smith, D, 2012, 'Governing the corporation: the role of 'soft regulation', *University of New South Wales Law Journal*, vol. 35, no. 1, pp. 378–403.

Klettner, A, Clarke, T & Adams, M, 2010, 'Corporate governance reform: an empirical study of the changing roles and responsibilities of Australian boards and directors', *Australian Journal of Corporate Law*, vol. 24, pp. 148–76.

Klettner, A, Clarke, T & Boersma, M 2016, 'Strategic and regulatory approaches to increasing women in leadership: multilevel targets and mandatory quotas as levers for cultural change', *Journal of Business Ethics*.

Lan, LL & Heracleous, L 2010, 'Rethinking agency theory: the view from law', *Academy of Management Review*, vol. 35, no. 2, pp. 294–314.

Lane, C 1998, 'Introduction: theories and issues in the study of trust', in C Lane & R Bachmann, *Trust within and between Organizations: Conceptual Issues and Empirical Applications*, Oxford: Oxford University Press.

Leblanc, R & Schwartz, MS 2007, 'The black box of board process: gaining access to a difficult subject', *Corporate Governance: An International Review*, vol. 15, no. 5, pp. 843–51.

Lobel, O 2004, 'The renew deal: the fall of regulation and the rise of governance in contemporary legal thought', *Minnesota Law Review*, vol. 89, p. 342.

Lorsch, JW 2011, 'Board challenges 2009', in W Sun, J Stewart & D Pollard (eds.), *Corporate Governance and the Global Financial Crisis: international perspectives*, Cambridge: Cambridge University Press.

Lynall, MD, Golden, BR & Hillman, AJ 2003, 'Board composition from adolescence to maturity: a multitheoretic view', *Academy of Management Review*, vol. 28, no. 3, p. 416.

Machold, S, Huse, M, Hansen, K & Brogi, M 2013, *Getting Women on to Corporate Boards: a snowball starting in Norway*, Cheltenham: Edgar Elgar Publishing.

MacLeod Hemingway, J 2007, 'Sex, trust and corporate boards', *Hastings Women's Law Journal*, vol. 18, pp. 173–97.

MacNeil, I & Li, X 2006, 'Comply or explain: market discipline and non-compliance with the combined code', *Corporate Governance: An International Review*, vol. 14, no. 5, pp. 486–96.

Majumdar, SK & Marcus, AA 2001, 'Rules versus discretion: the productivity consequences of flexible regulation', *Academy of Management Journal*, vol. 44, no. 1, pp. 170–79.

Marshall, S & Ramsay, I 2012, 'Stakeholders and directors' duties: law theory and evidence', *University of New South Wales Law Journal*, vol. 35, pp. 291–316.

Matolsky, Z, Stokes, D & Wright, A 2004, 'Do independent directors add value?', *Australian Accounting Review*, vol. 14, no. 32, pp. 33–40.

Ntim, CG, Opong, KK & Danbolt, J 2012, 'The relative value relevance of shareholder versus stakeholder corporate governance disclosure policy reforms in South Africa', *Corporate Governance: An International Review*, vol. 20, no. 1, pp. 84–105.

Perrault, E 2015, 'Why does board gender diversity matter and how do we get there? The role of activism and legislation in deinstitutionalizing old boys' networks', *Journal of Business Ethics*, vol. 128, no. 1, pp. 149–65.

Pye, A 2001, 'A study in studying corporate boards over time: looking backwards to move forwards', *British Journal of Management*, vol. 12, p. 33.

Roberts, J, McNulty, T & Stiles, P 2005, 'Beyond agency conceptions of the work of the non-executive director: creating accountability in the boardroom', *British Journal of Management*, vol. 16, pp. S5–S26.

Roche, OP 2009, *Corporate Governance & Organisational Life Cycle*, New York: Cambria Press.

Schoorman, FD, Mayer, RC & Davis, JH 2007, 'An integrative model of organizational trust: past, present and future', *Academy of Management Review*, vol. 32, no. 2, pp. 344–54.

Seidl, D, Sanderson, P & Roberts, J 2013, 'Applying the 'comply-or-explain' principle: discursive legitimacy tactics with regard to codes of corporate governance', *Journal of Management and Governance*, vol. 17, no. 3, pp. 791–826.

Spira, LF & Page, M, 'Regulation by disclosure: the case of internal control', *Journal of Management and Governance*, vol. 14, pp. 409–33.

Sundaramurthy, C & Lewis, M 2003, 'Control and collaboration: paradoxes of governance', *Academy of Management Review*, vol. 28 no. 3, p. 397.

Teigen, M 2012, 'Gender quotas for corporate boards in Norway: innovative gender equality policy', in C Fagan, M C Gonzalez Menendez & S Gomez Anson (eds.), *Women on Corporate Boards and in Top Management: European trends and policy*, New York: Palgrave-MacMillan, pp. 70–90.

Todnem, R 2005, 'Organisational change management: a critical review', *Journal of Change Management*, vol. 5, no. 4, pp. 369–80.

Van Ees, H, Gabrielsson, J & Huse, M 2009, 'Toward a behavioural theory of boards and corporate governance', *Corporate Governance: An International Review*, vol. 17, no. 3, pp. 307–19.

Vogel, D 2005, *The Market for Virtue: the potential and limits of corporate social responsibility*, Washington: The Brookings Institute.

von Nessen, P 2003, 'Corporate governance in Australia: converging with international developments', *Australian Journal of Corporate Law*, vol. 15, pp. 1–36.

Weil, D 2002, 'The benefits and costs of transparency: a model of disclosure based regulation', Transparency Policy Project, A. Alfred Taubman Centre for State and Local Government, Kennedy School of Government Working Paper.

Weil, D, Fung, A, Graham, M & Fagotto, E 2006, 'The effectiveness of regulatory disclosure policies', *Journal of Policy Analysis and Management*, vol. 25, no. 1, pp. 155–81.

Zattoni, A, Douglas, T & Judge, W 2013, 'Developing corporate governance theory through qualitative research', *Corporate Governance: An International Review*, vol. 21, no. 2, pp. 119–22.

INDEX

For Product Safety Concerns and Information please contact our EU
representative GPSR@taylorandfrancis.com Taylor & Francis Verlag GmbH,
Kaufingerstraße 24, 80331 München, Germany

Printed and bound by CPI Group (UK) Ltd, Croydon, CR0 4YY
12/05/2025
01866947-0002